"A GLORIOUS EXAMPLE."

ABLE-BODIED CIVILIAN (*to Territorial*). "THAT OUGHT TO GIVE YOU A GOOD LEAD, MATE."

TERRITORIAL. "YES—AND I MEAN TO TAKE IT! WHAT ABOUT *YOU*?"

TERRITORIALS

COURTESY OF IMPERIAL TOBACCO

MILI'TIA   *n. s.* [Lat.]
The trainbands, the standing force of a nation.

> Let any prince think soberly of his forces, except his *militia* be good and valiant soldiers. *Bacon.*

> The *militia* was so settled by law, that a sudden army could be drawn together. *Clarendon.*

> Unnumbered spirits around thee fly,
> The light *militia* of the lower sky. *Pope.*

TE'RRITORY   *n. s.* [*territorium,* law Lat. *territoire* Fr.]
Land ; country ; dominion ; district.

> Linger not in my *territories* longer than swiftest expedition will give thee time to leave our royal court. *Shakspeare.*

To VOLUNTEE'R   *v. n.*   To go for a soldier.

DR SAMUEL JOHNSON LL D
A Dictionary of the English Language, 1740.

EDITOR   Colonel Alastair Bruce of Crionaich
DESIGN   Major John Skliros TD RIFLES
PICTURES   Ms Liz Heasman
TYPOGRAPHY   Em Quad

© 2008 TA 100.

All rights reserved. No part of this publication may be reproduced or transmitted in any form or by any means, electronic or mechanical, including photocopying, recording or by any information storage and retrieval systems except as permitted by the UK Copyright, Designs and Patents Act 1988, without prior permission of the copyright owner.

First published April 2008 by DRA Publishing of 14 Mary Seacole Road, The Millfields, Plymouth, PL1 3JY on behalf of TA 100.

Printed and bound in the UK.

ISBN 978-0-9557813-1-5

Whilst every effort has been made to ensure the accuracy of the names and events in this book, the no liability can be accepted for any omissions or inaccuracies therein.

IAN F. W. BECKETT

TERRITORIALS

A CENTURY OF SERVICE

ABOVE *Private Child of the 1st Battalion, The Herefordshire Regiment taking advantage of a lull in the fighting to catch up on some reading in a captured German slit trench near Sonsbeck, 6th March 1945. In recognition of its wartime services, the Regiment was awarded the title of The Herefordshire Light Infantry in 1947.*

COURTESY OF THE HEREFORDSHIRE LIGHT INFANTRY MUSEUM, HEREFORD.

FOREWORD

BY PROFESSOR RICHARD HOLMES CBE

I T IS HARD to believe that it is well over 40 years since I slipped into 304 (Essex Yeomanry RHA) Field Regiment RA (TA) as a wholly unremarkable private soldier. The TA became an inseparable part of my life—part hobby and part job, part personal quest and part public duty—but always, start to finish, a passionate commitment which saw me imperil both private life and day job in a balancing act which as I look back at it, rather amazes me. I read Ian Beckett's wonderful book with enormous interest. It tells me much, as a Territorial, about the organisation in which I served, and it is odd to see the pivotal events of my career as historical facts rather than personal crises. It also tells me a good deal, as a military historian, that I did not know about Britain's army reserves.

I am struck by themes that emerge. There is indeed an 'essential continuity' linking today's Territorials with their ancestors, although we must be careful not to romanticise it. Haldane's 1908 Territorial Force subsumed militia and volunteers, both reserve forces, but with very different characters and traditions. The former had become a 'draft-finding body for the Regular Army', its ranks filled by men without serious employment, while the latter attracted men with a stake in society, prepared to do their bit in national emergency, but less eager to imperil careers unless they were sure that such an emergency existed.

The TA of my own times became a 'broad church,' containing, on the one hand, those who were happy to volunteer for an operational tour and, on the other, those who were content to accept mobilisation when necessary, but felt that the Regular Army should be able to cope with day-to-day demands without them. If we fail to offer the young and the bold the chance of operational service they will lose interest and, at the same time, the TA cannot justify its cost if it does not make a practical contribution to an over-stretched army.

It is always tempting to look at the settled part of the congregation as a target for cuts, but it is precisely this element that gives the TA its strongest links with civil society. Nobody should remain in the TA if they do not accept that, one day, the brown envelope might come through *their* letter box. Jettisoning the volunteer tradition to concentrate on the militia tradition would, though, be a grave mistake.

"The TA made me feel valued and valuable, and it has done the same for tens of thousands of those who have passed through its ranks."

"We live in a society that does not know the difference between a brigadier and a bombardier, a brigade and a battalion; that is deluged by flash-floods of reportage that depicts soldiers as heroes one minute and villains the next..."

OPPOSITE *An inter-war recruiting poster by Harry Woolley, published in June 1920 stresses the extra-curricular benefits of joining the TA at a time when memories of the Great War kept recruits in short supply.*

[IWM PST 13512]

COURTESY OF THE IMPERIAL WAR MUSEUM

Ian Beckett makes it clear that the relationship between the army and society, in which the reserve forces play a crucial role, is a complex and changing one. Over the past two centuries, it was only during the post-Waterloo rundown that the Regular Army was actually smaller than it is today while, if we look at the proportion of the population with personal experience of military service of any sort, then never, since the beginnings of the Regular Army in the 1660s, has a smaller percentage of Britons worn their country's uniform. We live in a society that does not know the difference between a brigadier and a bombardier, a brigade and a battalion; that is deluged by flash-floods of reportage that depicts soldiers as heroes one minute and villains the next; and, because it is itself increasingly preoccupied with its own interests, finds it hard to grasp that good armed forces are ultimately driven by values, old-fashioned virtues such as courage, loyalty, mutual respect and self-sacrifice. The TA made me feel valued and valuable, and it has done the same for tens of thousands of those who have passed through its ranks. One important reason for maintaining the Territorial Army's regional footprint of training centres (the drill halls of my youth) is to provide military presence in the community when the nearest regular soldier may be 50 miles away. The greatest challenge posed to the army at the beginning of this century is not military defeat, doctrinal inadequacy or technological insufficiency, but being fundamentally misunderstood by the society upon whose support it ultimately relies.

Basil Liddell Hart tells us that the TA is 'one of the hardiest of British plants', and the army in which I served underwent substantial, and generally positive, changes in size, structure and function. We would be rash to assume that the plant is as hardy as it once was. There are many other things that people can do in their spare time and, for those in employment, leisure time is itself often under pressure. A Territorial volunteers every time he or she reports for training, and seeks challenge backed by organisation, resources and commitment. Starve the TA of these—however sound the financial logic for doing so—and the plant will wither. Despite its occasional capacity to irritate, confuse and disappoint, we would, as this book so masterfully demonstrates, have been infinitely poorer without this uniquely British organisation.

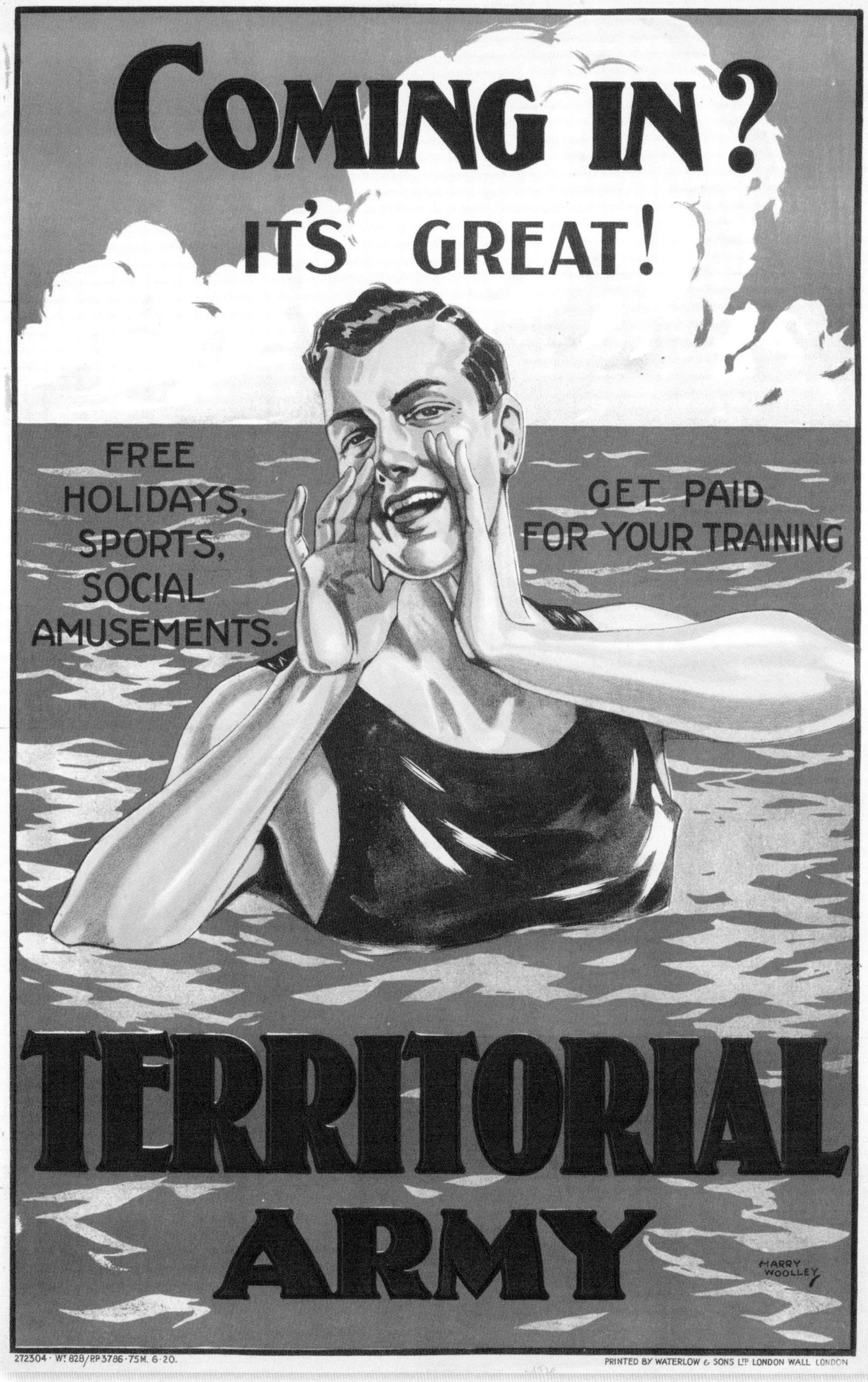
COMING IN?
IT'S GREAT!
FREE HOLIDAYS, SPORTS, SOCIAL AMUSEMENTS.
GET PAID FOR YOUR TRAINING
TERRITORIAL ARMY
HARRY WOOLLEY
272304 · WT. 828/P.P. 3786 · 75M. 6·20.
PRINTED BY WATERLOW & SONS LTD LONDON WALL LONDON

"Fathers and sons, husbands and brothers, left families, homes, the work and business of their lives almost at an hour's notice to go on active service abroad. It seems to me that we have not realised what these men were asked to do...

I sometimes wonder if the eyes of the country will ever be opened to what these Territorials of ours have done."

FIELD MARSHAL SIR JOHN FRENCH, 1915.

Contents

Subaltern. "Between ourselves, sir, there'll be trouble with this Territorial Captain. He's insufferable."
Major. "What of it? They said that about me."
Subaltern. "Ah, yes, sir. But you're a Regular. That's different."

COURTESY OF PUNCH MAGAZINE

ABBREVIATIONS

AA	Anti-Aircraft		FAL/FN	Fusil Automatique Léger/ Fabrique Nationale
AAC	Army Air Corps		FTRS	Full-time Reserve Service
ACF	Army Cadet Force		GC	George Cross
AGC	Adjutant General's Corps		GHQ	General Headquarters
ATS	Auxiliary Territorial Service		GOC	General Officer Commanding
BAOR	British Army of the Rhine		HAA	Heavy Anti-aircraft
BBC	British Broadcasting Corporation		HAC	Honourable Artillery Company
BEF	British Expeditionary Force		IFOR	Implementation Force
BLESMA	British Limbless Ex-service Men's Association		ISAF	Internal Security Assistance Force
CBRN	Chemical, Biological, Radiological and Nuclear		KFOR	Kosovo Force
			KOYLI	King's Own Yorkshire Light Infantry
CCRF	Civil Contingency Reaction Force		LAA	Light Anti-aircraft
CGS	Chief of the General Staff		LDV	Local Defence Volunteers
CID	Committee of Imperial Defence		LIAG	Land Information Assurance Group
CIGS	Chief of the Imperial General Staff		MC	Military Cross
CIMIC	Civil-Military Co-operation		MLRS	Multi-Launch Rocket System
CinC	Commander-in-Chief		MOD	Ministry of Defence
CSM	Company Sergeant Major		NAO	National Audit Office
CTA	County Territorial Association		NATO	North Atlantic Treaty Organisation
CVHQ	Central Volunteer Headquarters		NBC	Nuclear, Biological, Chemical
DCLI	Duke of Cornwall's Light Infantry		NCO	Non-commissioned Officer
DGHG&TA	Director General, Home Guard and Territorial Army		NEAB	National Employer Advisory Board
			NELC	National Employers' Liaison Council
DGTA	Director General, Territorial Army		NHS	National Health Service
DGTA&C	Director General, Territorial Army and Cadets		OCP	Operational Commitments Plot
			OCTU	Officer Cadet Training Unit
DRC	Defence Requirements Sub-committee		OTC	Officer Training Corps
			PAC	Public Accounts Committee
DRFC	Director, Reserve Forces and Cadets		PRT	Provincial Reconstruction Team
DTA&ACF	Director, Territorial Army and Army Cadet Force		PSI	Permanent Staff Instructor
			PUE	Pre-stocked Unit Equipment

PWRR	Princess of Wales's Royal Regiment	RVC	Rifle Volunteer Corps
RA	Royal Artillery	SaBRE	Supporting Britain's Reserves and Employers
RAC	Royal Armoured Corps		
RAF	Royal Air Force	SAS	Special Air Service
RAMC	Royal Army Medical Corps	SDR	Strategic Defence Review
RAOC	Royal Army Ordnance Corps	SFOR	Stabilisation Force
RAPC	Royal Army Pay Corps	SLR	Self Loading Rifle
RASC	Royal Army Service Corps	SSAFA	Soldiers, Sailors, Airmen and Families Association
RCT	Royal Corps of Transport		
RE	Royal Engineers	TA	Territorial Army
REME	Royal Electrical and Mechanical Engineers	TAER	Territorial Army Emergency Reserve
		TAVR	Territorial Army and Volunteer Reserve
RFCA	Reserve Forces and Cadet Association		
		TAVRA	Territorial Army and Volunteer Reserve Association
RFA	Royal Field Artillery		
RGA	Royal Garrison Artillery	TF	Territorial Force
RHA	Royal Horse Artillery	TUC	Trades Union Congress
RLC	Royal Logistic Corps	UDR	Ulster Defence Regiment
RMP	Royal Military Police	UN	United Nations
RN	Royal Navy	UNPROFOR	United Nations Protection Force
ROSO	Regimental Operations Support Officer	VAD	Voluntary Aid Detachment
		VC	Victoria Cross
RSOI	Reception, Staging and Onward Integration	VTC	Volunteer Training Corps
		WRAC	Women's Royal Army Corps
RTMC	Reserves Training and Mobilisation Centre		

ABOVE *A guard detail of the Staffordshire Militia at Windsor Castle in 1804. The yellow uniform of the Drum Major reflects the Regimental facing colour while the musicians wear the traditional white for bandsmen at this time with yellow facings and plumes. This painting is attributed to Arthur William Devis.*

COURTESY OF THE NATIONAL ARMY MUSEUM.

CHAPTER 1
ANTECEDENTS
PRE-1908

> "We believe that the volunteers are utterly unfit in respect of their training, their equipment, and their organisation to cope with continental soldiers. Either the volunteer force must be made what it ought to be, or the conscription [*sic*] must be introduced."

CAPTAIN H SPENSER WILKINSON MA,
20TH LANCASHIRE RIFLE VOLUNTEERS
Citizen Soldiers, 1884.

FOLLOWING THE EXAMPLE of their Victorian predecessors, with regard to earlier local military forces, Edwardian writers often used to begin narratives of the history of the Territorials by claiming the origins lay in the army gathered by Cassivelaunus to oppose Caesar's second invasion of Britain in 54BC. Such speculative excursions were pure flights of fancy, but most of these older works did correctly sense the essential continuity of English and British history.

It tends to be forgotten just how much the fear of invasion has shaped the story of these islands. Mayors of Sandwich in Kent, for example, still wear a black gown in commemoration of a predecessor killed in a French raid on the town in August 1457. The threat from the Spanish Armada in 1588 is well enough known, but not perhaps the Spanish raid on Mounts Bay in Cornwall in 1595. For many years, indeed, one of the public houses in Mousehole used to display the sword of a former landlord and the cannonball that supposedly took off his head in the raid. The Dutch landed in the Medway in Kent in 1667 while, in April 1778, the American privateer, John Paul Jones, raided Whitehaven in Cumbria. The following year saw the threat of a combined French and Spanish descent on the Isle of Wight, and it was about this time that the fishermen of Hartlepool in Cleveland famously hanged as a French spy a monkey that came ashore from a shipwreck. A monkey is still the symbol of the rugby club there.

During the 22 years that Britain was at war with Revolutionary and Napoleonic France, between 1793 and 1815, there were many scares. Indeed, the French landed at Fishguard in Pembrokeshire on 23rd February 1797, largely by mistake because they were driven off course when aiming for Bristol. They then surrendered to the local military forces, so it is said, because they saw Welsh women wearing red capes on the cliffs and took them for advancing regulars. A rather similar story is told at Ilfracombe in Devon, past which the French had sailed earlier, but here one Betsy Gannon, waving her red bloomers, supposedly prevented them from landing. The said bloomers are displayed in the museum there. Although the naval victory at Trafalgar in October 1805 clearly substantially blunted the threat, it was not entirely removed until about 1810.

ABOVE *Portrait of a Captain of the Ipswich Trained Bands, circa 1620, painted by Tobias Blosse.*

COURTESY OF COLCHESTER AND IPSWICH MUSEUM SERVICE.

OPPOSITE *The First Bucks Rifle Volunteers, ca. 1890.*

COURTESY OF THE OXFORDSHIRE AND BUCKINGHAMSHIRE LIGHT INFANTRY MUSEUM, OXFORD.

"A something in the City—a shopman or a clerk,
A fellow with a pen behind his ear,
A journalist, a lawyer, or an idler in the Park,
Is the ready-when-he's-wanted Volunteer."

HAROLD HARDY
The British Volunteer, 1900.

Victorian Britain saw three successive invasion panics in the 1840s and 1850s when, again, it was thought that the French might invade. The popular Victorian poet, Martin Tupper, captured the flavour during the second scare in 1852:

Think of the rapine, the flame and the slaughter,
If the fierce Algerine Frenchman here stood,
Think if you dare of your wife and your daughter,
Think of your little ones choked in their blood.

Just before the Great War, the *Daily Mail* estimated that the number of German spies and fifth columnists in Britain could be as many as 350,000 and memorably suggested that 'if your waiter says he is a Swiss, demand to see his passport'. There was a major invasion alert in the autumn of 1914 and, initially, two regular divisions were kept back from joining the British Expeditionary Force in Flanders as a precaution. Of course, the threat facing Britain in the summer of 1940 is still within popular memory although it may have been forgotten that there was also a belief that the Germans might launch suicide raids on Britain as a spoiling tactic prior to or immediately after D Day in 1944.

Traditionally, the main line of defence against invasion was the Royal Navy and, in consequence, the existence of a large standing Regular Army was distrusted as both unnecessary and even dangerous in that it might promote military despotism. Thus, there was a preference for raising amateur and temporary soldiers—the auxiliary military forces—brought into existence as needs dictated, both for defence against invasion and, indeed, for other purposes. While they frequently stretched the bounds of historical realism, the Victorians and Edwardians were therefore right to trace the antecedents of the auxiliary forces to military obligations of the Anglo-Saxon kingdoms dating from the seventh and eighth centuries AD, notably the 'common burdens' whereby all able-bodied freemen were liable when called upon to do so to build fortifications, repair bridges and undertake military service in the *fyrd*.

The precise nature of the *fyrd*—the 'Old English' word for 'army'—is disputed, but it survived in some form until at least the 12th century. Moreover, the actual principle of the freeman bearing arms in defence of the community was enshrined in successive medieval statutes, such as the Assize of Arms in 1181 and the Statute of Westminster in 1285, and was then effectively incorporated into the first so-called militia statutes in 1558. Thereafter the militia had a

PLAYER'S CIGARETTES

CASTLEMARTIN YEOMANRY,
1797

COURTESY OF IMPERIAL TOBACCO

ABOVE *The Presentation of Colours to the Bank Volunteers at Lord's Cricket Ground, 2nd September 1799, by George III. Painted by Thomas Stothard.*

COURTESY OF THE GOVERNOR AND COMPANY OF THE BANK OF ENGLAND

formal statutory existence until 1601, from 1648 to 1735, from 1757 to 1831, and from 1852 until 1908 when it was abolished. Even the absence of legislation did not, however, mean the militia had ceased to function. In 1642, therefore, King Charles I claimed the 1558 militia statutes were still in full force despite being repealed 38 years previously. Similarly, although the militia was abolished in 1908, the authority to raise it remained on the statute book until 1953.

The militia was always an institution of the state and implied a distinct element of compulsion for at least a section of society, but the basis of that obligation varied from time to time. Because of this, different epithets were attached to the militia at various times, such as the 'Exact Militia' of the 1620s, or the 'New Militia' of the 1750s. Essentially, prior to 1757, the militia obligation was one imposed upon property on a sliding scale, with those of wealth required to supply men to serve on their behalf and to equip them accordingly. After 1757, however, with the creation of the New Militia, militia service was a tax, as it were, on manpower, with each county raising a quota of men on the basis of its proportion of the total male population and that quota was found by compulsory ballot. It was not genuine conscription since exemption was widely available and the burden fell largely on the poorest elements of society. It was so unpopular, indeed, that there were widespread anti-militia riots in 1757 and again in 1796 when the 'Supplementary Militia' was raised and the last actual ballot took

place in 1829. Thus, when the force was revived in 1852 as a result of the French threat, it was raised on the basis of voluntary enlistment, and that remained the case until its abolition in 1908.

Depending upon the period, a man would serve around three years in the militia and, in that time, would undertake a number of days of compulsory training at a central county depot. In Elizabethan England, it was an average of ten days a year, usually between Easter and Whitsun. It became the practice, from 1573 onwards, to call out only a portion of the eligible manpower in so-called 'Trained Bands'—a term which remained in general usage until the Restoration Militia was created in 1663, although it was still used to describe the militia of London until 1793. The Stuart militia served 12 days on average. From 1762, however, the annual training period became a continuous 28-day period of training in summer. That is how it remained until 1852, when it became 21 days, but it was restored to 28 days in 1875 and could be extended to 56 days in times of crisis. In wartime the militia was embodied for permanent service, as during the Seven Years War (1756-63), the American War of Independence (1775-83), the French Revolutionary War and Napoleonic Wars (1793-1815), the Crimean War (1854-56) and the South African War (1899-1902). The term militia was revived briefly in 1921 in the sense that the Special Reserve, which had replaced it in 1908, was again called militia, but this was absorbed into the Supplementary Reserve in 1924. The term was also used to describe those conscripted under the Military Training Act of May 1939, but only one group was called up before the National Service (Armed Forces) Act introduced general conscription in September 1939.

Volunteer forces existed at other periods when the militia was in abeyance or simultaneously with the militia. Although most of the armies of the English Civil Wars (1642-45, 1648 and 1651) were volunteers rather than pressed men, true volunteer bodies, in the sense of defending their local communities, first appeared in the 1650s and, briefly, after the Restoration in 1660. Thereafter, volunteers were raised at times of great emergency, such as during the Jacobite invasions of England in 1715 and 1745, when legal difficulties made it problematic to call out the militia and, again, between 1778 and 1782 when the French and Spanish allied with the American rebels. The first specific volunteer legislation

ABOVE *Light Infantry Volunteers, 1804. A cartoon by Thomas Rowlandson who, together with James Gillray, regularly lampooned the military pretensions of the 'middling' classes serving in the volunteer movement during the Napoleonic Wars.*

COURTESY OF CHRIS BEETLES, LONDON/THE BRIDGEMAN ART LIBRARY.

OPPOSITE *Sergeant H Gordy, an old Wiltshire Rifle Volunteer, Malmesbury.*

COURTESY OF THE RIFLES (BERKSHIRE AND WILTSHIRE) MUSEUM, SALISBURY.

ABOVE *Men of the Devon*
Royal Garrison Artillery
Militia 'hamming it up' with
a Nordenfeldt three-barrel
(Land Pattern) machine-gun in
Plymouth.

COURTESY OF
THE ROYAL ARTILLERY MUSEUM, WOOLWICH.

dates from 1782. Volunteers, however, are primarily associated with the French Revolutionary and Napoleonic Wars, with volunteer infantry units and mounted volunteer units known as yeomanry—many of the latter appearing for the first time in 1794—with most of the infantry appearing for the first time in 1797 and 1798. Many of these infantry units were transferred in 1808 to a new semi-balloted force called the Local Militia but this was suspended in 1816. The legislation for the Local Militia was renewed annually until 1836 and did not finally lapse until 1875, but the Local Militia never reappeared after 1816.

A very few volunteer infantry units survived the end of the Napoleonic Wars, as did most of the yeomanry regiments. Indeed, the Volunteer Consolidation Act (1804) continued to govern the yeomanry until 1901 and volunteers until 1863. There was a new Volunteer Act in 1863 because, just as the militia was revived as a result of one French invasion scare in 1852, so the volunteers were revived as a result of another French invasion scare in 1859. Most were rifle volunteer corps, but there were some artillery volunteer corps, a few engineer volunteer corps and a handful of light horse and mounted rifle volunteers. A Railway Volunteer Staff Corps appeared in 1865, a Volunteer Medical Staff Corps in 1885 and just two volunteer transport companies in the 1890s. With the abolition of the militia in 1908, the volunteers and yeomanry were then combined into the new Territorial Force.

"...to make confusion worse confounded, there is no higher organisation than the battalion; no known plan of mobilisation; and, apparently, no existing store of equipment for a campaign."

CAPTAIN H SPENSER WILKINSON MA, 20TH LANCASHIRE RIFLE VOLUNTEERS
Citizen Soldiers, 1884.

The feature of all these volunteer forces, as opposed to the militia, was that they were supposedly self-sufficient though, in practice, most soon took state assistance and thus became subject to state control. It is all but impossible to summarise the many varied conditions under which volunteer forces served. In the Napoleonic Wars volunteer corps, or associations as they were sometimes called, frequently set their own rules and regulations. The Frampton Volunteers in Gloucestershire, for example, specified in 1798 that, in the event of a French invasion, they were prepared to serve up to eight miles outside the village; for the Hitchin Association in Hertfordshire it was only three miles. Volunteer officers in both the 1790s and the 1860s were often elected, and there was often proposing and seconding of members, entrance fees and annual subscriptions. In one new unit being formed in Edinburgh in 1860 it was decided that all those who wanted to be elected as officers should leave the room to be voted on by the remainder: all but three men left and they then elected themselves.

BELOW *Rifle Volunteers mounted on penny farthings ride in formation down George Street, Edinburgh in 1884.*

COURTESY OF THE NATIONAL WAR MUSEUM OF SCOTLAND, EDINBURGH.

ABOVE *Men of the 1st Volunteer Battalion, The Oxfordshire Light Infantry at camp circa 1890. This battalion later became the Oxford University Officers' Training Corps in 1908. One of a series of glass plates rescued from an Oxford skip in 2002.*

COURTESY OF THE OXFORDSHIRE AND BUCKINGHAMSHIRE LIGHT INFANTRY MUSEUM, OXFORD.

OPPOSITE *Company Officer of The 6th Battalion, The Gordon Highlanders, 1861.*

COURTESY OF THE NATIONAL WAR MUSEUM OF SCOTLAND, EDINBURGH.

Training times also varied. Volunteers raised in 1794 could be paid for two days' training a week, those raised in 1797 were not paid at all, those raised in 1798 were paid for one day a week and those raised in 1803 had two entirely different sets of conditions applied. All was consolidated in 1804 with pay for 24 days' training a year. In the Victorian revival, a capitation grant was paid for nine days' training a year and attendance at an annual inspection. Yeomanry did eight days a year, usually at times of agricultural convenience. In practice, most volunteers and yeomen did far more, and annual camps of 8 or 14 days became fashionable in the 1860s, with summer camps becoming compulsory in 1901.

A few specifically wartime creations are often confused with the auxiliary forces but actually stood apart from them. In 1796 a Provisional Cavalry was raised on the pre-1757 militia concept of an obligation upon property, requiring the wealthy to provide one man and one horse for every ten or more horses kept for riding or carriage drawing. Only six units were actually embodied, of which the Worcestershire Provisional Cavalry briefly served in Ireland, and they were all absorbed into the yeomanry in 1800. The Supplementary Militia, to which reference has already been made, was a force of 60,000 men raised by ballot and trained for 20 days a year in contingents of one twentieth of total strength. In effect, it greatly increased the militia quotas levied on counties and it continued in force until 1803.

Rifle volunteers were only permitted to wear silver lace on their uniforms as gold lace was deemed to be the exclusive mark of regular soldiers. Far from being taken as a snub, the volunteers welcomed the ruling since it would ensure that they would not be mistaken for the 'dregs of society'.

ABOVE *Trooper J R P Haig of the Imperial Yeomanry in South Africa,*
painted by William Skeoch Cumming in 1904.

COURTESY OF THE NATIONAL WAR MUSEUM OF SCOTLAND, EDINBURGH.

Another idea was for a French-style *levée en masse*—the calling out the whole able-bodied male population in the event of an invasion. The idea was first tried in Dorset in 1797 when the High Sheriff proposed to list all those eligible in a revival of the ancient *posse comitatus*, literally meaning the civil power of the county. Lists were also made in Buckinghamshire and Northumberland in 1798, and the idea then attracted government support through the Defence of the Realm Act of 1798, requiring all counties to list inhabitants, livestock and vehicles. The idea was revived in 1803 by two successive Defence Acts in June and July, again requiring returns to be made—the first of men from 15 to 60 and the second of men from 17 to 55. Three years later, in 1806, the Training Act also proposed calling up all able-bodied males between 16 and 40 and training them in batches of 20,000 for 26 days a year.

Yet further improvisations were enacted. The Army of Reserve, also called the Additional Army of England, was raised in 1803 and sought to find 50,000 men to serve for five years through a ballot. Subsequently, the Permanent Additional Force Act in operation from 1804 to 1806 absorbed both the Army of Reserve and the Supplementary Militia. It was not to be raised by ballot, but parishes were to find recruits and were fined if they did not meet their quota. In both the American War of Independence and the French Revolutionary and Napoleonic Wars, fencibles were also raised, but these were actually regular troops raised for home defence only, the majority of units being raised in Scotland. In the South African War, two new forces were raised for service in South Africa, primarily because legislation made it difficult to accept direct offers from volunteers and yeomanry. The City Imperial Volunteers was a small force raised by the Lord Mayor of London, while the Imperial Yeomanry was a much larger mounted force raised in three separate contingents. Rather

ABOVE *Cyclists of the Hampshire Rifle Volunteers, circa 1890. They are armed with .303-inch Lee Metford Mk II rifles which were the last rifle in British service to use black powder as a propellent. It was hoped that the introduction of the bicycle would not only draw the growing number of keen cyclists into the volunteers but also prove a useful military innovation since, unlike a horse, it needed no forage and could be taken into the firing line. The need for good roads suggested practical limitations on campaign.*

COURTESY OF THE ROYAL HAMPSHIRE REGIMENT MUSEUM, WINCHESTER.

ABOVE *The helmet plate of the 4th Volunteer Battalion, The Hampshire Regiment. The device in the centre shaped like a stirrup is a dog gauge. Residents of the New Forest were permitted to keep dogs as long as they were small enough to fit through the gauge; larger dogs were deemed to be a threat to the King's deer.*

COURTESY OF THE ROYAL HAMPSHIRE REGIMENT MUSEUM, WINCHESTER.

confusingly, the name Imperial Yeomanry was then also attached to the domestic yeomanry force as a whole between 1901 and 1908.

Invasion may have been the *raison d'être* for this astonishing range of local auxiliary forces, but they were not just intended as a defence against invasion. They were also a safeguard against internal disorder. To use the example of Buckinghamshire in the Napoleonic Wars, the articles of enrolment of the Bucks Yeomanry in 1794 emphasised not just invasion but the 'suppression of riots and tumults'. Almost at once, they were helping to suppress food riots in 1796 at High Wycombe and escorting food convoys at Stony Stratford. The Royal Bucks King's Own Militia, like most other militia regiments when on embodied wartime service, largely fulfilled the purpose of internal security, serving in the north of England during the Luddite disturbances. After 1815 the yeomanry in particular was clearly intended as a constabulary. The suppression of a political rally in Manchester ('Peterloo') in 1819 was primarily the work of the Manchester and Salford Yeomanry. The Swing riots in southern England in 1830 were another occasion on which yeomanry regiments were called out, as they were in the Chartists' disturbances in the 1840s. Even in the 1860s the volunteers could still be represented as making property secure, although the prospect of volunteers firing on crowds was something that, by the 1860s, governments wished to avoid. Fortunately, the gradual extension of police forces by the permissive provisions of the Rural Constabulary Act (1839) and the mandatory provisions of the County and Borough Police Act (1856) made such a prospect increasingly unlikely.

Not too far distant from preserving the status quo, there was also what might be termed a role in social control. It was the perennial desire of successive councils in Elizabethan and Stuart England—and even governments in the early 18th century—that men of property and respectability should serve in person in the militia. It was a hope never realised and, if anything, the militia tended to be depicted as liable to ruin a man for civil occupation. The poet William Cowper, for example, described a militiaman as a 'pest where he was useful once'. Certainly, once the militia was balloted after 1757, it was expected that it would consist of the worst elements of society since they alone would be unable

to escape the ballot. By the 1850s it was hoped that the militia might prove a means of generating social benefits through the provision of regimental schools, religious instruction and so on. It was, some said, a 'halfway house between a Sunday school and a superior mechanics' institute'. The Victorian volunteers were enthusiastically supported by men such as Thomas Hughes, Samuel Smiles and Thomas Arnold for the same reason and, in the 1880s and 1890s, the Boys Brigades and Church Lads Brigades were both started by volunteer officers. It was suggested that the habits of discipline and orderliness imparted by service in the volunteers made better employees.

The auxiliary forces also existed as a supplement to and an alternative to regular standing armies. The militia was often called the 'old constitutional force' and its survival after 1660 owed much to the parliamentary view of it as a counterweight to a standing army. Indeed, the fundamental issue of the control of the militia had been one of the causes of the outbreak of civil war in the summer of 1642. By the 18th century there was less mileage in the idea of the militia as a check on military despotism and it was much more a case of how far the militia could genuinely supplement the army. Unfortunately, from the point of view of the army, it was often illegal to use the auxiliaries overseas. As early as the Elizabethan period, the trained bands had been illegally raided for men for overseas expeditions. What was supposed to be a temporary expedient of recruiting militiamen into the army in 1799 was repeated frequently throughout the rest of the Napoleonic Wars and it is often said that many of the men at Waterloo were still wearing militia uniforms. The same thing happened in the Crimean War and, by the 1870s, it was accepted that the militia was simply a draft-finding body for the army.

As far as volunteer forces was concerned, it was a matter of special legislation. There was one near mutiny in the Tetbury Volunteers in Gloucestershire in 1806 when their colonel suggested they might all like to volunteer for the expedition

ABOVE *The Marquis of Salisbury, Lord Lieutenant of Hertfordshire, commissioned Richard Livesay to produce this painting of the Royal Review of the county's militia, yeomanry and volunteers at Hatfield Park on 13th June 1800. A total of 1,065 officers and men were reviewed by King George III, who was accompanied by Queen Charlotte, the Prince of Wales, and the Dukes of York and Cumberland. The King is shown mounted on a white horse at centre, taking the salute of the volunteer infantry, the yeomanry having already passed in review. After making sketches on the day, Livesay recorded accurately the uniforms of the various units, representative of whom were summoned subsequently to Hatfield House for the purpose.*

COURTESY OF THE MARQUESS OF SALISBURY.

ABOVE *Members of the Wiltshire Rifle Volunteer Corps, including two men from the 20th Foot (East Devons) later the Lancashire Fusiliers, at a shooting match in 1868. The range is thought to be Semington near Melksham. The weapons are Enfield Percussion Rifles but at least two have been converted to the Snider breech loading device.*

COURTESY OF THE RIFLES (BERKSHIRE AND WILTSHIRE) MUSEUM, SALISBURY.

"The army appears to be the only institution in the kingdom which is outside of the people. They know nothing of it, take no interest in it, and express no opinion on it."

JOHN HOLMS
The Nineteenth Century, 1878.

to Buenos Aires in Argentina. Victorian volunteers, however, were often more willing to go and offers were made to serve overseas during international crises in both 1878 and 1882. Men of the 24th Middlesex (Post Office) Rifle Volunteers did perform postal and telegraph duties in the expeditionary forces sent to Egypt in 1882 and eastern Sudan in 1884, and some volunteers from the 1st Newcastle and Durham Engineer Volunteers and 1st Lancashire Engineer Volunteers also helped construct a railway in eastern Sudan. Any wider mobilisation, however, would have needed special legislation and this is why the City Imperial Volunteers and the Imperial Yeomanry were raised as separate forces for the South African War. Nonetheless, composite service companies were found for regular battalions from the volunteer force.

The existence of the auxiliary forces also meant, effectively, that the army could not be enlisted by conscription and, apart from temporary legislation in the early 18th century to impress debtors, vagrants and criminals, there was no conscription for the army until 1916. The militia ballot was unpopular enough, and men joined the volunteers and the yeomanry in the 1790s in part because that meant exemption from the ballot. It was widely believed by government after 1836 that to reintroduce conscription would be equivalent to committing political suicide and, in fact, a number of attempts to bring back conscription were defeated in parliament in the years leading up to 1914.

In drawing into voluntary service those who would have resented compulsion, however, the auxiliary forces were also serving to inculcate military values throughout society. Militia officers were always drawn from the landed and, indeed, had to fulfil a property qualification to hold a commission until 1869. The rank and file, however, as already suggested, were invariably from the lower elements of society. In the Elizabethan and Stuart period, this meant miners and fishermen in Cornwall, agricultural labourers in Northamptonshire, and 'mechanicals' in Wiltshire. This was even truer of the militia as raised by

ABOVE *A depiction in folk art style of the surrender of the 1,400 strong French* Legion Noire *to the Castlemartin Yeomanry (in the foreground), Fishguard Fencibles and Pembrokeshire Militia at Goodwick Sands near Fishguard, Pembrokeshire on 24th February 1797. The Castlemartin Yeomanry thereby earned the unique battle honour of 'Fishguard' (awarded in 1853) and the incident also fostered the myth that the French had surrendered after mistaking the red capes of local women for approaching regulars.*

COURTESY OF CARMARTHENSHIRE MUSEUM SERVICE

the ballot between 1757 and 1831, for the wealthier could pay a £10 fine to be exempted for a year or find a substitute to serve the full three years on their behalf. There was a brisk trade in substitutes, invariably farm servants or farm labourers, so that few other than the casually employed would end up serving in person. On occasions, substitutes would renege on their agreements. In Buckinghamshire in 1803, for example, a labourer was brought to court by a grocer who alleged he had hired him in a pub one night as a substitute for 22 guineas with five shillings in advance, three shillings worth of ribbons and all Stevens could drink, only for him not to appear. There were even militia insurance clubs. Men paid a subscription and, if their name was drawn in the ballot, the fund would provide enough money to hire a substitute. The cost of hiring a substitute invariably rose throughout the Napoleonic period. The poet John Clare referred to the Northants Local Militia in 1808 as a 'more motley multitude of lawless fellows [that] was never seen in Oundle before'. With the revival of the militia on a voluntary basis in 1852, it was dependent once more on the casually employed.

By contrast, volunteer forces were always likely to be more middle class or artisan in composition. The yeomanry as a mounted force was always strong among farmers and those connected to horse trades because, of course, they had to find their own horses although the landed might often horse their tenants. Volunteer infantry, whether in the 1790s or the 1860s, initially had a

ABOVE *A New Year card depicting a Volunteer armed with a Lee Metford rifle, prior to embarking for the South African War, 1900.*

COURTESY OF THE ROYAL HAMPSHIRE REGIMENT MUSEUM, WINCHESTER

substantial number of professional men and tradesmen although, as the novelty wore off, most tended to rely upon those in regular employment, as opposed to the casually employed. In Buckinghamshire, for example, the rifle volunteer force by the end of the 19th century was dependent largely upon chairmakers from High Wycombe, printers from Aylesbury and the employees of the London and North Western Railway Company Carriage Works at Wolverton. In Northamptonshire, it was said the rifle volunteers were mostly shoemakers and strawplaiters. There were corps of shipyard workers and shipping clerks in Liverpool, mill hands in Nottingham and silk spinners in Huddersfield. Quite often, volunteer corps were formed by the employees of one particular firm, such as the Mersey Iron Works in Liverpool, or the London Lead Company at Middleton in County Durham. In 1861 the Risca Colliery disaster in Monmouthshire led to the deaths of 100 volunteers and at Seaham Colliery in County Durham in 1880 another 36. There were 'ethnic' corps such as the Liverpool Welsh and London Irish while the metropolis also boasted exclusive units such as the Inns of Court and the Artists Rifles.

These local military units were always far more visible to society as a whole than the Regular Army, which was literally out of sight and out of mind in that it was small and mostly serving overseas. The administration of the local forces was a constant burden on county, hundred[1] and parish officials, not least in terms of the militia when the ballot had to be organised and the families of serving militiamen maintained at parish expense. The pages of local newspapers in the 19th and early 20th centuries all have very full reports on local forces for they provided spectacle, attracting large crowds to such events as the presentation of new colours to the Wiltshire Yeomanry, which attracted 20,000 spectators in 1798, or the 150,000 who saw one volunteer review at Knowlsley in Cheshire in 1860. Thousands regularly attended the great Easter volunteer reviews held in the 1860s and 1870s, usually at resorts such as Brighton.

While being far more visible than regulars, however, the auxiliaries also bore the brunt of popular anti-militarism. There were the anti-militia riots in the 18th century, but Victorian volunteers attracted hostility over their need for drill space and rifle ranges. Thus, volunteers clashed with mobs in Regent's Park,

COURTESY OF IMPERIAL TOBACCO

1. A common law geographical subdivision of an English shire introduced in Saxon times for military, administrative and judicial purposes.

"There is no better proof of the spirit of volunteers than that a percentage of them persevere in shooting at 800 yards with the Enfield rifle, of which an Ordnance Committee reported twenty years ago that at that range it could not be trusted to make a hit within 3ft. of the point where it ought to hit."

CAPTAIN H SPENSER WILKINSON MA, 20TH LANCASHIRE RIFLE VOLUNTEERS
Citizen Soldiers, 1884.

London in 1861 and with cricketers in the same venue in 1875. Tynemouth Town Council complained that the volunteer artillery was making too much noise and driving away holidaymakers in the North East in 1883. Ridicule was often a weapon used against the auxiliaries, often because they did have military pretensions. Dryden spoke of the militia as 'mouths without hands maintained at vast expense' while the cartoons of Gillray regularly satirised the Napoleonic Volunteers, as did *Punch* in the 1860s. Yet, in other circumstances, the prestige of the community could become bound up with that of the auxiliaries. There was fierce opposition, for example, in Berkshire in 1809 when the Reading Volunteers were disbanded after an altercation with the Berkshire Local Militia. Similarly, the disbanding of one Hampshire rifle corps after a lapse of discipline at the Guildford Review in 1864 caused uproar in its hometown of Basingstoke.

Of course, much depended upon the actual conduct of the auxiliaries and there was constant emphasis in all units upon maintaining dignified conduct. In June 1795 Lord Delaval noted in his pocket book of the presence of the West Yorkshire Militia on his estate, 'disturbance – noise – drums – poultry – intrusions – depredations – profligacy with servants – camp followers – interruptions – marauding – how to be protected – compensation – recompense'. Many unit histories contain increasingly repetitive testimonials of good conduct received from towns, an emphasis which says much of the significance of good conduct. But, despite the possibility of bad behaviour, auxiliaries were mostly welcome in that their presence was bound to increase trade. The uniforms of yeomanry and volunteers were provided mostly by local tradesmen rather than central government. Between 1794 and 1827 the London and Westminster Light Horse Volunteers spent almost £64,000 on its premises alone in terms of rent and leases. The rifle volunteers were given very favourable terms by railway companies who competed for custom in carrying men to the Easter reviews, and it was said that Volunteers and their families spent £50,000 in Brighton in one weekend in 1863. Aristocrats commanding yeomanry regiments spent vast sums locally in equipping their units. The Earl of Dudley spent at least £4,000 a year on the Worcestershire Yeomanry between 1854 and 1871, while the expense of the Bucks Yeomanry Cavalry helped bankrupt the 2nd Duke of Buckingham and Chandos in 1848.

Spending money locally begins to suggest a certain interdependence between auxiliaries and society, and there was

BELOW *An 1881 Pattern Other Ranks' Home Service Helmet of the Oxfordshire Rifle Volunteers. Adopted in imitation of the German army, the Home Service Helmet remained part of the British army's full dress until the Great War.*

COURTESY OF THE OXFORDSHIRE AND BUCKINGHAMSHIRE LIGHT INFANTRY MUSEUM, OXFORD.

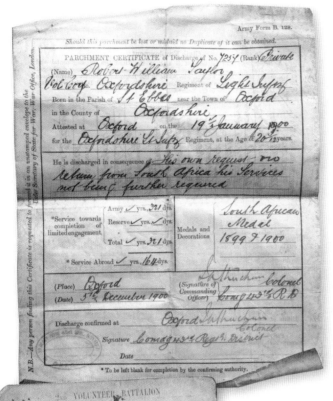

ABOVE *The discharge paper [top] of Private Robert Taylor of the 2nd Volunteer Battalion, The Oxfordshire Light Infantry from the volunteer service company that joined the regular 1st Battalion in South Africa in 1900. Shown together with Taylor's certificate of authority (bottom), dating from 1897, allowing him to keep his rifle and bayonet at home.*

COURTESY OF THE OXFORDSHIRE AND BUCKINGHAMSHIRE LIGHT INFANTRY MUSEUM, OXFORD.

also that dependence in terms of the relationship of the auxiliary to his employment. They were civilians temporarily in uniform and the ability to fulfil training commitments rested on the state of a man's employment. Even in the militia, which would only attract the casually employed, it was custom on embodied wartime service to allow men home on furlough for work on the land at harvest time. The yeomanry was especially associated with the unchanging nature of the agricultural year which governed when its training occurred. Tradesmen or artisans in volunteer units had equal commitments, hence the increasingly close relationship with employers in the 19th and 20th centuries. Victorian volunteers were also instrumental in supporting parliamentary legislation on Half Day Holidays and Early Closing.

Mention of parliamentary agitation raises the political link between the auxiliaries and society. They were frequently a major issue in national politics as in the outbreak of the Civil War. Auxiliaries were often very well represented in parliament. The Crown often gerrymandered the Lieutenancy for political purposes since local commissions were solely the province of the Lieutenancy until 1871, while the granting of commissions was also frequently used for local political purposes. Indeed, generally, the auxiliary forces provided opportunities of various kinds. At one level this might only be the opportunity of experiencing something different, of enjoying recreational facilities or a comradeship that might not otherwise be attainable. On a different level, it could be a conscious commitment to the status quo, a demonstration of loyalty to country or perhaps to landlord or employer. It might be, too, a means of upwards social mobility, of becoming respectable. There might be major obstacles to using the auxiliaries as a route into the landed society, as when the Marquis of Salisbury remarked of one hapless applicant for a militia commission in 1852 that employment by the General Screw Steam Navigation Company was an 'insuperable obstacle'. Similarly, a common saying in the 1860s of the volunteers was a greengrocer presented with a volunteer commission was not an officer but a greengrocer pleased. Yet the yeomanry was clearly a major *entrée* to local society, so many aspiring Jewish families entering the

Royal Bucks Hussars in the late 19th century, including the Rothschilds, that the regiment's nickname was the 'Flying Foreskins'.

It can be seen, therefore, that in 1908 the Territorials were following in a proud 'amateur military tradition' of great longevity. Auxiliaries always embraced a very wide section of society. Figures are difficult to assess for earlier periods, but around 336,000 men were serving in the yeomanry and volunteers alone in 1806, representing about 3.5 per cent of the population as a whole and there were perhaps another 135,000 in the militia. In 1877 the auxiliaries represented 6.3 per cent of the male population of military age and, by 1903 about 3.6 per cent of the male population as a whole. This may seem insignificant but, to put it into perspective, 953,000 men passed through the militia between 1882 and 1904 and there was rarely less than 250,000 men serving in the yeomanry and volunteers at any one time. At the height of the Great War, in which 5.7 million men passed through the British Army, this still represented only 22.1 per cent of the male population and 10.7 per cent of total population.

Few of these men would have come into contact with the army in any other way. In the process, they absorbed and, in turn, transmitted military values to society as a whole, both favourable and, on occasions, unfavourable. Above all, they were ever-present and part of the very fabric of Britain at the county and community level. Before the 20th century they were not often tested in war, of course, but even in merely existing they were a focus and an outlet for many who wished to demonstrate their commitment to their country or community for whatever reason and, in so doing, to enjoy in the words of one historian of the later Home Guard, the 'incommunicable satisfaction of a job whose value lies beyond questioning'.

ABOVE *The Lord Mayor's reception in the Guildhall for the City Imperial Volunteers upon their return from service in the South African War, 29th October 1900, as painted by John Henry Frederick Bacon. The CIV had been raised on the initiative of the Lord Mayor, Sir Alfred Newton, in December 1899. The Court of Common Council voted £25,000 for the purpose with further large sums donated by banks, livery companies and other firms.*

COURTESY OF THE GUILDHALL ART GALLERY, CITY OF LONDON

THE HONOURABLE ARTILLERY COMPANY

ABOVE *A Priest 105mm self-propelled gun of 11th Royal Horse Artillery (Honourable Artillery Company), serving with the 1st Armoured Division in Tunisia, 22nd April 1943.* [IWM: NA 2313]

COURTESY OF THE IMPERIAL WAR MUSEUM.

A GOOD ILLUSTRATION OF the longevity of the auxiliary forces is the Honourable Artillery Company (HAC), which has had a continuous existence since August 1537, being only predated by the Yeomen of the Guard (1486) and the Honourable Corps of Gentlemen at Arms (1509). The HAC originated as the Guild of St George, established by charter of incorporation to maintain the 'science and feate of shootinge' with bows and handguns at a time when martial pursuits became fashionable within the City of London. Originally based at Spitalfields, the HAC moved to the present Artillery Garden in Finsbury in 1641, the headquarters building of Armoury House dating from 1735. Other similar military gardens and martial yards had been created both in London and the provinces in the first two decades of the 17th century but failed to survive.

It became the custom for the HAC, which received the 'Honourable' title in 1685, to supply officers and non-commissioned officers for the London Trained Bands. It is still closely linked with the City of London, providing the Lord Mayor

ABOVE *A depiction of the 'Gordon Riots' in the City of London on 7th June 1780 shows the London Military Foot Association, subsequently incorporated into the Honourable Artillery Company, firing on the mob. The riots were occasioned by popular agitation against the Catholic Relief Act, led by an extremist Protestant, Lord George Gordon. A march by an estimated 60,000 people to petition Parliament on 2nd June degenerated into five days of rioting, in which public buildings as well as property owned by prominent Catholics were attacked. Over 280 people were killed before regulars, militia and volunteers restored order. The still nightly military guard on the Bank of England was instituted during the riots.*

COURTESY OF THE HONOURABLE ARTILLERY COMPANY

Regarded as the premier unit of the revived volunteer force after 1859, the HAC provided a battery for the City Imperial Volunteers in the South African War armed with four Vickers-Maxim 12½-pounder, quick-firing guns.

OPPOSITE *HAC soldiers cleaning their Short Magazine Lee Enfields in the trenches near St Eloi, 1915.* [IWM Q 49364]

COURTESY OF THE IMPERIAL WAR MUSEUM.

COURTESY OF IMPERIAL TOBACCO

with an escort on civic occasions, such as the annual Lord Mayor's Show on the second Saturday in November, and (since 1924) firing the Royal Salute from the Tower of London on the Sovereign's official birthday, as well as other royal and state occasions. The uniform of the Company of Pikemen and Musketeers, formed from former members of the HAC in 1925 for ceremonial duties, still reflects that of the era of the Civil War, precipitated by the issue of whether Crown or Parliament should control the London Trained Bands. A similar HAC Light Cavalry ceremonial unit was formed in 1979, a light cavalry reconnaissance unit having previously existed between 1861 and 1891.

Regarded as the premier unit of the revived volunteer force after 1859, the HAC provided a battery for the City Imperial Volunteers in the South African War armed with four Vickers-Maxim 12½-pounder, quick-firing guns. Upon the formation of the Territorial Force in 1908, it was originally intended that the HAC become a battalion of the London Regiment but, in the event, while becoming formally part of the Territorials, it remained an independent unit. Two HAC infantry battalions and five artillery batteries served overseas in the Great War and three Royal Horse Artillery (RHA) regiments in the Second World War. HAC members won three Victoria Crosses (VCs) in the Great War and one in the Second. Edward Heath, Prime Minister from 1970 to 1974, commanded the 2nd Regiment HAC (HAA) from 1947 to 1950. The HAC's current role is to provide surveillance and target acquisition patrols for the NATO Allied Command Europe Rapid Reaction Corps.

The HAC is not considered first in precedence within the TA since The Royal Monmouthshire Royal Engineers (Militia), while only claiming a continuous existence since 1539, is regarded as having an unbroken period of loyalty to the Crown, whereas the HAC fought for Parliament in the Civil War. Moreover, whereas the HAC took precedence over all militia units in 1883, the Special Reserve, which the Royal Monmouthshire entered in 1908, then took precedence next after all regular units. While the Royal Monmouthshire entered the Supplementary Reserve in 1926, it retained its former militia status and precedence over Territorial units, which now included the HAC. The Royal Monmouthshire became formally part of the TA in 1953, its precedence over the HAC being confirmed in 1957.

❖

CHAPTER 2
HALDANE'S ARMY
1908-1914

"The problem, as it presents itself to my mind, is how to reorganise the military forces of this country in such a fashion as to give the whole nation what is really a National Army, not separated from itself by artificial barriers of caste and class, but regarded by the people as something that is their very own."

RICHARD BURTON HALDANE, SECRETARY OF STATE FOR WAR 1906-1912
25 April 1906.

ABOVE *Richard Burton Haldane,*
1st Viscount Haldane, painted by
Philip Alexius de László in 1928.

COURTESY OF NATIONAL PORTRAIT GALLERY,
LONDON.

THE SOUTH AFRICAN War proved the catalyst for the military reforms that led to the creation of the Territorial Force. When war broke out between Britain and the Boer republics of the Transvaal and the Orange Free State in October 1899, there was little expectation that the potential reserve of military experience represented by the militia, yeomanry and volunteers would be called upon. Britain, after all, was the world's most powerful empire and its military and naval might was unlikely to be threatened by 'a handful of farmers'. In the event, Britain suffered three successive defeats in the 'Black Week' of December 1899 and it required the deployment of 448,000 men from Britain and its empire to defeat the Boers by May 1902.

The early setbacks had been a profound shock to the extent that it raised real concerns about the possibility of a deterioration of the imperial race. This prompted the emergence in response of such varied organisations as the National Service League, which advocated conscription, the National Social Purity Crusade and the Boy Scouts. Influential works such as *The Times History of the War in South Africa* proclaimed the army a 'sham' as a fighting machine. In reality, the lessons of the war were by no means clear cut and much disputed but it brought about a sweeping series of administrative reforms including the abolition of the post of Commander-in-Chief; the creation of the Chief of the General Staff and, in due course, the establishment of a General Staff. There were also attempts at organisational reform between 1901 and 1905 by St John Brodrick and Hugh Arnold-Forster as Secretaries of State for War amid the beginnings of a reorientation of British strategic interests, driven partly by the cost of the war and partly by fears arising from British diplomatic isolation during the war and the effort required to meet global commitments.

The militia, yeomanry and volunteers had made a considerable contribution to the war effort. Over 45,000 militiamen had served in South Africa or overseas garrisons and a further 74,000 had enlisted in the Regular Army. More than 19,000 volunteers served in South Africa in active service companies attached to regular battalions, with some 7,000 enlisting in the Regular Army. The three contingents raised for the Imperial Yeomanry, though certainly far from recruited exclusively from the domestic yeomanry, totalled over 34,000 men. The domestic volunteer force also increased by more than 19,000 men amid renewed, if irrational, fears of invasion and it was freely acknowledged that, with virtually all the Regular Army overseas, it was the only available means of home defence should an enemy land on British shores. That very fact, however,

OPPOSITE *Men of the 4th*
Battalion, Alexandra, Princess of
Wales's Own (Yorkshire Regiment)
on exercise in 1908. White cap
bands were invariably worn on
manoeuvres and exercises in the
pre-war army.

COURTESY OF THE GREEN HOWARDS MUSEUM,
RICHMOND.

ABOVE *Gunner John Gamble,*
2 Kent Battery, Royal Field
Artillery TF, at an artillery
practice camp in Shorncliffe
in 1914. One of the battery's
15-pounders can be seen in the
middle distance on the right.

COURTESY OF THE ROYAL ARTILLERY MUSEUM,
WOOLWICH.

coupled with often unjustified criticism of the military performance of some of the auxiliaries in South Africa, led to the belief that the auxiliary forces, too, must be reformed. Much of the disparagement was aimed at the Imperial Yeomanry and, admittedly, many of the second contingent reaching South Africa in 1901 could not ride since few were recruited from the domestic yeomanry. Lord Chesham, the Inspector General of the Imperial Yeomanry, came across one such trooper leading his horse on two successive days and, assuming the man was sparing the animal because of a sore back or some similar reason, commended him on his care. The trooper replied that he had lost his left stirrup so Chesham suggested he simply mount the animal on the other side, receiving the incredulous reply: 'Get along with you! Why, if I did that I'd be facing the wrong way!'

A succession of witnesses—albeit mostly regulars—to a Royal Commission in 1903 chaired by the 15th Duke of Norfolk and set up to determine the minimum standards of efficiency required of militia and volunteers, claimed that neither militia nor volunteers could be safely entrusted with the defence of the country unaided due to deficiencies of training. The commission, dominated by advocates of conscription, concluded in May 1904 that neither force was fit to take the field. Brodrick and Arnold-Forster, therefore, drew up reform plans for the auxiliary forces as part of their wider proposals which aroused particular hostility from the representatives of the auxiliary forces in Parliament. Indeed, it was opposition from MPs who were volunteers that did most to wreck Arnold-Forster's plans.

Brodrick and Arnold-Forster were Unionists but, in December 1906, a new Liberal government took office with Richard Burdon Haldane appointed Secretary of State for War. A Scottish barrister, Haldane had a powerful intellect —he was one of many politicians who have been characterised as 'too clever by half'—but with an inability to make himself easily understandable that often left those of lesser accomplishment floundering. A lifelong devotee of German philosophy, he left his military advisers somewhat bemused by announcing at one of their first meetings that his vision was one of a 'Hegelian[1] army'. There

....

1. Georg Wilhelm Friedrich Hegel, a German philosopher created a fundamentally influential system of thought. His view of man's mind as the highest expression of the Absolute is expounded in *The Phenomenology of Mind* (1807).

Leo Amery remarked that Haldane's explanation of his scheme to the House of Commons 'in which he explained at terrific speed, but with great suavity, that the more battalions and batteries he scrapped the stronger he made the Army, always reminded me a little of a conjurer's patter'.

was a personal charm about him, however, leading one volunteer colonel to remark after dining with the Secretary of State that 'he felt exactly like a calf well licked over by a boa constrictor as a preliminary to deglutition'.

In later years, Haldane liked to claim that his reforms were driven by the need to make Britain ready for the continental war that he clearly foresaw. Regulars and auxiliaries were thus reshaped alike to produce an expeditionary force and the means by which it could be sustained in the field. Far from being a result of any perception of future strategic need, the reform package as a whole was the consequence of the demand for greater military economy. Placing a ceiling upon expenditure that he deemed acceptable to a majority in Cabinet and Parliament, Haldane had to find a means of reorganising existing resources sufficiently to meet a range of commitments at home and abroad. Indeed, the much-vaunted six infantry divisions of the expeditionary force were organised on Indian army divisional scales and determined simply by what troops were available in Britain, eight 'surplus' regular battalions then being disbanded. Leo Amery, a Conservative politician noted for his interest in military preparedness, remarked that Haldane's explanation of his scheme to the House of Commons 'in which he explained at terrific speed, but with great suavity, that the more battalions and batteries he scrapped the stronger he made the Army, always reminded me a little of a conjurer's patter'.

Nonetheless, Haldane did have a wider encompassing vision of the purpose of the auxiliary forces, which owed something to the belief that reform was an alternative to the compulsory service that was anathema to him. As originally outlined in a memorandum in February 1906, Haldane wanted to create out of the auxiliaries a 'real national army, formed by the people' that would weld a new unity of army and society. This would be the Territorial Force. The idea of educating the nation in its military responsibilities was then carried further in another memorandum in April 1906, which suggested that, as well as raising, supplying and administering the Territorials, new County Territorial Associations would also promote military virtues in schools through encouraging drill, physical exercise, cadet units

BELOW *Bashing spuds at the 4th Battalion, Alexandra, Princess of Wales's Own (Yorkshire Regiment) annual camp in 1908.*

COURTESY OF THE GREEN HOWARDS REGIMENTAL MUSEUM, RICHMOND.

"The Militia was rural in character, the Territorial Army is essentially urban; the one was manned largely by agricultural labourers and officered by country gentlemen; the other tends to be manned by artisans and clerks and officered by business men."

BREVET-COLONEL W E GREEN DFC TD
The Territorial in the Next War, 1939.

COURTESY OF IMPERIAL TOBACCO

and rifle clubs. Haldane was aware that attachment to military virtues did not necessarily run deep within British society and, therefore, his proposals were intended as a long-term programme for a 'nation in arms' that would be subtly different from that resulting from the conscript systems of the great continental powers. Few of the Liberals were much interested in this programme except in so far as it avoided the possibility of conscription, and what mattered to them was that the estimated annual cost of this new Territorial Force would only be £2.8 million rather than the £4.4 million the auxiliaries were currently costing.

In some respects, the Territorial Force represented the fulfilment of older schemes by Victorian volunteers who had advocated the establishment of a genuine reserve army. There would now be a definite term of four years' enlistment terminable on three months' notice (on penalty of a fine), with the possibility of re-engaging for a further four years. There would be an ability to enlist in the Regular Army at any time, the entire force would be under military law, and there would be between eight and 15 days' annual camp with pay. Embodiment for service anywhere in the United Kingdom would be possible in the event of imminent national danger or grave emergency and, in such circumstances, there was an obligation to be embodied for a year in addition to the normal term of engagement. There would be no role in aid of the civil power, however, although individuals might combine to use their military knowledge under the common law, and weapons might be used in defence of armouries.

RIGHT *The South Midland Brigade Company Army Service Corps en route to The Bustard on Salisbury Plain in 1910. Raised from the cyclist sections of the 1st Bucks and 1st Berks Rifle Volunteers, the ASC should have confined its other recruitment to Taplow and Burnham but its novelty attracted men from other areas. Captain Barron, the Officer Commanding, had served with the Volunteer Service Company in South Africa.*

COURTESY OF THE BUCKINGHAMSHIRE MILITARY
MUSEUMS TRUST.

Sussex Manoeuvres 1910 Head Quarters Signallers In Lewes

The War Office would now be placed firmly in control of finance, training and command but, by way of concession, all papers relating to the force would be referred to a new Director General of the Territorial Force before decision, and the Territorials would be represented on the Army Council by the Parliamentary Under-Secretary of State for War.

The Territorial Force would comprise 42 infantry brigades organised into 14 infantry divisions (East Anglian, East Lancashire, Highland, Home Counties, 1st London, 2nd London, Lowland, North Midland, Northumbrian, South Midland, Welsh, Wessex, West Lancashire, and West Riding) with full supporting services, including a Territorial Royal Field Artillery, and the designation of those parts of the Imperial Yeomanry not required for the expeditionary force—all but six regiments—as the mounted arm, organised into 14 cavalry brigades. There had been cyclist companies in some former volunteer battalions and, by 1914, each division had a designated cyclist battalion, such as the Huntingdonshire and Kent cyclist battalions. In the case of the artillery, each infantry division would have nine batteries armed with four 15-pounder field guns, two with four 5-inch howitzers and one with four 4.7-inch guns. The 14 cavalry brigades would also each have a battery of Territorial Royal Horse Artillery with four 15-pounder, quick-firing guns. In addition, since many of the existing artillery volunteer corps were garrison artillery manning fixed coastal defences, there would be 81 companies of Territorial Royal Garrison Artillery. The 182 horse and field batteries would all require supporting ammunition columns at brigade level, while there would also need to be a considerable expansion of existing engineer volunteer corps to provide sufficient Territorial Royal Engineers and Royal

ABOVE *These men are members of the 4th Battalion, Royal Sussex Regiment's Signalling Section on exercise near Lewes in 1910. Battalion is in the barn and the signallers are using an electric lamp and telescope.*
[IWM HU 94584]
COURTESY OF THE IMPERIAL WAR MUSEUM.

ABOVE *The 1st Queen's Westminster Rifles, complete with 1903 pattern bandolier equipment and the Long Lee Enfield, leaving Yaverland Camp in July 1909.*

COURTESY OF THE IMPERIAL WAR MUSEUM

COURTESY OF IMPERIAL TOBACCO

Signals companies, and the provision of entirely new Territorial Army Service Corps companies at divisional level. There would also be Territorial units of the Royal Army Medical Corps[2] and Army Veterinary Corps. There was even a short-lived London Balloon Company. One anomaly was that a single volunteer battalion—the 7th (Isle of Man) Volunteer Battalion of The King's (Liverpool Regiment)—survived to be attached to the West Lancashire Division.

In all, the Territorial establishment would amount to 314,094 officers and men. Taking to heart the criticism of the Norfolk Commission, Haldane intended that the Territorial Force should both support and also expand the Regular Army. As outlined in yet another memorandum in November 1906, they would garrison naval ports, replace regular garrisons and provide defence against hostile raids. But, after six months' training upon mobilisation, the Territorials would also be ready for overseas service.

It was here that the vision began to become blurred by political compromise. The militia opposed absorption into either the Regular Army or the Territorial Force, Haldane making three unsuccessful attempts over the course of the summer and autumn of 1906 to reach agreement with militia commanding officers. As a consequence, Haldane resolved to abolish the militia and create instead the Special Reserve, which was intended to supply drafts to fill gaps in regular battalions upon mobilisation. There was also opposition from many volunteers, particularly those commanding officers who believed that County Territorial Associations would encroach upon their independence and, at one

---

2. 42 Field Ambulances, 14 Mounted Brigade Field Ambulances, 23 General Hospitals and 2 Sanitary Companies

point, Haldane seriously considered removing the associations' proposed financial powers. He did remove his original idea that there should be an elective element on the associations found from county and borough councillors. Other volunteers opposed the six months' liability upon mobilisation, believing that this would be unacceptable to employers.

Given the size of the Liberal majority in the Commons, the result was hardly in doubt should Haldane win the support of his parliamentary colleagues. That, however, involved a further crucial compromise. In presenting the annual estimates to the House in February 1907, Haldane still spoke of the overseas role of the Territorial Force but, on the first reading of the Territorial and Reserve Forces Bill just eight days later, the entire emphasis was upon home defence in an attempt to forestall radical opposition. The Bill now provided only for the embodiment of the Territorials after the call-out of the Army Reserve and only for service in the United Kingdom unless units or individuals volunteered to serve abroad. Haldane was thus left with the hope that sufficient Territorials might be prepared to volunteer for overseas service if called upon to do so, the so-called Imperial Service Obligation being subsequently introduced in 1910 to give effect to this. Similarly, radical and Labour opposition led to Haldane dropping proposed financial assistance for cadets on the part of the associations though, subsequently, it was agreed that cadets could be supported

ABOVE *The London Rifle Brigade passing Brighton Pier at the end of their London to Brighton March, 18th April 1914, covering the 52½ miles in 14 hours and 23 minutes. They beat the previous record set by the London Scottish in 1911.*
[IWM HU 65446]
COURTESY OF THE IMPERIAL WAR MUSEUM.

LEFT *Buglers of the 4th Battalion, The Royal Berkshire Regiment sounding 'Warning for Parade' at The Bustard on Salisbury Plain, 1910.*

COURTESY OF THE RIFLES (BERKSHIRE AND WILTSHIRE) MUSEUM, SALISBURY.

ABOVE *The Territorial Force Efficiency Medal awarded to Sir Alexander Fleming [rim inscription below]. The Nobel prize-winning scientist served as a private soldier in the London Scottish from 1900-1914 and won many prizes for shooting and swimming. He served in the RAMC during the Great War, reaching the rank of Captain, and was awarded a Mention in Despatches.*

COURTESY OF THE NATIONAL WAR MUSEUM OF
SCOTLAND, EDINBURGH.

RIGHT *The machine-gun section of the 25th London (Cyclists) Battalion with its newly supplied private vehicles photographed at Oulton Broad, 1914. Like the Volunteers before them, Territorials routinely purchased equipment which was not otherwise officially available.*

[IWM HU 70701]

COURTESY OF THE IMPERIAL WAR MUSEUM.

"...most of our association are businessmen and are unable to understand why it takes ten weeks and upwards to reply."

GLOUCESTERSHIRE COUNTY ASSOCIATION
Comment on War Office responses to specific questions. September, 1910

by associations from non-public funds. With these compromises made, the Territorial and Reserve Forces Bill received its Royal Assent on 2nd August 1907 and the Territorial Force formally came into existence on 1st April 1908.

With the militia no longer to be incorporated into the Territorials, an establishment in excess of 314,000 looked highly ambitious given that the volunteers could muster 224,000 men at most if all willingly transferred. There were 55 regiments of yeomanry, some of recent origin since some new 'urban' regiments such as the Westminster Dragoons and the Surrey Yeomanry had been raised in only 1901. Familiarity with horses, however, was declining, as was the country's horse population under the impact of the motor car, and the yeomanry had rarely exceeded 10,000 men since the 1870s.

Haldane had hoped that his new Officers' Training Corps (OTC), which had emerged as part of the overall reform package in 1907 as a means of reorganising the university and public school cadet corps, could furnish at least 800 officers a year, but for the Special Reserve rather than the Territorials. Just reaching establishment would thus be a crucial test of the reforms. Haldane certainly energetically campaigned from the beginning, with an exhausting round of dinners and other gatherings to drum up support from among the existing auxiliaries. The volunteers were even offered the ability to enlist up until 30th June 1908 for just one year rather than four. By June 1908, however, only 144,620

ABOVE *A route march casualty from the 5th Battalion, Alexandra, Princess of Wales's Own (Yorkshire Regiment) is treated by the roadside, Scarborough 1909.*

COURTESY OF THE GREEN HOWARDS MUSEUM, RICHMOND.

officers and men had transferred to the new force and less than a third had enlisted for the full four years.

One problem was the additional commitment required compared to that in the volunteers or yeomanry—attendance at a minimum of 40 drill periods being required of recruits in the first year, as well as attendance on at least eight days of the full 15 days' camp, and 20 drill periods per annum thereafter. Moreover, compared to the four-year term of engagement, volunteers and yeoman had been able to resign on just 14 days' notice. It has been argued that the pecuniary rewards of camp pay, a boot allowance and discretionary payments of up to a shilling a day throughout the rest of the year that were now being offered actually deterred those who had previously served as a 'labour of love'. Haldane himself erred in expressing a preference for those under the age of 24, though the permitted age range of enlistment was from 17 to 35, thus discouraging many existing older volunteers and yeomen. Purely local factors were also at work. Employers in Birmingham, such as BSA, the Dunlop Rubber Company and Mitchell & Butler, actively supported the Territorials. W D & H O Wills in Bristol promised Territorials in their employ a full 21 days' annual leave on full pay to attend camp and fulfil other obligations, while Colman's of Norwich also promised support, albeit for no more than 100 of its employees. In London, the Alliance Assurance Company and the Westminster Fire Office attracted unwelcome publicity for insisting that their employees be Territorials, while one departmental head in the civil service invariably enquired of newcomers if they had a hobby: 'Failure to give a satisfactory reply elicited the advice that

the youngster should join the Civil Service Rifles'. But other employers were notably hostile, including both Hull and Bradford corporations and the North Eastern Railway Company. Smaller firms often could not be as generous as larger concerns in the matter of a second week's camp.

Where new units were being raised, such as Army Service Corps (ASC) companies, they sometimes proved more attractive than existing infantry units. Khaki was adopted as the standard service dress for the Territorial Force, with the wearing of full dress strictly controlled and often confined to officers. A 'walking-out' uniform could be provided for other ranks to wear on certain parades and when off duty, and it was suggested in some areas that the uniform of the Army Service Corps companies or Royal Field Artillery batteries was regarded as superior to that of some infantry units, especially where gold lace or gilt badges, previously unknown in the volunteers, were authorised. One gentleman in Twickenham hit on the idea of offering a pair of kid gloves to any lady who persuaded a man to join the Territorials, but it is not recorded how successful this proved.

Associations pressed for more rewards and, in 1912, separation allowances were extended to all married other ranks if they attended a full 15 days' camp while, in the following year, men at camp were relieved of the necessity of paying both their own and their employers' national insurance contributions. After a vigorous campaign by the Territorials, the government also announced in March 1914 that a £1 bounty would be paid to those attending the full 15 days' camp. Seaside camps proved popular but, fearing that these did not always

COURTESY OF IMPERIAL TOBACCO

"In Yeomanry Cavalry units a complication arises sometimes with regard to saddlery, for the men need to keep their saddlery on leaving camp in order to ride home. This privilege is however as a rule naturally restricted to good men who are known to be such as can be trusted to keep their saddlery in good order and not to use it on the farm or for other non-military purposes."

COLONEL G R CODRINGTON CB DSO OBE TD
The Territorial Army, 1938.

provide the best training opportunities, the Army Council restricted units in February 1912 to only one such camp every three years.

Unfortunately the Territorials came under sustained assault from a variety of quarters. The failure to reach the establishment targets generated criticism and, in turn, generated more disillusionment. Regulars had no more confidence in the Territorials than they had shown in their predecessors. The likely efficiency of the new Territorial artillery provoked a major controversy in which the army's former commander-in-chief, Field Marshal Earl Roberts, played a prominent role in denigrating Territorial achievements. The exercise was a cynical one, for Roberts had become president of the National Service League in November 1905. Initially, the League had not been overtly critical and had seen the force as a possible organisational basis for compulsion. Roberts, however, stepped up his attacks on the force immediately prior to introducing a bill for compulsory military service in the House of Lords. Thereafter, the League's growing frustration[3] resulted in increasing attacks, to which a number of serving regulars close to Roberts contributed.

OPPOSITE TOP & BELOW
The Duke of Lancaster's Own Yeomanry on Brigade Camp in Lowther Park, May 1912. Yeomanry brigade camps had been instituted in 1893 but then discontinued in 1898. The principle was revived in 1908.

COURTESY OF THE ROYAL ARTILLERY MUSEUM, WOOLWICH.

3. Five parliamentary bills were lost between 1908 and 1914.

"There is no country on the face of the earth to which the principle of citizen-soldiership is so well adapted as our own, for the freedom possessed by Britons is of so general and real a character as to cause the humblest in the land to feel deeply the necessity of preserving the safety and independence of the nation of which he is a part."

The Volunteer's Book of Facts, 1863.

In April 1913, the Army Council as a whole embraced the idea of some form of compulsory military service. Even some Territorials became sufficiently despondent to advocate conscription, ten associations calling for it by April of that year and 17 backing a thinly veiled recommendation for compulsion in the Council of County Territorial Associations in the January. Territorial MPs also often criticised the force, and the chairman of the County of London Association, Viscount Esher, penned one of the most damaging attacks in the columns of the pro-conscription *National Review* in September 1910.

Standards of training, attendance at camp, the high annual manpower wastage of 12.5 per cent and the attainment of musketry standards all came under close scrutiny, and younger regulars often resisted being posted as adjutants of Territorial units for fear that it would damage their careers. No proper mobilisation scheme existed for the Territorials as late as 1912 and, in any case, as might be expected, priority was accorded to the expeditionary force since regulars questioned the validity of expending scarce resources on formations that had no clear liability to overseas service. In 1914, Territorials had still not been armed with the most modern version of the Lee Enfield rifle, while the 15-pounders and 5-inch howitzers were now obsolescent. Finding sufficient horses for artillery batteries was also a constant difficulty since each required between 50 and 60 animals. In Hertfordshire, where there were three batteries and a brigade ammunition column, the association had managed to purchase 15 horses by April 1909, lodging them with farmers who were able to

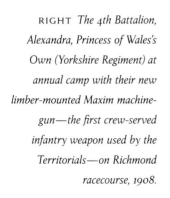

RIGHT *The 4th Battalion, Alexandra, Princess of Wales's Own (Yorkshire Regiment) at annual camp with their new limber-mounted Maxim machine-gun—the first crew-served infantry weapon used by the Territorials—on Richmond racecourse, 1908.*

COURTESY OF THE GREEN HOWARDS MUSEUM, RICHMOND.

ABOVE *Men of F Company, 4th Royal Sussex at musketry practice at Arundel, 31st August 1912. they are using the Long Lee Enfield.*
[IWM HU 94583]
COURTESY OF IMPERIAL WAR MUSEUM

use them except when required for training or camp. The remainder had to be hired or borrowed, mostly from breweries. As one local newspaper commented in 1912, the different horses taken to camp each year 'very much resented being used for war-like purposes and there was many a tough tussle between man and beast'. Doubts about the effectiveness of the Territorials thus resulted in the Committee of Imperial Defence recommending in October 1908 that two of the six regular infantry divisions of the expeditionary force be kept back in Britain upon mobilisation, a recommendation reiterated in April 1914.

The Trades Union Congress (TUC) made its hostility to the Territorials clear in 1909 and Haldane also miscalculated in presenting a virtual ultimatum to uniformed youth organisations in 1910 to affiliate to the associations or risk forfeiting War Office assistance. The Church Lads Brigade did affiliate, but the Boy Scouts resisted and the Boys Brigades rejected affiliation by an overwhelming 87 per cent to 13 per cent in January 1911. By 1913, the Territorial Cadet Force had some 41,000 members. More successful, however, was the augmentation after August 1909 of the new Territorial Force Nursing Service by locally organised Voluntary Aid Detachments (VADs), the latter having some 26,000 mostly female members. The VADs became part of the Territorial Technical Reserve but were not under actual Territorial control. It might be added that the aristocratic First Aid Nursing Yeomanry, formed in 1907, had no official connection either to the yeomanry or the Territorials. The Technical Reserve itself was intended to recruit specialists, such as electrical or railway engineers, who would not train in peacetime but would be available for service upon mobilisation.

ABOVE *The 4th Battalion,
Alexandra, Princess of Wales's
Own (Yorkshire Regiment) at
annual camp on Richmond
racecourse, 1908.*

COURTESY OF THE GREEN HOWARDS MUSEUM,
RICHMOND.

The VADs recruited best at a time of a renewed invasion scare in 1909 and this also boosted Territorial numbers as Haldane sought to lend particular emphasis to the home defence role. There was a conscious attempt to exploit the popularity of Guy du Maurier's topical invasion play, *An Englishman's Home*, which opened in London in January 1909. A recruiting booth was established in the theatre and, in all, 30,000 recruits were obtained in just seven weeks before the scare began to subside. Meeting criticism of the Lord Chamberlain, who had attempted to suppress satirical versions of the play, Haldane defended what he characterised as 'modern methods of recruiting'. He also sponsored a history of the county lieutenancies in the Revolutionary and Napoleonic Wars by Sir John Fortescue, which presented an unflattering image of the role of the auxiliaries in the past in a way calculated to enhance his own reforms. Even King Edward VII was pressed into service, a meeting of lords lieutenant at Buckingham Palace in October 1907 seeing the culmination of a campaign to secure the co-operation of the lieutenancy. On 19th June 1909, too, there was a glittering ceremony at Windsor at which the King presented Colours and Guidons to 108 Territorial units.

Neither invasion scare nor royal support, however, could achieve more than a temporary increase in strength or offset the criticism being directed at the force. It declined from 268,000 officers and men in June 1909 to 245,000 by September 1913. Even more significantly, such large numbers had chosen not to re-engage on the expiry of their original term of service in 1912-13 that 80 per cent of the force had less than four years' service experience. The social composition of the Territorials had become broader than in the volunteers of old as a result of the award of pay, with working class as well as 'cuff and collar' units, but the average age had also dropped and, in 1913, some 40,000 Territorials

"The first two or three years after 1908 it was found that men in the large cities—London in particular—found it difficult to do their annual course of musketry. Saturday afternoons were the only time available. Large numbers of those serving found it difficult, if not impossible, to get away from their work and travel twenty or thirty miles to the rifle ranges. The introduction of musketry on Sundays solved this problem. This innovation was the result of one Major General Commanding a Territorial Division being brave enough to risk the displeasure of those who thought it wicked to do anything of the sort on the Sabbath."

COLONEL EVELYN WOOD CB DSO OBE
Constitution of The Territorial Army, 1938.

were under the age of 19 at which service overseas became legally possible. A third of the force had failed the modest musketry requirement[4] of firing off 23 rounds in 1910 and, in 1912, only 155,000 men had camped for the full 15 days. Haldane's emphasis on home defence had also had its impact, with only 1,090 officers and 17,788 men—barely seven per cent—having taken the Imperial Service Obligation by September 1913. The force as a whole was 63,000 men short of establishment in January 1914.

Other aspects of the reforms had been similarly disappointing. Of the 18,000 young men who had passed through the OTCs by March 1912, only 238 had joined the Special Reserve. The Special Reserve itself had attracted about 60 per cent of the militia in 1908, but the momentum was not sustained and it was between 16 and 18 per cent short of its 80,300 establishment and 50 per cent short of subalterns. A Territorial Force Reserve was established in 1909 for men who had served at least one year in the Territorials, and a Veteran (later the National) Reserve in 1910. The latter was aimed at men aged over 45 years of age capable of filling Territorial vacancies upon mobilisation or performing sedentary duties. The National Reserve was relatively successful and had more than 190,000 men registered by January 1913, but the Territorial Force Reserve proved a failure. In 1910 the City of London Association recorded just five officers and five men in the Territorial Force Reserve. Two years later Derbyshire with one of the strongest contingents had but three officers and 23 men.

By 1914, therefore, the Territorials had fallen a long way short of Haldane's vision, fatally weakened by his political expediency. It did offer a far better organisational framework than the auxiliaries of old and was far stronger in its range of supporting services. Unfortunately, perceived weaknesses had undermined its status as a means of expanding the army. When war broke out in August 1914, the pre-war record was to determine its employment to such an extent as to result in a long and deep-felt sense of grievance.

❖

ABOVE *Bandmaster Smith of The Buckinghamshire Battalion succumbs to the fresh air and finds himself unwittingly 'incriminated' by fellow Territorials.*

COURTESY OF THE OXFORDSHIRE AND BUCKINGHAMSHIRE LIGHT INFANTRY MUSEUM, OXFORD.

4. A stark contrast to the more exacting Hythe Musketry Test of 15 aimed rounds per minute used as a minimum qualifying standard for Regular Army recruits at the time.

ABOVE *In the foreground officers and clergy wait for Edward VII to present Colours to the Territorial Force battalions at Windsor on 19th June 1909. The Colours to be presented are held by the Household Division. The 108 receiving units are formed up to the right, while their Ensigns wait to take the Colours from the King in the middle*

COURTESY OF THE ROYAL REGIMENT OF WALES MUSEUM, BRECON.

OPPOSITE *Recruiting poster for the 25th (County of London) (Cyclist) Battalion, The London Regiment, 1912. Many Pre-Great War recruiting posters played on the idea of the 'nobility' of uniformed service to make a direct appeal to the generation of recruits that had been raised on a literary diet of G A Henty and Rudyard Kipling.*

COURTESY OF THE IMPERIAL WAR MUSEUM

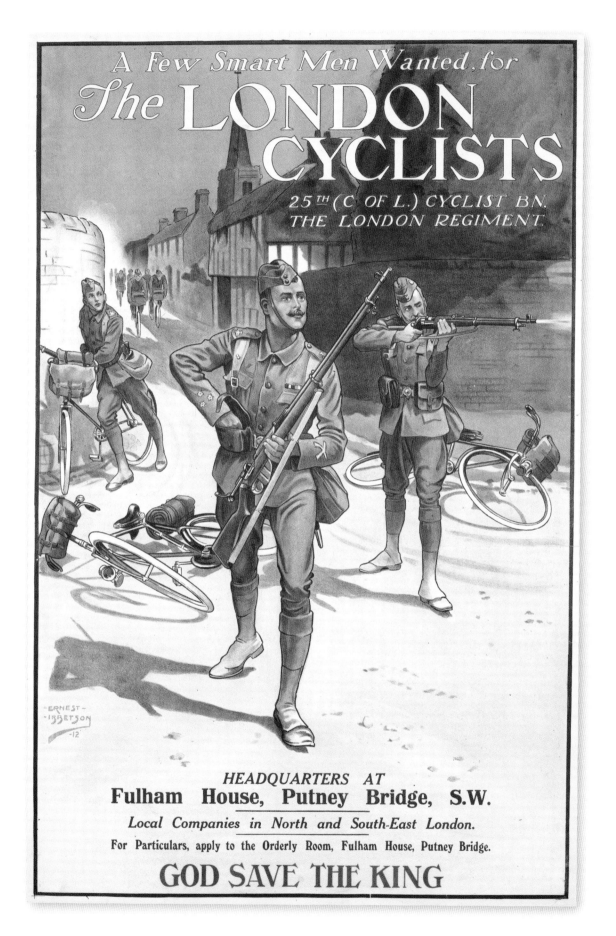

"Consequently the basis of our whole military fabric must be the development of the idea of a real national army, formed by the people and managed by specially organised local Associations."

R B HALDANE
1st February 1906.

COUNTY ASSOCIATIONS

OPPOSITE & BELOW

In contrast to more conceptually sophisticated continental posters, British inter-war recruiting posters generally stuck to the traditional illustrative approach. Some [opposite] tried to convey as much literal detail as possible whereas those aimed at the national audience [below] tended to focus on a single issue.

COURTESY OF THE IMPERIAL WAR MUSEUM

THE 94 (LATER 104) County Territorial Associations were intended to form a key element in forging the new unity of army and nation, building a 'military structure which shall have its foundations in the nation itself'. The title of County Association itself was consciously borrowed from that of the associations that had administered those counties under parliamentary control during the Civil War and ultimately formed the financial basis for the maintenance of the New Model Army. Centralised War Office command over the force would be firmly separated from local administration—the associations to be chaired by lords lieutenant and to include not only *ex officio* representatives from the Territorials but, in the original scheme, also to have elected members from local councils. Indeed, one of the proponents of the scheme, Viscount Esher, saw the associations breaking the former 'trade unionism' of the volunteer force by promoting regional groups with conflicting interests and competing aims. In administering and supplying the Territorial Force, however, the associations would also free commanding officers from crippling financial burdens and the responsibility of providing ranges, training grounds, uniforms and equipment.

As already indicated, the elective element was removed from the final legislation though not the financial powers and associations were able to assume control of drill halls and other premises formerly owned by volunteer or yeomanry units. Moreover, by way of offsetting the distrust of many former volunteer commanding officers regarding the powers of the associations, with the King's support, Haldane was successful in winning the support and participation of 'natural leaders' within the counties. A total of 115 peers had joined associations by November 1909, although a number of lords lieutenant were members of the National Service League, and the Duke of Bedford, a former militia colonel, resigned as lord lieutenant of Middlesex in opposition to the Territorial scheme. Former regulars or auxiliaries, appointed or elected by the associations, but approved by the Army Council, often filled the important role of secretary to the association.

The size of association membership and the number of sub-committees depended upon the number of units administered, the War Office determining the number and type of units on the basis of one Territorial per 112 of total population in a given area, according to the 1901 census. The Anglesey and Kinross Associations had only to provide a single infantry company each, but West Lancashire administered 44 units. Some associations, therefore, faced formidable challenges in recruitment, let alone subsequent retention.

One of the greatest challenges was that of the new City and County of London Associations. In the old volunteer force, the consolidation of individual rifle corps into battalions in the 1860s and 1870s had been followed, as elsewhere, by affiliation as volunteer battalions of regular regiments in 1881, but the London battalions had been divided between The Duke of Cambridge's Own (Middlesex Regiment), The Queen's (Royal West Surrey Regiment), The East Surrey Regiment, The Queen's Own (Royal West Kent Regiment), The Rifle Brigade, The Royal Fusiliers, and The King's Royal Rifle Corps. In 1908 there was a major reorganisation through the creation of the London Regiment, to which all the former volunteer battalions of the capital were now affiliated, eight battalions being administered by the City of London Association and 18 by the County of London Association. Rather similarly, a new Cambridgeshire Regiment (TF), and Hertfordshire Regiment (TF) emerged to be followed shortly by the 1st Battalion, The King's Shropshire Light Infantry being transformed into The Herefordshire Regiment (TF).

A Council (originally Federated Association) of County Territorial Associations comprising presidents, chairmen and vice chairmen of the CTAs, was also established on 4th June 1908. Led initially by the Earl of Dartmouth, it campaigned generally on behalf of the Territorials, as did the National Defence Association, which had emerged in May 1906.

"Many units advertise for recruits by means of posters and publicity in the local Press, while other units there are who would no more employ such methods than would a good Regular Regiment advertise for officers."

COLONEL G R CODRINGTON
CB DSO OBE TD
The Territorial Army, 1938.

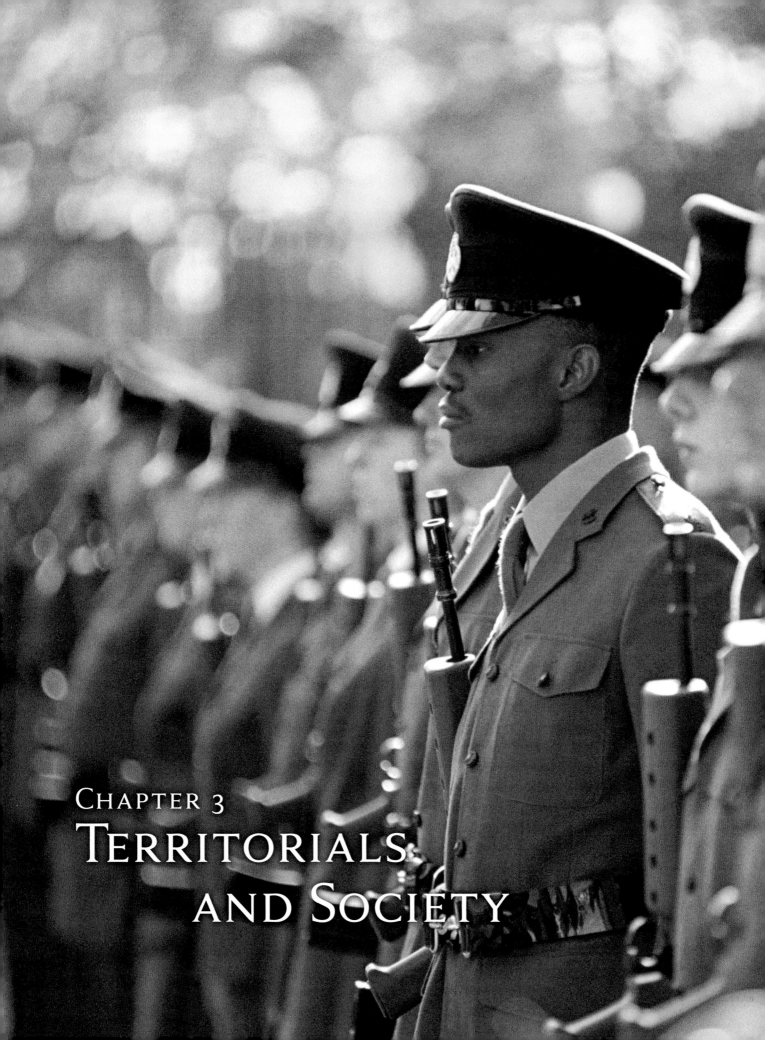

CHAPTER 3
TERRITORIALS AND SOCIETY

"In these days, most of the Regular battalions are concentrated in one or other of our great military training areas—Aldershot, Salisbury Plain, or Catterick. The Militia is no longer in existence, and there are large areas of the land that would be without any visible sign of the existence of the British Army were it not for the local Territorial Army unit."

LIEUTENANT COLONEL J K DUNLOP MC TD
The Problems and Responsibilities of the Territorial Army, 1935.

I T WAS ONCE commonplace to suggest that armies mirrored their parent societies. This always seemed to fit uneasily into the British context, and it is now more often suggested that there may be a concept of 'strategic culture' or of a specifically national 'way of warfare' in reconciling military means with political objectives. There are limitations to this concept since continuity may simply be a consequence of strategic environment and circumstances may change over time through adjustment of frontiers, demographic variations, technological advances or even for ideological reasons. Nonetheless, in the case of Britain there was long continuity of it being an island under fairly constant actual or perceived threat of invasion. The resulting primary reliance upon the Royal Navy underlined the peripheral nature of the army in society—the role primarily assigned it within an overseas empire being out of sight and usually out of mind. It was not unexpected, therefore, that given the preference for the voluntary spirit over continental-style conscription, there was a ready recourse to the auxiliary forces whenever danger most threatened and that enlistment into the Regular Army should so often reflect what Field Marshal Lord Nicholson once characterised as the 'compulsion of destitution'.

The auxiliary forces, therefore, were always likely to attract a far wider section of society than the Regular Army and to represent military values within local communities to a much greater extent than regulars. In the Victorian and Edwardian periods, Britain was far more conditioned to accept military activity than often supposed, but this was still militarism in mild form and Haldane's concept of a 'nation in arms' based on the Territorials fell well short of the kind of genuine mass citizen army that existed in Switzerland. Yet, just as in the case of the auxiliaries of old, the Territorials undeniably continued to project military values to society at least until the end of the Second World War. Their role in so doing was naturally circumscribed by the greater national mobilisation implied by wartime conscription in two world wars. Nonetheless, it can be noted that, in the highly successful wartime propaganda film *The Way Ahead* (1944), scripted by Eric Ambler and Peter Ustinov, the newly minted lieutenant forging the assorted group of conscripts into being part of a modern national army is based on a pre-war Territorial called Jim Perry—a former garage mechanic commissioned after seeing service in the 1940 campaign—even if David Niven seems an unlikely mechanic. The continuation of national service until the early 1960s was then viewed by some as a more suitable means of establishing essential links between army and society.

OPPOSITE *The Guard formed by The 5th (Volunteer) Battalion, The Royal Green Jackets listen to the address given by Lieutenant General Sir Christopher Wallace whilst exercising the Freedom of Aylesbury on 25th October 1998. The granting of the freedom of a city or town to a unit with the accompanying custom of marching through the streets with bands playing, bayonets fixed and colours flying dates from the earliest origins of the British army. It remains a significant link between a unit and its local community. The Freedom of Aylesbury was originally granted to The Oxfordshire and Buckinghamshire Light Infantry in October 1945.*

COURTESY OF THE MILITARY PICTURE LIBRARY

ABOVE *200 (Sussex Yeomanry)*
Field Regiment RA (V) being
granted the Freedom of Lewes on
26th June 1984.

COURTESY OF THE ROYAL ARTILLERY MUSEUM,
WOOLWICH.

As suggested by government announcements in recent years, there is still an expectation that Territorials can provide such a link between army and society as in the past, and there is some evidence that they do represent wider society. About 20 per cent of the TA is now female although this reflects a general trend. A survey in 2002 suggested that, whereas the top aspiration for boys aged 16 in the 1950s was to enter the forces but a military career held no attraction for girls, a service career in 2002 did not figure anywhere in the top ten aspirations for boys but at number three for girls. It would appear that there is greater ethnic representation in the TA than in the Regular Army. The Public Accounts Committee also found in 2007 that the number of Territorials commissioned from the ranks had increased from 37 per cent in 2003-2004 to 55 per cent in 2005-2006. Moreover, in a preface to the report of the All-Party Parliamentary Reserve Forces Group in 2007, Richard Holmes testified to the continuing social value of the TA as a 'superb leveller and mixer and a way of making men and women—so often left directionless by social pressures—both feel valued and become valuable'.

The change in the attitudes of young women towards military service, however, is a reminder that society and its mores are not constant. Other social changes have not been as beneficial. Since the end of national service, familiarity with the armed forces has declined sharply. Arguably, there has been

LEFT *The Busman's Holiday.*
Sergeant de Gay, a member of the
44th Royal Tank Regiment and
a bus driver by day, drives his
Mk 6 Cromwell Tank down his
normal Bristol town centre route
in May 1951.

COURTESY OF SOLDIER MAGAZINE.

more military visibility in the sense that, since the 1960s, the growth of media has made conflict seem more immediate. Yet, certainly until 2003, conflict either seemed distant (at least to those on the mainland in the case of Ulster) or less lethal from the emergence of new technologies producing a kind of sanitised 'virtual' war so far as western societies were concerned. In 1905 one well-known military writer, F N Maude, lamented on the reaction to losses in the South African War commenting that the British 'did not know that bloodshed was a usual consequence of the armed collision of combatants'. What Churchill called the 'blood test' was then experienced with a vengeance between 1914 and 1918, and the 'people's war' between 1939 and 1945 equally conditioned a new generation. Arguably, there has been a growing unwillingness in recent decades to accept casualties even of far less magnitude than in the past. Tempered by perceptions of political deceit, the reaction to contemporary conflicts, therefore, has been a less ready acceptance of the application of military force and a desire to avoid conflict altogether. That said, auxiliaries have always confronted a strain of anti-militarism. In the 1980s The Royal Monmouthshire Royal Engineers (Militia) constructed a footbridge to a church so reducing the congregation's journey from five miles to a few hundred yards but, as they had also moved plant on a Sunday, were denounced from the pulpit as 'Soldiers of

ABOVE *Lord Raglan, Lord Lieutenant of Monmouthshire and Honorary Colonel of the Regiment with Alderman Partridge, the Mayor of Monmouth, inspects the Royal Monmouthshire Regiment in 1953.*

COURTESY OF THE CASTLE AND REGIMENTAL MUSEUM, MONMOUTH.

OPPOSITE *Members of 101 Field Regiment, Royal Engineers line the route of George VI's funeral cortége, 1952.*

COURTESY OF THE ROYAL ENGINEERS MUSEUM, CHATHAM.

Satan'. As the unit historian puts it, 'so far as is known the congregation still use the footbridge'.

Allied to the declining perception of the value of military force, the 'footprint' of the TA within local society is now so reduced in comparison with the ubiquity of the presence before the Second World War and even into the early 1960s that it is difficult to envisage how it might truly recapture a central role in the projection of military values and the provision of the civil and social benefits still envisaged. In some respects, the auxiliaries always lacked status in the wider population beyond what might be regarded as the traditional county community, but when the public profile dwindles so does the ability of the Territorials to play the important role they once did within society. To many, indeed, despite the current high level of deployment, knowledge of the TA is confined to the television series, *All Quiet on the Preston Front*, first broadcast in 1994, and the character, Gareth in *The Office*, first broadcast in 2001. In some respects these are in a comic tradition that stretches back to Francis Beaumont's satirical treatment of the London Trained Bands in *The Knight of the Burning Pestle* (c. 1607), but in the 17th century and, indeed, arguably right up until the 1960s, few would have been unaware of the existence and purposes of the Territorials and their predecessors.

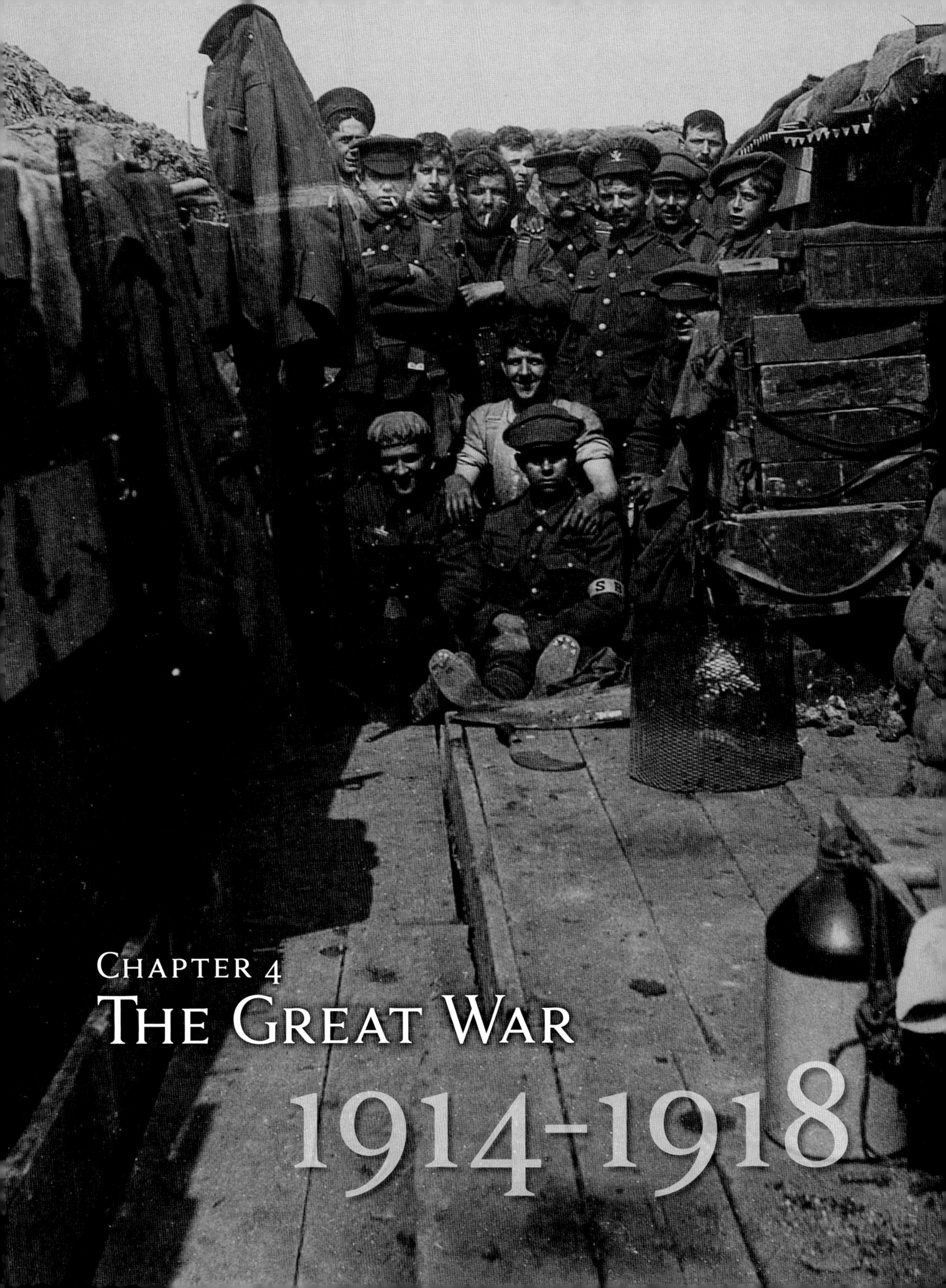

CHAPTER 4

THE GREAT WAR

1914-1918

"We arrive at Le Havre and got to wait until evening to get off. November 7th 1914—how excited we all are. Let's hope it don't finish before we get off the boat. If we can only step off the boat we can get a medal. Let's hope they don't send us straight back before we have a bit of a do."

C P HEARE
The War Diary of Private C P Heare, 2nd Monmouthshire Regiment TF.

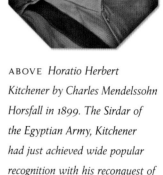

ABOVE *Horatio Herbert Kitchener by Charles Mendelssohn Horsfall in 1899. The Sirdar of the Egyptian Army, Kitchener had just achieved wide popular recognition with his reconquest of the Sudan in 1898.*

COURTESY OF THE NATIONAL PORTRAIT GALLERY, LONDON.

O F THOSE EUROPEANS who found themselves at war in August 1914, the British had the least time to react, the preoccupation with the Irish Home Rule crisis having ensured that most were unaware of the impending dangers of a European war until almost the end of July. The news of the German ultimatum to Belgium reached London on the morning of Bank Holiday Monday, 3rd August. Many Territorials had only just returned from summer camp when units received mobilisation orders on the early evening of 4th August 1914. Special service sections had gone directly from camp to precautionary period stations to guard vulnerable points. Britain's own ultimatum to Germany expired at 11 pm on 4th August. The first telegram to arrive at the War Office declaring completion of all of its units' mobilisation—from the Renfrewshire Association—was recorded at 2.30 pm on Wednesday 5th August. In theory, seven divisions were to be allocated to local defence and seven to a central force poised to resist any invasion.

Though the idea of overseas service for the Territorial Force had been somewhat stifled by Haldane's compromises, the assumption in 1914 was still that it would proceed overseas after six months and be the basis for any wartime expansion of the army. No one had reckoned on Field Marshal Earl Kitchener of Khartoum becoming Secretary of State for War.

Haldane had become Lord Chancellor in 1912 and his successor at the War Office, J E B Seely, had been forced to resign in March 1914. The Prime Minister, Asquith, temporarily took over the office himself but, on 5th August, Kitchener was appointed, this great imperial proconsul happening to be on home leave from his appointment as effective ruler of Egypt. The very morning he arrived at the War Office, Kitchener remarked that 'he could take no account of anything but regular soldiers' and preceded to ignore the machinery of the county associations by raising his 'New Army' directly through the War Office.

Undoubtedly, there was a measure of prejudice. Contemporaries recorded his distrust of 'amateur' soldiers from the time he had observed one of the French citizen armies during the Franco-Prussian War as well as his experience of sometimes undisciplined irregulars during the South African War. Pre-war Territorials could claim far more acquaintance with military knowledge than a new wartime recruit but Kitchener preferred them to those with 'a smattering of the wrong thing'. Knowing nothing of the home army, for he had served continuously overseas since the 1880s and nothing of Haldane's pre-war plans, Kitchener also referred to the Territorials as a 'town clerk's army', implying a

OPPOSITE *One of Captain Evelyn Byrde's haunting pictures of his men from the 2nd Battalion, The Monmouthshire Regiment taken near Le Bizet shortly before the Second Battle of Ypres in April 1915. Byrde sent the roll of film to his wife in Usk where it was placed in an envelope and forgotten.*

Byrde lost a leg to a German bullet on 8th May 1915 and was invalided home. A few weeks later, the Battalion lost nearly half its strength in a single action.

Sixty years later, Byrde's grandson discovered the undeveloped film at the back of a drawer.

COURTESY OF THE ROYAL REGIMENT OF WALES MUSEUM, BRECON.

COURTESY OF IMPERIAL TOBACCO

5TH (CUMBERLAND) BATTALION,
THE BORDER REGT. 1914

distrust for the potential independence of the associations and of possible local nepotism.

There was more, however, to his reasoning than simply bias. There were no actual plans for expansion through the associations and he appears to have believed that they would be swamped by rapid augmentation and the effort required to recruit and train men simultaneously. Of course, there was the problem of the Imperial Service Obligation and Kitchener also seems to have been reluctant to put pressure on married men to volunteer to go overseas. Many Territorials were either too young for overseas service at 19 years old because of the ability to enlist at 17, or considered too old. Many older men had family commitments. Most significantly, Kitchener was pre-occupied with the fear of invasion against which the Territorials remained the principal defence although, in line with the agreed pre-war policy, two regular divisions were initially kept back for home defence.

There is no doubt that the Imperial Service Obligation was a drawback. Only five complete units had volunteered for overseas service prior to 1914. On 10th August an invitation was extended to the remainder, with an announcement on 21st August that units where 80 per cent of men volunteered could complete to war establishment and others could combine to form service units. It was not at all uncommon to find units in which 80 or 90 per cent of men did indeed immediately volunteer but this was not always the case, hence a more

ABOVE *A daylight patrol from The London Irish leaving their trench to enter the town of Albert, 6 August 1918. Of the patrol of seven, one was killed and three were wounded.* [IWM Q 6898]

COURTESY OF THE IMPERIAL WAR MUSEUM.

realistic setting of the bar at 60 per cent on 31st August. In some instances, commanding officers made commitments on behalf of their men that proved wildly optimistic when individuals actually came to signify their assent on paper. In the 51st (Highland) Division, the initial figure of 75 per cent acceptance fell significantly, one entire brigade that had supposedly volunteered to a man subsequently opting for home service. There could be wide discrepancies even within a single unit. Fitness was also a factor with, for example, 15 per cent of the Montgomeryshire Yeomanry declared unfit for service and 20 per cent of

ABOVE *An extraordinarily rare action image of the 1/10th Battalion, The Kings (Liverpool Regiment) (Liverpool Scottish) under fire during their attack at Hooge on 16 June 1915. The scene was captured by Private F A Fyfe while he was lying wounded. A pre-war journalist, Fyfe had concealed a pocket camera he had previously used for police court work in his bandolier. Of 542 men who went into action, almost 400 became casualties.*

COURTESY OF THE IMPERIAL WAR MUSEUM, LONDON.

the 1/6th West Yorkshire. The 1/6th Royal Welsh Fusiliers were passed only after multiple teeth extractions and the promise of dentures that actually failed to materialise for another year. In the case of the 42nd (East Lancashire) Division, medical inspection upon mobilisation found it full of 'all sorts of crocks' and it was then filled with 'any loafer or corner boy they could find to make up the numbers'. Others took the view that they had enlisted only for home defence. The Chancellor of the Exchequer, David Lloyd George, subscribed to this view, urging his son not to be bullied into volunteering from his Welsh Territorial unit.

Having taken his decision to bypass the County Territorial Associations, Kitchener would not be swayed. On 13th August, however, he did indicate to Lord Esher that he would be prepared to use those Territorials who did take the Imperial Service Obligation. Some Territorials, therefore, began to go overseas in September 1914, but they were meant to release regulars from imperial garrisons rather than to afford the Territorials real opportunities for active service. Accordingly, the 42nd (East Lancashire) Division sailed for Egypt on 10th September with the 43rd (Wessex) Division sailing for India on 9th October. Two more divisions, the 44th (Home Counties) and 45th (2nd Wessex) also went to India in December 1914, while some individual units were despatched to Gibraltar, Malta, Cyprus and Aden. Those sent to such imperial garrisons came to feel that they had actually been penalised for early readiness, and those sent to India in particular were immensely dissatisfied with the conditions under which they were to continue to serve there until 1919 and even 1920 in violation of Kitchener's categorical promise that they would be brought back to serve in France and Flanders within a year. The outbreak of the Third Afghan War in May 1919 resulted in many Territorials awaiting transportation home being hastily sent north in ad hoc service units and, not perhaps surprisingly, those counties that had supplied men for these divisions faced notably greater recruiting difficulties when the force was reconstituted in 1920.

Kitchener was rather more reluctant to allow Territorials to 'fill the gap' on the Western Front in the winter of 1914-1915 before his 'New Army' was ready to take the field. Sheer necessity, however, forced his hand as the British Expeditionary Force (BEF)—already heavily dependent upon reservists to fill its ranks—suffered large casualties in the opening campaign. There had been an assumption that wastage would run at 40 per cent in the first six months of any major war. The actual rate was 63 per cent in the first three months. The first two units sent to France, the 1/14th London (London Scottish) and the 1/1st Queen's Own Oxfordshire Hussars, were despatched on 16th and 22nd

BELOW Major J B Gilliat leading his squadron of the 2/1st Hertfordshire Yeomanry during a mounted exercise on Hartham Common, Hertford in mid-1915. No second line yeomanry units went overseas, their function being to supply drafts to the first line units on active service.

COURTESY OF THE HERTFORDSHIRE YEOMANRY AND ARTILLERY HISTORICAL TRUST.

September 1914 respectively, ostensibly only as lines of communication troops. The 1/1st Northumberland Hussars, acting as divisional cavalry for the regular 7th Division, landed at Zeebrugge on 7th October. All were soon pressed into action and, with additional pressure from the BEF's commander-in-chief, Sir John French, seven yeomanry, three engineer, one medical and 22 infantry units had arrived by December 1914. As fears of invasion subsided, the total number of Territorial infantry battalions in France and Flanders rose to 48 in February 1915, with the first complete division—46th (North Midland)—arriving that same month. The first complete brigade to go into action was 149 (Northumberland) Brigade from 50th (Northumbrian) Division in April 1915. As it happened, some Territorials also saw action at home, with men of the Durham Royal Garrison Artillery manning the Heugh and Lighthouse 6-inch coastal batteries at West Hartlepool engaging cruisers of the German High Seas Fleet that shelled the town, together with Scarborough and Whitby, on 16th December 1914. The cruiser *Blücher* was hit; nine seamen were killed and two of its own 6-inch guns put out of action.

Some explanation is required of the nomenclature of individual Territorial units and of divisions. On 21st August 1914 it had been announced that, where 80 per cent of men in a unit had volunteered for imperial service, units could

ABOVE *'Over the Top' by John Nash is one of very few officially commissioned works depicting a specific action. It commemorates the 1/28th London (Artists' Rifles) involvement in an attack at Welsh Ridge, near Marcoing south west of Cambrai on 30th December, 1917. The unit was recalled from 'rest' in response to a German attack and hastily committed to action, suffering heavy casualties. This profoundly affected the artist, the simplicity and directness of the image visually complementing the accounts in the unit history and war diary.* [IWM ART 1656]

COURTESY OF THE IMPERIAL WAR MUSEUM.

THE LONDON EXPRESS ON FIRE. *Gretna Green Disaster, May 22nd, 1915*

COURTESY OF THE NATIONAL WAR MUSEUM OF SCOTLAND, EDINBURGH.

BELOW A corporal of the 1/5th London (1st London Rifle Brigade) clips a colleague's hair behind the lines at Ploegsteert, December 1914. [IWM HU 65452]

COURTESY OF THE IMPERIAL WAR MUSEUM

complete to war establishment and others combine to form service units. From 15th August associations were authorised to raise new units to replace those volunteering, enabling the 'first line' units to complete from 'second line' units and to return their own home service men to the second line. 'Third line' units were then raised in November 1914 as first line units went abroad. Third line units were then authorised for all remaining regiments which had not as yet gone abroad in March 1915, at which time responsibility for supplying reinforcing drafts to the first line passed from the second to the third line units. The nomenclature adopted in January 1915, therefore, was 1/1st, 2/1st and 3/1st for battalions in the respective lines. Thus, the original pre-war 5th Battalion, The Hampshire Regiment became the 1/5th Battalion, its second line unit the 2/5th Battalion, The Hampshire Regiment and its third line unit the 3/5th Battalion, The Hampshire Regiment. In May 1915, too, the original 'Territorial' designations of higher formations were also discontinued so that the pre-war East Lancashire Division became 42nd (East Lancashire) Division and its pre-war Lancashire Fusiliers, East Lancashire and Manchester Brigades the 125, 126 and 127 Brigades respectively. The original 14 Territorial divisions were numbered 42nd to 44th and 46th to 56th, with divisions formed from second line units being numbered 45th and 57th to 69th, with a 74th (Yeomanry) Division—the 'Broken Spur' Division—later being formed in Egypt from dismounted yeomanry. The Territorials also eventually formed five mounted divisions.

In numerical terms, the eventual contribution of the Territorial Force to the war effort was considerable, with 318 battalions and 23 infantry divisions serving overseas. As already related, three served in India[1]. Eight served in the Mediterranean and the Middle East[2]. Four of these divisions later transferred to France[3]. Ten divisions served solely on the Western Front[4]. One division (59th) served in Ireland before transferring to the Western Front. One division, (48th) served on the Western Front and then subsequently in Italy, while another (60th) also served on the Western Front before serving in Salonika and Egypt. This

1. 43rd, 44th and 45th Divisions.
2. 42nd, 46th, 52nd, 53rd, 54th, 74th, 2nd Mounted, and Yeomanry Mounted Divisions.
3. 42nd, 46th, 52nd and 74th Divisions.
4. 47th, 49th, 50th, 51st, 55th, 56th, 57th, 58th, 60th, 61st, and 66th Divisions.

LEFT *Second Lieutenant John B L Hill, the future father-in-law of Field Marshal Sir John Chapple, with No 1 Troop of the 1st County of London Yeomanry at Aylsham in Norfolk, circa 1915.*

COURTESY OF SIR JOHN CHAPPLE.

BELOW *Men of the York & Lancaster Regiment prepare to conduct a trench raid near Arras in 1918. Trench raids were highly controversial, costing many lives yet arguably maintained the 'offensive spirit', and often provided valuable field intelligence.*

COURTESY OF THE IMPERIAL WAR MUSEUM.

compared favourably to the 404 battalions and 30 divisions of the 'New Army' that served overseas. By 1918, moreover, 692 Territorial battalions had existed compared to 267 regular or reserve and 557 New Army service battalions. When voluntary enlistment in the Territorial Force ended in December 1915, some 725,842 men had enlisted since August 1914, or approximately half the number enlisted in Kitchener's New Army during the same period.

Second line units were raided for men when first line units went overseas and, with insufficient men available to send to second line units from the third line, efficiency suffered. Second line units were soon being characterised as

ABOVE & INSET *Men of the 1/4th Battalion, The Suffolk Regiment at Neuve Chapelle, 1915. The offensive at Neuve Chapelle in March 1915 marked the British Army's first attempt to break through the German lines on the Western Front. Innovations, including aerial reconnaissance and a short opening barrage, achieved a breakthrough to a depth of 1,000 yards but experimental telephone communications broke down and exploitation opportunities were missed. The offensive was closed down after two days, having cost over 12,000 casualties.*

COURTESY OF THE GANZONI FAMILY/SUFFOLK REGIMENT MUSEUM.

'sucked oranges'. To give one example, when the 178 (2nd Notts and Derby) Brigade of 59th (2nd North Midland) Division was sent to Ireland during the Easter Rising in April 1916, so many men had been sent as drafts to France that the majority of those remaining had only three months' training and had not yet fired a full-bore rifle. In August 1916 the brigade was then again stripped of men for France, with one commanding officer describing this as 'heartbreaking as it meant masses of new recruits, beginning training all over again and many months before the Brigade would be fit for service'. Whereas it had taken just eight months to prepare most first line units for active service, the average was 27 months for second line units. The latter frequently lacked equipment, the supposed 'Emergency Battery' formed by 67th Division in September 1915, for example, possessing no rifles and no ammunition for its 15-pounders. The 2/2nd (Welsh) Heavy Brigade, RFA only managed to acquire guns by purloining those of the 2/1st Heavy Brigade when railway officials mistakenly attached a wagon to the wrong train. County Territorial Associations could and should have been used more constructively, but the War Office showed scant sympathy for the special legislative difficulties

ABOVE *Sergeant F W Giles of the 1/4th Battalion, The Royal Berkshire Regiment in the line at Hébuterne in 1915, engaged in sniping—a task he excelled at and could be found doing even when off-duty.*

COURTESY OF THE RIFLES (BERKSHIRE AND WILTSHIRE) MUSEUM, SALISBURY.

LEFT *The men of the 1/6th Battalion South Staffordshire Regiment (46th Division) are issued winter clothing before entraining for the front line in March 1915.* [IWM Q 60526]

COURTESY OF THE IMPERIAL WAR MUSEUM.

ABOVE *The 1/1st Buckinghamshire Battalion attacking Poziéres on the Somme, 22 July 1916,
painted by W B Wollen. Participating in an operation mounted by 48th Division and the 1st
Australian Division, the battalion successfully secured the village—situated on a low but
commanding ridge and the subject of four earlier unsuccessful attacks—on the following day at
the cost of 242 casualties.*

COURTESY OF THE NATIONAL ARMY MUSEUM.

COURTESY OF IMPERIAL TOBACCO

that complicated the use of Territorials and the grievances that arose as a result.

The challenge of expanding a small Regular Army to meet the exigencies of a modern 'total' war would have presented enormous difficulties in any case. It was perhaps understandable, therefore, if the War Office found aspects of existing Territorial legislation irksome. Apart from the question of the Imperial Service Obligation, there was the ability of men to continue to enlist for home service only until March 1915. Indeed, there were enough home service Territorials to form 68 Provisional (later Home Service) Battalions for anti-invasion duties in April 1915 while still leaving more than 80,000 home servicemen on the rolls. The provision was finally eradicated by the first of the Military Service Acts which introduced conscription in January 1916, with those under the age of 41 being obliged to take the Imperial Service Obligation or resign and become liable to conscription. The same legislation also removed the ability of pre-war Territorials to seek their discharge at the end of four years plus the automatic one year extension imposed by the war. More than 159,000 men would have been eligible for such a discharge between 1914 and 1917. Those whose services were compulsorily retained were offered a furlough where possible and a

LEFT *The five Liebermann brothers [LR: William, Harry, Charlie, Leonard and Fred] who served together during the Great War in the 4th Battalion, The Oxfordshire and Buckinghamshire Light Infantry. All survived the war and three (William, Charlie and Leonard), together with two younger cousins, landed in France with the BEF in 1940.*

COURTESY OF
THE OXFORDSHIRE AND BUCKINGHAMSHIRE
LIGHT INFANTRY MUSEUM, OXFORD.

ABOVE *The 2/4th Hampshire Regiment in Baluchistan. Part of the 45th (2nd Wessex) Division, the battalion found itself despatched to India in December 1914 to enable regular battalions to be brought back for service on the Western Front. Indian service, which lasted until 1920 in some cases, proved highly unpopular..*

COURTESY OF THE ROYAL HAMPSHIRE REGIMENT
MUSEUM, WINCHESTER.

OPPOSITE *'Sentry-go'; The 1/4th Battalion, The Royal Berkshire Regiment near Hébuterne, 1915.*

COURTESY OF THE RIFLES (BERKSHIRE AND
WILTSHIRE) MUSEUM, SALISBURY.

bounty, but the War Office refused to bring back retained time-expired men from India to complete service at home.

A still greater difficulty was that the 1907 legislation had made it illegal to transfer Territorials between units, or to amalgamate or disband units. It was clearly stated on the form Territorials signed in accepting overseas service that an individual would remain with his own unit. As casualties began to exceed all expectations, such a guarantee became increasingly problematic. 'Exceptional' measures were taken in June 1915 to take trained men from second line units to supply drafts to the first line instead of drafts for both coming from the third line depots. The War Office briefly attempted to issue a new form but, with the realisation that this was meeting resistance, clauses were then included in the second Military Service Act of May 1916 to authorise transfers. In any case, as already indicated, direct recruiting into the Territorial Force had been suspended in December 1915 except for a handful of specialist units.

Increasingly, units protested that the special character of the Territorial Force was being jeopardised by haphazard drafting. To some extent, the character of units was something of a fiction in many instances. The novelist Patrick MacGill, for example, claimed he and the commanding officer were the only genuine Irishmen in the 1/18th London (London Irish). The original character of a unit would also change as men went home time-expired or through acceptance for commissions or became sick, let alone the casualty rate. The latter, of course, was the factor most likely to determine a unit's survival as a recognised entity. In the case of the 1/7th Royal Scots, the process began even before they left Britain, with 227 officers and men being killed and 246 injured in the worst-ever British railway accident near Gretna Green in May 1915 while they were en route to embark for Egypt. Much depended upon how soon a unit proceeded on active service and, once there, on the relative periods spent in quiet or active sectors or on actual operations. Charles Carrington, who served with 1/5th Royal Warwicks in 143 Brigade, recorded that in 1916 he spent only 65 days in the front line, although 36 days were spent in close support and 120 in reserve. A further 73 days were spent 'at rest' and 72 on leave, while sick, travelling or attending schools of instruction. The 48th Division, of which 143

TOP *The charge of 1/1st The Queen's Own Dorset Yeomanry against Senussi tribesmen and their Turkish officers at Agagia in the Libyan Desert, 26th February 1916, as painted by Lady Butler. The Senussi broke and their leader, Gaafar, surrendered to Lieutenant J H Blaksley. All the regiment's officers were exact portraits but Lady Butler remarked that their own mothers would not recognise them 'in the heat, dust and excitement of a charge'.*

COURTESY OF DORSET COUNTY COUNCIL/THE KEEP
MILITARY MUSEUM, DORCHESTER.

ABOVE *The 1/4th Battalion, The Hampshire Regiment entering Baghdad, 13th March 1917. Having reorganised the Mesopotamia Expeditionary Force, General Sir Stanley Maude had begun his advance on Baghdad in December 1916, the city falling just two days before the entry of the Hampshires. General Maude died nine months later of cholera contracted from tainted milk.*

COURTESY OF THE ROYAL HAMPSHIRE REGIMENT MUSEUM, WINCHESTER.

Brigade was part, occupied a relatively quiet sector of the line around Hébuterne for 12 months between July 1915 and July 1916. Accounts of the period such as that by Frederick Grisewood, later a well-known broadcaster, who served with 1/4th Oxfordshire and Buckinghamshire Light Infantry, indicate what has been termed 'live and let live'. From Hébuterne, however, the division moved to the Somme and only 25 men of the 1/4th Oxford and Bucks served continuously with the battalion from 1914 through to the armistice—16 of them in the signals or transport sections and just nine riflemen. In the case of 56th Division, its wartime service in France and Flanders comprised 330 days at rest, 195 days in quiet sectors, 385 days in active sectors and only 100 days of actual active operations. Indeed, generally, the semi-mobile warfare of 1914 and 1918 cost far more casualties than the static warfare of 1915-17 even taking into account the great offensives of the Somme and Third Ypres.

Even static trench warfare, of course, meant a steady toll of losses, and change naturally accelerated with the heavy losses on the Somme in the summer and autumn of 1916. On 1st July 1916, of the 13 divisions committed by the Fourth Army, none were Territorial but 48th and 49th Divisions were both in immediate reserve. Both Third Army divisions committed, however, were Territorials, namely the 46th and 56th Divisions. Moreover, through the course of the battle as a whole, Territorial units suffered more than 83,000 casualties.

ABOVE *Breakfast in the front line at Armentiéres, 1915. Taken from the album of Lieutenant N B N Goode, 1/4th Battalion, Northumberland Fusiliers.*

COURTESY OF THE NORTHUMBERLAND FUSILIERS MUSEUM, ALNWICK.

BELOW *The 2/8th Battalion London Regiment (Post Office Rifles) at bayonet practice using staves and sheathed bayonets at Cuckfield, Sussex, May 1915.*
[IWM Q 53715]

COURTESY OF THE IMPERIAL WAR MUSEUM

ABOVE *[l-r] Privates Martinnant,
Latham, Morton, Baldwin, Furrell,
Smith, Trendle and Moran of
the 1/5th London (London Rifle
Brigade) at Ploegsteert, 1915.*
[IWM HU 65493]

COURTESY OF THE IMPERIAL WAR MUSEUM.

PLAYER'S CIGARETTES

4TH/5TH BN., THE BLACK WATCH
(ROYAL HIGHLANDERS), 1917

COURTESY OF IMPERIAL TOBACCO

Drafts, of which the 1/5th London (London Rifle Brigade) received 11 between July and October 1916, might fortuitously maintain the Territorial element or they might not. At one point during the Somme campaign, the 1/16th London (Queen's Westminster's) were said to have men from 17 different regiments, included kilted units, serving in it. For the 1/6th West Yorkshire, the Somme 'smashed up a good deal of this "Territorial" influence' so that what was 'narrow and local' was said to have 'died' there. The distinguished military historian, C R M F Cruttwell, who served in the 1/4th Royal Berkshires, also noted that, by the end of 1916, the battalion had 'lost its exclusive Berkshire character which, at the beginning of the war, had been its unique possession'. In some cases, units were able to retain a degree of pre-war identity longer, this certainly applying to units in Lancashire where at least a regional identity was assisted by the structure of Western Command, confined to Lancashire, Cumberland and Westmoreland, and the influence of the Earl of Derby, the 'King of Lancashire', who became Secretary of State for War in 1916.

Units also faced the possibility of being amalgamated or disbanded. Temporary amalgamations followed heavy losses in early 1915 in the case of the 1/1st, 2/1st and 3/1st Monmouthshire Regiment. In 1916, however, amalgamations became more permanent and, in 1918, second line units took the brunt of the reductions consequent upon a reorganisation of the BEF. The 50th (Northumbrian) Division was reduced to cadre and then reconstituted without a single original unit and only one Territorial battalion, while the 53rd (Welsh)

and 60th (2/2nd London) Divisions, serving in Palestine, were completely reorganised by despatching all but one battalion of each brigade to France and replacing them with Indian battalions. During the war, two other Territorial divisions were reduced and reconstituted, a further four reconstituted, and two broken up. Regular and New Army formations equally faced drafting and amalgamations, but the Territorials felt it keenest because it appeared that the military authorities had a patronising and even hostile attitude towards them. London units particularly figured in the criticism of the drafting system, which reached a crescendo in the House of Commons in March and April 1916 even before the onset of the heaviest casualties, it being said that the military authorities intended the 'gradual extinction' of the Territorials.

Haldane had promised that Territorials would receive higher command appointments but, in 1914, no Territorial commanded a division and only three

ABOVE *The 1/7th Battalion of The Manchester Regiment practice on a range at the 47th Division's camp at Suez in Egypt, circa June 1916.* [IWM HU 63571]

COURTESY OF THE IMPERIAL WAR MUSEUM

LEFT *The 1/1st Queen's Own West Kent Yeomanry on Gallipoli, possible at Fusilier Bluff Cove, Cape Helles. The yeomanry regiments in the 2nd Mounted Division were compelled to leave their horses in Egypt when ordered to the Gallipoli peninsula. Subsequently, they were reunited with their mounts for the campaign against the Senussi tribe, allies of the Turks, in the Libyan Desert.* [IWM Q 98298]

COURTESY OF THE IMPERIAL WAR MUSEUM

ABOVE *Second Lieutenant William Wedgwood Benn, Liberal* MP *for the Tower Hamlets [left], serving with the 1/1st County of London Yeomanry (Middlesex, Duke of Cambridge's Hussars), on the quay at Alexandria in 1915 about to taste the hardtack biscuits supplied for the day's rations on landing.* [IWM Q 13217]

COURTESY OF THE IMPERIAL WAR MUSEUM.

commanded brigades. In February 1917 it was stated in the House of Commons that only 18 Territorials had risen above the rank of lieutenant colonel at the front and three at home, though it was claimed in mitigation that Territorials and New Army candidates together now filled more than a third of all places on staff courses. In January 1918 Lord Derby claimed that four Territorials had now commanded divisions and 52 had commanded brigades, while 61 Territorials below the rank of Lieutenant in 1914 had risen to that of Lieutenant Colonel. What Derby did not care to say was that most of the higher commands had been only temporary, and at home, and it was admitted in the following month that only ten Territorials currently commanded brigades. The situation was exacerbated by the pre-war convention that Territorials ranked junior in precedence to regulars of the same rank, which left many older and experienced Territorials subordinate to younger regulars and, worse, temporary wartime officers of the New Army. Territorials also got less pay and allowances, and some accounts indicate that some removed the 'T's from their tunics as they felt it a badge of inferiority.

COURTESY OF IMPERIAL TOBACCO

BELOW *An officer of 1/7th Battalion, The Manchester Regiment carries out a routine rifle inspection in Gallipoli.*

COURTESY OF THE IMPERIAL WAR MUSEUM.

Few regulars appear to have expected much from the Territorials. The Army Council had concluded before the war that a notional calculation that two Territorial divisions was equal to one regular division would not be attained even after the six months' continuous training period envisaged before deployment overseas. One regular officer was also heard to complain that Territorials were too intelligent and had too much imagination to make good soldiers. However, those such as the first Commander-in-Chief of the BEF, Field Marshal Sir John French, who had been adjutants to the auxiliaries in the past, were more sympathetic. French, indeed, was highly complimentary of the Territorial performance on the Western Front and even contemplated using 50 Territorial battalions in a projected amphibious assault on Zeebrugge. French's successor, Sir Douglas Haig, also favoured the early employment of the Territorials. Less than objective reports, however, from both France and India in December 1914 and April 1915 respectively concluded that Territorials knew little of interior economy

COURTESY OF IMPERIAL TOBACCO

and, in France, had been slow to move. It was widely believed that they had fewer recuperative powers than regulars and one post-war committee concluded they were better in static defence than attack. It must be borne in mind, however, that Territorials remained poorly equipped, arriving in France even into 1915 with obsolete rifles and artillery. Nonetheless, Territorials showed no lack of courage. Attention has often been drawn to Captain W P Nevill sending his company of the 8th East Surreys, a New Army battalion, over the top at the Somme on 1st July 1916 by kicking footballs towards the German lines, but the Territorials had done it first. At Loos on 25th September 1915 members of the football club within 1/18th London (London Irish) had done exactly the same and broken into the German front line.

Regulars also complained of what they regarded as the lax discipline of the Territorials, though this was primarily a failure to understand the traditional ethos of the amateur soldier, the recurrent imagery in so many wartime Territorial memoirs being that of a 'family' or 'club' relying on a strong sense of self-discipline and the free intercourse of social equals. The discipline of the 1/5th London (London Rifle Brigade), for example, was characterised as 'exceptional' but 'incomprehensible to a critical outsider'. This is not to imply that there were not problems, the very closeness of some units causing difficulty for newcomers. Moreover, there was sometimes rivalry between

RIGHT *A working party from one of the Territorial battalions of the York & Lancaster Regiment moving defence stores up to the trenches held by the 62nd Division in the Oppy-Gavrelle Sector, January 1918.*
[IWM Q 8436]

COURTESY OF THE IMPERIAL WAR MUSEUM

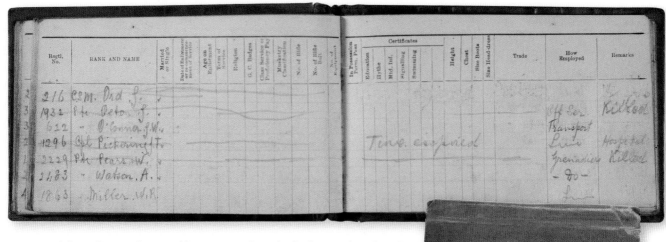

personnel from first and second line units when drafted to each other. It is also a misapprehension to suppose that all Territorials were primarily 'class' corps. Thus, the 1/8th Royal Scots and 1/8th Scottish Rifles were described as 'slum battalions' while troopers of the 1/2nd County of London Yeomanry (Westminster Dragoons) found their journey to Egypt aboard the same vessel as the men of the 1/9th Manchesters particularly trying from the latter's inclinations to spit and swear. Indeed, the Manchesters were 'the commonest lot of men' the yeomen had ever encountered. Nonetheless, it would appear that Territorial units were far less affected by military crime than regulars or New Army formations, only ten Territorials being numbered among the 312 men executed under the provisions of the Army Act between August 1914 and March 1920. Ironically, too, the Territorials provided large numbers of candidates for wartime commissions in regular and New Army units. French asked the 1/28th London (Artists' Rifles) to provide 50 subalterns—the 'Suicide Club'—for immediate employment with the regular 7th Division in November 1914 and, subsequently, the Artists had 10,256 men commissioned. The Inns of Court OTC, also nominally a Territorial unit, found more than 11,000 officers for the wartime army. Other OTCs similarly produced officers throughout the war, with 4,218 men being commissioned from the University of London OTC.

Faced with what appeared to be an intention on the part of the authorities to destroy the character of the Territorial Force, their representatives fought back. London units were especially prominent in criticising the drafting system, with concerns surfacing in the House of Commons as early as November 1914 and reaching a climax in the spring of 1916. Scottish associations also attempted to fight battlefield amalgamations that same spring but received little support from those yet to experience the problem. The ability of the associations to exercise statutory powers, however, was being steadily eroded. They had found themselves in direct competition with the War Office and those corporations, firms and individuals trying to secure equipment for units of the New Army— the duplication of effort damaging to both the Territorials and the New Army.

ABOVE *An extract from the Roll Book of D Company, 1/6th Battalion, Northumberland Fusiliers. The hastily scribbled notes reveal the fates of three men; Private James Octon: killed 11th September 1916; Private William Pears: killed 11th April 1916; and a Corporal J Pickering who—being listed as 'time expired'—appears to have made it back to 'Blighty'.*

COURTESY OF THE NORTHUMBERLAND FUSILIERS MUSEUM, ALNWICK.

ABOVE *Two men from the*
2/10th Londons relax beside a
German machine-gun captured
by their battalion near Sailly
Laurette during the Battle of
Amiens, 8th August 1918.
[IWM Q 6911]

COURTESY OF THE IMPERIAL WAR MUSEUM.

Expenditure in such circumstances was much greater than anticipated. East Lancashire, for example, was administering 49,000 men after seven months when its pre-war establishment had been just 18,000. It had spent more than £37,000 on uniforms and equipment alone in the first month of war. By April 1915 the West Riding Association had spent almost £350,000. There were also increasing amounts of wartime separation allowances to pay, Worcestershire supporting more than 14,000 wives and children, Warwickshire some 16,000, East Lancashire more than 60,000 and the County of London more than 78,000. The Territorial Cadet Force also continued to be administered by associations, a system of capitation grants being instituted. Around 2,000 cadet units existed by 1918.

Initially, Kitchener had requested co-operation from the associations and, on 7th September 1914, the Midleton Committee also turned to the associations for help in housing and training recruits of the New Army. Seven days later, the committee was dismissed and the invitations to the associations rescinded. Associations were again called upon for help in December 1914, and Cambridgeshire and the Isle of Ely, Denbighshire and the East Riding actually raised 11 units for the New Army. With the cessation of direct recruiting for the Territorials in December 1915, however, associations were further reduced in significance. Responsibility for clothing their units was taken away, although they remained distribution agents. In early 1916 control was also lost over Territorial ASC units and over the National Reserve, the latter now incorporated into the Royal Defence Corps. Alarmed by the implications, association representatives met Derby in January 1917. He denied further powers would be curtailed without parliamentary sanction but, in March 1917, the War Office centralised depots, closing many Territorial ones and, later in the year, closed Territorial record offices. In September 1917 the Council of County Territorial Associations met for the first time in three years to protest against the 'whittling away' of their responsibilities and the 'gradual extinction' of the force amid rumours that even payment of separation allowances would now be taken from them. Another delegation met Derby in October 1917 with the result that the payment of separation allowances remained with associations and remaining depots were given a stay of execution. Derby's hint, however, of a major role in demobilisation was not forthcoming and the only additional wartime role was the highly unpopular administration of a new manifestation of the volunteer spirit in the form of the revived volunteer force or Volunteer Training Corps (VTC).

Originating as a private response to the invasion scare in the autumn of 1914, the VTC was officially recognised in November 1914, with new volunteer legislation in 1916 placing the force on a more formal footing. The Director

ABOVE *Sergeant Turland of the Northamptonshire Yeomanry watering his horse, Italy, December 1918.*
[IWM Q 26142]

LEFT *A Squadron of the 1/1st Northamptonshire Yeomanry, commanded by Captain J C Lowther, crosses the river Piave while in patrol in northern Italy, December 1918.* [IWM Q 26139]

COURTESY OF THE IMPERIAL WAR MUSEUM

ABOVE *The 1/4th Suffolks at
Neuve Chapelle, March 1915.*

COURTESY OF COLCHESTER AND IPSWICH MUSEUM
SERVICE

General of the Territorial Force became the Director General of the Territorial and Volunteer Force. The associations, however, were reluctant to see any role in administration as a substitute for the erosion of their statutory powers. Indeed, the County of London Association protested in November 1917 that the new volunteer force 'had no history, no continuity, and consists of those too old or too young for active service, or of exempted men who for the most part, at any rate, are not the keenest fighting men'. The strictures on the military value of the new volunteers were widely shared among the associations, Hampshire denouncing them as a 'colourable substitute' for Territorials. Traditional ridicule of auxiliaries resurfaced with the 'GR' armband worn by the VTC prior to the issue of full uniform bringing forth such epithets as 'George's Wrecks', 'Grandpapa's Regiment' and 'Genuine Relics'.

In fact, despite many difficulties, the VTC did contribute special service companies for coastal defence duties in 1918 when the German spring offensives on the Western Front revived fears of possible invasion. They also released trained soldiers from guarding prisoners, bridges, factories and aerodromes; dug defences around London; helped gather the harvest and manned anti-aircraft defences. They were placed in suspended animation with little thanks for their efforts in February 1919. It was a familiar story for auxiliaries. Indeed, Territorial associations, which had themselves contributed to the volunteers' difficulties, had reason to believe that their efforts had been equally ignored.

Between 1914 and 1920 Territorial units had sustained 577,016 casualties in all theatres. There had been notable achievements, not least the crucial role in 'filling the gap' in 1914-15. Disembodiment, however, which began in December 1918, was marked by the Army Council resolving not to issue any special decoration to those who had taken the Imperial Service Obligation in 1914. Moreover, the Territorials did not fit easily into War Office perceptions of the post-war military situation and the requirements of imperial defence. To some, indeed, the role of the Territorials appeared superfluous.

COURTESY OF IMPERIAL TOBACCO

BELOW *The 1/8th Battalion, The King's (Liverpool Regiment) (Liverpool Irish) entering Lille, 18th October 1918, the city having been in German hands since August 1914.* [IWM Q 9574]

COURTESY OF THE IMPERIAL WAR MUSEUM.

THE LONDON SCOTTISH AT MESSINES

ABOVE *The Stand of the 1/14th London (London Scottish) at Messines on 31st October 1914, painted by Richard Caton Woodville.*

COURTESY OF THE LONDON SCOTTISH MUSEUM

THE 1/14TH LONDON (London Scottish) arrived in France on 16th September 1914, initially tasked with lines of communication work. They still had the old eight-company organisation and received the Short Magazine Lee Enfield rifle only on 25th September. Unfortunately, since this was the SMLE Mark I and the ammunition issued was for the Mark VII, they were incapable of rapid fire since rounds had to be inserted singly. The Hodden Grey kilts frequently caused a stir among French civilians. A patrol on policing duty in Paris was surrounded by a curious crowd every time they stopped to ask men for their passes. Suddenly moved up to Ypres in open-top buses, they were quartered in the Cloth Hall on 29th October. Marched up to Sanctuary Wood on the following day, they were promptly marched back again, the men singing their own version of *Pop Goes the Weasel*: 'Up and down the Menin Road, in and out the Eagle, what a way to run a war and what a bloody fatigue O'.

"Passing concealed artillery batteries as they opened fire, one man remarked they were 'airborne for a few seconds... one of the occasions when breeches can claim superiority over the kilt'."

Then, on 31st October 1914, came a summons to Messines, this time to reinforce British cavalry under enormous pressure from the German attempt to break through to Ypres. Passing concealed artillery batteries as they opened fire, one man remarked they were 'airborne for a few seconds... one of the occasions when breeches can claim superiority over the kilt'. Moving in short rushes over the crest of a hill into open beet fields, since it was assumed an attack was intended, they came under intense artillery and machine gun fire, forcing them to find what cover they could. The London Scottish held on with the other defenders of Messines, but took 640 casualties in the process. One was the future Hollywood actor, Ronald Colman, then a 23 year-old shipping clerk, whose ankle was fractured by shellfire. He was discharged as unfit for further service in May 1915. Another future Hollywood actor, Claude Rains, also enlisted in the London Scottish before being commissioned in the Bedfordshire Regiment. Yet another, Basil Rathbone, was also a wartime Territorial, winning the Military Cross with another 'Scottish' unit, the 1/10th King's Liverpool (Liverpool Scottish), though Rathbone's later claim to have been personally shot at in No Man's Land by aircraft flown by both Manfred von Richthofen (the 'Red Baron') and Hermann Goering stretches credulity.

ABOVE *The future Hollywood star, Basil Rathbone* MC, *who served with the 1/10th Battalion, The Kings (Liverpool Regiment) (Liverpool Scottish).*

COURTESY OF THE LIVERPOOL SCOTTISH MUSEUM

BELOW *The roll call of the London Scottish on the morning after their epic stand at Messines.*

COURTESY OF THE LONDON SCOTTISH MUSEUM

TERRITORIALS AND THE DARDANELLES

THE INITIAL LANDINGS on the Gallipoli peninsula in Turkey on 25th April 1915 were undertaken by the regular 29th Division, the Royal Naval Division and, of course, the Australian and New Zealand Army Corps (Anzac). Progress in the imaginative but doomed enterprise soon foundered in the face of the terrain, lack of sufficient technical means of achieving a breakthrough—not least in effective artillery support—and a resolute enemy. A bitter struggle for the high ground ensued through April, May and June, to which the 42nd (East Lancashire) Division was committed in May and the 52nd (Lowland) Division in June. On 28th June 1915, 156 (Scottish Rifles) Brigade of 52nd Division, attached to the 29th Division, received little artillery support in one attack and had a casualty rate of 70 per cent among its officers and 50 per cent among other ranks.

In an attempt to give new impetus to the campaign, a new amphibious landing was undertaken at Suvla Bay on 6th August 1915. The five divisions committed included the 53rd (Welsh) and 54th (East Anglian) Divisions. The 2nd Mounted Division was also then deployed at Suvla, moving from

Egypt without its horses, while six more dismounted yeomanry brigades arrived in September and October. This sector, too, became a struggle for the high ground of Chocolate, Scimitar and Green Hills. On 12th August the 1/5th Norfolks, famously containing a company raised from the King's Sandringham estate, advanced beyond its supports around Tekke Tepe and was surrounded and slaughtered. According to some supposed witnesses, the 'vanished battalion' disappeared into strange clouds from which it never emerged, their true fate only gradually becoming known. On 21st August, the 2nd Mounted Division took 30 per cent casualties in a frontal assault towards Scimitar Hill in broad daylight and against a well entrenched and numerically superior Turkish force, Brigadier Generals Lord Longford and Paul Kenna VC both being killed.

The commander of the Mediterranean Expeditionary Force, General Sir Ian Hamilton, praised the courage of the Territorials, as in the case of the 1/1st Herefordshire Regiment in its attack on Hetman Chair and Kaslar Chair from Suvla on 9th August, but he largely failed to appreciate the problems of Territorial formations. In particular, criticism of the 53rd and 54th Divisions failed to recognise the impact of the constant loss of trained men to other formations prior to their despatch to Gallipoli.

OPPOSITE *1/1st The Herefordshire Regiment attacking towards Hetman Chair and Kaslar Chair at Suvla Bay, Gallipoli on 9th August 1915. According to Sir Ian Hamilton, commanding the Mediterranean Expeditionary Force, the attack was pressed with 'impetuosity and courage'. Unfortunately, the battalion had been committed as soon as it landed without any clear intelligence on the Turkish positions and was soon ordered to withdraw.*

OPPOSITE INSET *A sun helmet bearing the recognition flash of the Herefordshire Regiment. These helmets were on general issue to all troops operating in hot climates as it was believed that malaria was caused by 'bad air' and that the design offered a degree of protection from the disease by improving air circulation about the wearer's head.*

COURTESY OF THE HEREFORDSHIRE LIGHT INFANTRY MUSEUM, HEREFORD.

LEFT *The 1/5th Royal Scots cleaning rifles after coming out of the line at Suvla Bay, 1915.*
[IWM Q 13645]

COURTESY OF THE IMPERIAL WAR MUSEUM

RIGHT *Second Lieutenant Geoffrey Harold Woolley VC.*

COURTESY OF THE IMPERIAL WAR MUSEUM.

BELOW *The Victoria Cross is the highest award for gallantry available to the soldiers, sailors and airmen of the British and Commonwealth armed forces. It was introduced at the end of the Crimean War at the behest of Prince Albert and instituted in January 1856. The facility for posthumous awards was made in 1902 and confirmed in 1907.*

COURTESY OF THE MILITARY PICTURE LIBRARY.

THE FIRST TERRITORIAL VICTORIA CROSS

S ECOND LIEUTENANT GEOFFREY Harold Woolley (1892-1968) of the 1/9th London (Queen Victoria's Rifles) won the first of the Territorial Force's 71 wartime VCs on Hill 60 at Ypres on the night of 20th-21st April 1915. The son of a clergyman, Woolley was educated at St John's School, Leatherhead, in Surrey, and Queen's College, Oxford, where he earned a reputation as a fine sportsman. About to be ordained when the war broke out, Woolley sought a commission instead and went overseas with his battalion in November 1914.

A prominent but artificial hill created before the war by spoil from a railway cutting at Zwarteleen, south-east of Ypres, Hill 60 (so named as it was 60 metres above sea level) was taken from the Germans with the assistance of a number of mines dug under their position on 17th April 1915. The Germans counter-attacked furiously and continuously over the next few days. On the night in question, all the other officers in Woolley's company holding the position were killed and he found himself leading the defence with a steadily dwindling number of men as casualties mounted. As his citation put it, Woolley 'successfully resisted all attacks on his trench and continued throwing bombs and encouraging his men till relieved. His trench during all the time was being heavily shelled and bombed, and was subjected to heavy machine gun fire by

"From that beginning the Territorials went on winning the confidence of the Army and of the Nation, till at the end their divisions were ranked by friend and foe alike as peers of the best."

MAJOR-GENERAL SIR FREDERICK MAURICE
The History of The London Rifle Brigade (1859-1919), 1921.

the enemy'. Woolley's award was gazetted on 22nd May 1915. After the war, he followed his original intended career as a clergyman.

Appropriately, there was a direct link with the auxiliaries of the past. The battalion was formerly the 1st Middlesex (Victoria and St George's) RVC, itself originating in the Royal Victoria Rifle Club, which had been authorised to establish a volunteer corps in 1853. In turn, however, the club had been formed in 1814 by members of the Duke of Cumberland's Sharpshooters as a means of preserving their military identity when other Napoleonic-era volunteers were disbanded.

Among the other Territorial VCs were two of only three men ever to have been awarded a bar to the supreme decoration. Both were members of the RAMC. Surgeon Major Arthur Martin-Leake had won his first VC with the South African Constabulary during the South African War. A Territorial, he gained his bar serving with 5th Field Ambulance, RAMC for various acts of bravery between 29th October and 8th November 1914. Captain Noel Chavasse, medical officer of the 1/10th King's Liverpool (Liverpool Scottish), won his first VC on 9th-10th August 1916 and the bar between 31st July and 2nd August 1917. He died of wounds on 4th August 1917. The last VC of the Great War was also won by a Territorial, Major Brett Cloutman, serving with 59th Field Company, RE on 6th November 1918.

LEFT *Even though Victoria Cross winners were not commonplace, less than a month after Second Lieutenant Woolley's VC, another Londoner—Lance Sergeant Douglas Belcher [right] of the 1/5th Londons—became the first Territorial 'other rank' to win the country's highest award for gallantry at St Julien on 13th May 1915.*

COURTESY OF THE IMPERIAL WAR MUSEUM.

"I did not before think much of Territorials, but by God they can fight."

BRIGADIER-GENERAL C B PROWSE
Commander 11th Brigade, 4th Division, July 1916.

CROSSING THE ST QUENTIN CANAL

I T IS NOW widely accepted among historians that, despite the persistence of the old 'lions led by donkeys' myth, the British army immeasurably improved in its operational and tactical methods during the course of the war. Although the learning curve was often uneven and practice often inconsistent, it was a reality. By 1917 artillery techniques had become ever more sophisticated through such developments as sound ranging, flash spotting, survey work and aerial reconnaissance, enabling greater accuracy in indirect and predicted fire, and far more refined creeping barrages and counter-battery fire. Equally, the introduction of light machine guns, light mortars and grenade launchers gave the infantry its own portable firepower for those occasions when artillery support was not available. Communication remained an enormous problem, but there was far more tactical flexibility than previously and a genuine all-arms concept of operations

was beginning to emerge although this still only facilitated a break-in to an opposing defensive position rather than a complete breakthrough.

It is sometimes suggested that Australian and Canadian divisions led the field in tactical innovation, but it was in fact shared by all British formations. Indeed, one of the most outstanding illustrations of the transformation of the Army was the crossing of the St Quentin Canal by the 46th (North Midland) Division on 29th September 1918 as part of the breaking of the Hindenburg Line. The Division itself had not had a particularly noteworthy record thus far, and had suffered heavy casualties assaulting the Hohenzollern Redoubt at Loos in October 1915 and the Gommecourt salient on the Somme on 1st July 1916. It was now commanded by Major General Gerald Farrell Boyd, who had begun his military career as a ranker. The task of spearheading the attack was given to 137 (Staffordshire) Brigade, the leading battalions being the 1/5th and 1/6th South Staffordshire and the 1/6th North Staffordshire.

The brigade commander was Brigadier General John Vaughan Campbell VC, known as the 'Tally Ho VC' from his encouragement of an attack with a hunting horn at Ginchy in September 1916.

The Germans had withdrawn part of their front line to the new defensive zone of the *Siegfriedstellung* (Siegfried position) between Arras and Soissons, popularly known as the Hindenburg Line, between February and April 1915. The formidable defences extended to between 6,000 and 8,000 yards in depth, with five lines of trenches, barbed wire entanglements, as well as concrete machine-gun and artillery positions. The St Quentin Canal itself was an additional obstacle, with a cutting 35 feet wide and 50 feet deep, and water or mud to a depth of ten feet in places. Immediate German reserves were also held in the Bellicourt tunnel, through which the canal passed at one point.

Meticulous preparation for the attack included provision of collapsible boats, scaling ladders, mud mats, rafts and 3,000 life belts obtained from cross-channel steamers while a supporting bombardment delivered 126 shells per 500 yards of German line per minute for eight hours. In all over 945,000 shells were fired on a 3,000 yard front or more than for the whole 22,000 yard front on 1st July 1916. Assisted by fog, the 1/6th Staffords rushed the key Riqueval Bridge and, within barely an hour and half, the formidable defences had been breached at Bellenglise, with the eventual advance penetrating to a depth of 6,000 yards. The 46th Division took 4,200 prisoners and 72 guns, suffering just 800 casualties itself. A famous series of photographs pictured Campbell addressing his men from the Riqueval Bridge on 2nd October 1918.

ABOVE *Brigadier General John Vaughan Campbell* VC *addressing his men from the Riqueval Bridge on 2nd October 1918.*
[IWM Q 9534]
OPPOSITE *A view of the canal where the crossing was effected.*
[IWM Q 9508]

COURTESY OF THE IMPERIAL WAR MUSEUM.

TERRITORIALS IN THE HOLY LAND

ABOVE *The Charge of the 1/1st Royal Bucks Hussars of 6 Mounted Brigade at El Mughar, 13th November 1917. The left-handed officer in the foreground is Major Crocker Bulteel, formerly clerk of the course at Newmarket, while to the far right is Lieutenant (later Captain) Cyrus Perkins, who described the sensation as one of being constantly knocked in the face by a pillow from the shell blasts.*

COURTESY OF THE JOINT SERVICES COMMAND AND STAFF COLLEGE, SHRIVENHAM.

THE DEFENCE OF Egypt and the subsequent Palestine campaign was, uniquely among the war's other campaigns, largely a Territorial achievement. Territorials suffered 32,274 casualties compared to the 29,072 suffered by British regular, Indian, Australian and New Zealand formations put together. Most of the infantry of the Egyptian Expeditionary Force that advanced into Palestine in 1917 were drawn from the 52nd (Lowland), 53rd (Welsh), 54th (East Anglian) and 60th (2/2nd London) Divisions. The 52nd, 53rd and 54th Divisions had all served at Gallipoli, while the 60th had initially served on the Western Front and then at Salonika. Apart from Dominion formations, the mounted troops were primarily yeomanry of the 1st and 2nd Mounted Divisions. The 74th (Yeomanry) Division was also formed in Egypt in February 1917 from 18 dismounted yeomanry regiments.

The campaign as a whole was one of enormous hardship, from the conditions encountered with contrasts of searing heat and bitter cold, ceaseless attention from flies and the concomitant risk of disease, including malaria, typhus and typhoid. It was also one that required an extraordinary logistic effort, with more

ABOVE *The 1/1st Hertfordshire Yeomanry and the Bikanir Camel Corps (in the background) are shown during a desert reconnaissance in Egypt, 14th February 1915. The Turkish 'Suez Expeditionary Force' had been easily repulsed when attempting to seize the Suez Canal on 3rd February and this reconnaissance would appear to be part of the British follow up operation.* [IWM Q15562].

COURTESY OF THE IMPERIAL WAR MUSEUM.

BELOW *Men of the 496th Field Company Royal Engineers, part of the 75th Infantry Division, building a road in Palestine, December 1917.*

COURTESY OF THE ROYAL ENGINEERS MUSEUM, CHATHAM.

than 135,000 native labourers being employed on such tasks as road making, railway construction, laying pipelines and construction of reservoirs. The availability of water, of course, was a major potential limitation on operations—not least in the case of mounted troops.

Attention has often been most drawn to the yeomanry, the Palestine campaign seeing some of the British army's last large-scale cavalry charges. Thus, at Huj on 8th November 1917, the 1/1st Warwickshire Yeomanry and 1/1st Queen's Own Worcestershire Hussars, attached to the Australian Mounted Division, charged a Turkish position that was holding up the advance, taking 11 field guns and four machine-guns. At El Mughar on 13th November 1917 the 6 Mounted Brigade, led by the 1/1st Royal Bucks Hussars and 1/1st Dorset Yeomanry, charged over an open plain devoid of cover against an unbroken Turkish position, capturing 1,400 prisoners, two field guns and 14 machine-guns.

Nonetheless, the contribution of the Territorial infantry divisions should not be overlooked. Indeed, the 60th Division, which broke the main Turkish defensive position, had the distinction of capturing Jerusalem, though the city's surrender on 9th December 1917 was a bizarre occurrence. Seeking to surrender the city after the Turkish army had fled, the mayor first encountered Privates Andrew and Church of the 2/20th London (Blackheath and Woolwich), who were searching for water. Feeling out of their depth, they moved on, at which point the hapless and increasingly desperate mayor, accompanied by a large crowd, approached Sergeants Sedgwick and Hurcomb of the 2/19th London (St Pancras) on outpost duty. Though often credited with doing so, they also proved reluctant to take the surrender, while two artillery officers merely promised to report to their superiors. In the end, Lieutenant Colonel Bayley of 303 Brigade, RFA finally accepted the city's surrender. General Sir Edmund Allenby entered Jerusalem in triumph two days later.

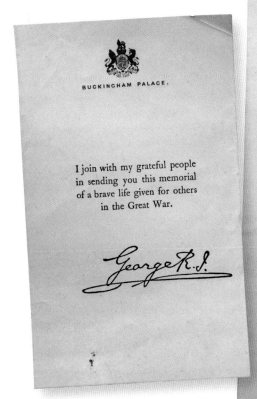

I join with my grateful people
in sending you this memorial
of a brave life given for others
in the Great War.

George R.I.

BUCKINGHAM PALACE.

GV R I

HE whom this scroll commemorates
was numbered among those who,
at the call of King and Country, left all
that was dear to them, endured hardness,
faced danger, and finally passed out of
the sight of men by the path of duty
and self-sacrifice, giving up their own
lives that others might live in freedom.
Let those who come after see to it
that his name be not forgotten.

Pte. Percival Charles Freeman
Oxf. & Bucks. L.I.

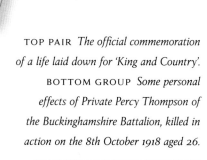

TOP PAIR *The official commemoration
of a life laid down for 'King and Country'.*
BOTTOM GROUP *Some personal
effects of Private Percy Thompson of
the Buckinghamshire Battalion, killed in
action on the 8th October 1918 aged 26.*

COURTESY OF THE OXFORDSHIRE AND BUCKINGHAMSHIRE
LIGHT INFANTRY MUSEUM, OXFORD.

THE ARMISTICE SIGNAL *'To 1st Bn MGC. Following from 9th Corps aaa Hostilities will cease at 11 hours today Nov 11th aaa Troops will stand fast on line reached at that hour which will be reported to Corps HQ as soon as possible aaa Defensive precautions will be maintained aaa There will be no intercourse of any description with the enemy until receipt of instructions from Corps HQ. aaa Further instructions follow Ends aaa Added Inf Bdes DA Nos 1, 2, 3, 4, 5, 6, 7, 8, 9, 10 and 12 List T and DADOS, DADVS and French Mission.'*

COURTESY OF THE NORTHUMBERLAND FUSILIERS MUSEUM, ALNWICK.

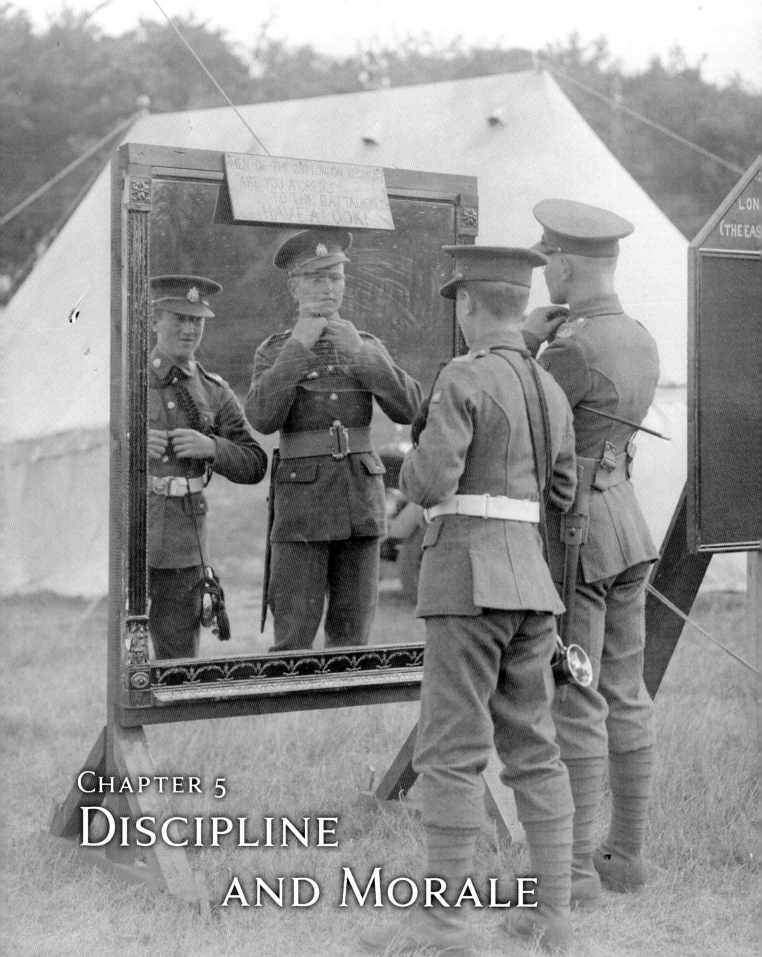

CHAPTER 5
DISCIPLINE
AND MORALE

"It may be said that in the Territorial Army discipline is neither enforced nor maintained, it just happens."

COLONEL G R CODRINGTON CB DSO OBE TD
The Territorial Army, 1938

FACED WITH INCREASING pressure to authorise the establishment of volunteer corps, the army's commander-in-chief, the Duke of Cambridge, remarked in 1857 that they would prove a 'very dangerous rabble' and 'unmanageable bodies that would ruin our Army'. Few regulars at the time believed volunteers could be disciplined sufficiently to meet trained continental troops on equal terms in the field. In part, it was a view reflecting a narrowly conservative belief in the need for rigid discipline when most army recruits were obtained from the lowest elements of society. By contrast, volunteers emphasised that 'what the Army lost in discipline it would gain in intelligence', given that most volunteers were of a higher social standing than army recruits and likely to be educated to a higher standard.

It was also argued that, being men of intelligence, volunteers would understand the value of discipline where it was necessary. As Sir Thomas Acland, a leading Devon volunteer, wrote in 1868, 'volunteers, for want of time, cannot form military habits; but they may be inspired by a military spirit, and they may end up where the soldier begins, by absolute obedience, that obedience being willingly rendered from a matured conviction of its necessity'. The view persisted into the Territorial Force, it being said of the 5th London (London Rifle Brigade) just prior to the Great War that 'it was always the discipline of men who knew by their upbringing when discipline was necessary'. Similarly, it was said of the HAC during the war that there was a 'dull indifference to discipline, yet a wonderful loyalty to duty'. It has to be said that these were both 'class corps', in which officers and men were frequently of the same social standing, and that wartime losses had an impact. Indeed, it was said of the London Rifle Brigade that its relaxed disciplinary system 'worked well until 1918 when most of the originals having become casualties, these methods were not understood by the replacements and orthodox disciplinary methods had to be introduced'. Nevertheless, there was generally a more relaxed attitude in the Territorials and certainly an *esprit de corps* derived from local identity equal to that derived from regular regimental tradition. In 1940, a report by the German IV Corps suggested that, while Territorials were less well trained than British regulars, they had proved their equal in morale.

ABOVE *Lance Corporal Leonie Barnard RAMC, visits Santa's Grotto in Camp Bastion during her six-month deployment with Salonika Company, Christmas 2007. Although this is a lighthearted example, considerable effort is put into getting the welfare package right for Territorials who do not have the advantages of the centralised resources available to their Regular counterparts.*

COURTESY OF 7 RIFLES

OPPOSITE *Territorials of the 23rd Battalion, The London Regiment adjust their dress before a parade at Annual Camp in 1928.*

COURTESY OF GETTY IMAGES

ABOVE *Cadets from the University of Oxford Officers' Training Corps undergoing basic foot drill.*

COURTESY OF OXFORD UNIVERSITY OFFICERS' TRAINING CORPS.

OPPOSITE *The handwritten caption on the reverse of this photograph of a group of friends from the 5th Battalion, The Green Howards (Alexandra, Princess of Wales's Own Yorkshire Regiment) taken in 1938 reads 'These were the grandest bunch ever'.*

COURTESY OF THE GREEN HOWARDS REGIMENTAL MUSEUM, RICHMOND.

Less happily, in an echo of the drafting controversies of the Great War, the greatest instance of collective disobedience during the Second World War illustrated the difficulties of the strong divisional identity forged by Douglas Wimberley in the 51st Division. He had told his men, 'if wounded and separated from your own units, do not allow yourselves to get drafted to other battalions, but see that you come back to us'. By mistake, an order for a reinforcing draft for 46th Division fighting at Salerno in Italy reached a transit camp in North Africa where 1,200 men from the 50th and 51st Divisions, some recovering from wounds or illness, understood that they were being sent back to their own units. At Salerno on 20th September, 300 refused to join 46th Division and 191 men persisted even after the corps commander admitted the error. Court-martialled for mutiny, most received suspended terms of imprisonment, three death sentences being commuted.

Territorials, through the nature of their voluntary commitment of time, remain different to professional soldiers who have chosen to pursue a full-time military career. There is also a sense in which a Territorial has to be 'recruited' for each training event. A lack of novelty or imagination when planning training can cause TA soldiers to vote with their feet which, with the exception of going absent without leave (AWOL) is a concept alien to the Regular Army. At least one Regular officer, genuinely puzzled as to why a TA battalion could not provide soldiers for a working party on a Divisional task asked a TA company commander why he couldn't 'just order them to turn up'. Consequently, they have always required understanding on the part of Regulars. As one TA officer remarked to US Colonel Wallace Earl Walker in 1989, it remained hard to explain to Regulars that the Territorial 'thinks differently, trains differently and that TA soldiers are more impatient with boredom than regular soldiers. The TA must be led in different ways than the Regulars'.

CHAPTER 6
CINDERELLA ARMY
1919–1939

> "Yet the Territorial Army survives. It is surely one of the hardiest of British plants, as it grows in financially stony soil without even being watered by moral encouragment."

BASIL LIDDELL HART
When Britain Goes to War, 1935.

THE BRITISH EMPIRE stood at its greatest extent at the end of the Great War through the seizure of German colonies in Africa and the Pacific, and the dismemberment of the Ottoman Empire in the Middle East. There were occupation duties to be performed, a campaign in Ireland to be waged and other nationalist disturbances with which to cope in India, Africa and the Middle East. All this, moreover, had to be accomplished amid the pressure for rapid demobilisation of the wartime army and for economic retrenchment following the heavy expenditure of waging a global conflict on a then unprecedented scale.

Yet, there was now clearly little risk of invasion, and part-time soldiers were unsuited to an imperial garrison and constabulary role. By adopting the so-called Ten Year Rule in August 1919, the Cabinet assumed no major conflict in the immediate future and the rule was renewed annually until March 1932, when it was abandoned in the aftermath of the Japanese invasion of Manchuria. In any case, the Committee of Imperial Defence concluded in 1922 that only a comprehensive mobilisation of all the state's resources would suffice if Britain became involved in another major war and, in the following year, the CID's manpower sub-committee established wartime conscription as a fundamental principle for the future. Given that a conscript army would wage a major war, this seemingly left a role for the Territorials only in medium-scale conflict falling short of that for which conscription might be considered necessary. Any consideration of such a role for the Territorials, however, required greater legislative flexibility on the key issues of obligation for general service and the integrity of units, which Territorials were in no mood to concede after their recent wartime experiences. Anything that rendered the Territorials virtually unusable, however, could only result in the War Office regarding them as the most expendable part of the army at a time of financial retrenchment. As Basil Liddell Hart, successively military correspondent of *The Daily Telegraph* and *The Times*, put it, the Territorials proved 'one of the hardiest of British plants' since they operated in 'financially stony soil, without even being watered by moral encouragement'.

In many respects, the battle lines over the precise conditions of post-war service were drawn up as early as January 1918 when, in disbanding many second line units, the War Office declined to guarantee that they would be reconstituted after the war. By early 1919 the War Office was under mounting

ABOVE *Although the TA were traditionally considered second line troops, the men of the two anti-aircraft divisions protecting London were classed as first line.*
[IWM 18-11]
COURTESY OF THE IMPERIAL WAR MUSEUM

OPPOSITE *Men of A Company, 6th (Duke of Connaught's Own) Battalion, The Hampshire Regiment firing the .303-in watercooled Vickers machine-gun at Tipnor ranges, 1933 under the supervision of Lieutenant Bell.*
COURTESY OF THE ROYAL HAMPSHIRE REGIMENT MUSEUM, WINCHESTER.

ABOVE *Machine-gunners of the 5th Battalion, The Green Howards (Alexandra, Princess of Wales's Own Yorkshire Regiment), 1928.*

COURTESY OF THE GREEN HOWARDS MUSEUM, RICHMOND.

COURTESY OF IMPERIAL TOBACCO

pressure to declare its hand before trained wartime Territorials lost interest in continuing their services. Understandably, the new Secretary of State for War, Winston Churchill, believed it better to establish wider military requirements before deciding on specific policies. It was clear to him, however, that a general service obligation was desirable on military grounds and, on 21st February 1919, the War Office issued an official defence of its wartime drafting policies, pointing out that military necessity had had to prevail over Territorial integrity since 'there have been times when it has been imperative to subordinate sentiment to military exigencies of an even more vital nature'.

The problem lay in finding some form of obligation that was acceptable to the Territorials, yet sufficiently flexible for the War Office to be able to deploy them overseas. In March 1919 a sub-committee on reconstitution chaired by the Adjutant General, Sir George Milne, recommended making Territorials liable for general service once conscription had been introduced and, while allowing them to proceed overseas in their own units, declining to guarantee integrity thereafter. Better pay and allowances would compensate for the loss of integrity. In outlining the proposals to Territorial representatives on 1st April 1919, Churchill also indicated that brigade commands would be opened immediately to suitable Territorials in an organisation corresponding to the pre-war structure of 14 infantry divisions and 14 mounted brigades.

Churchill promised to meet the representatives again before the terms of service were finally agreed. When he did so in May 1919, however, nothing had been settled. It was not until January 1920 that the Cabinet finally debated the issue and then lack of agreement delayed any decision until 27th January. Three days later Churchill announced that recruiting would begin on 1st February 1920 for a force to be raised on a four-year term of engagement with provision for re-engagement for between one and four years up to the age of 40 (50 for NCOs). All aged under 35 would be liable to serve overseas, but only after army reserves

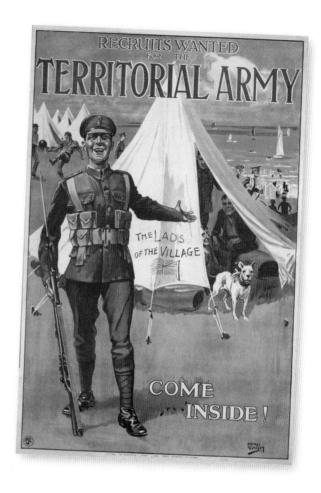

Sir,—Permit me to appeal to the public through your columns on the necessity of raising further recruits in this district for the Territorial Army. It might be mentioned that a Platoon of the 4th Oxfordshire and Buckinghamshire Light Infantry is operating with headquarters in Chipping Norton, with an establishment of 45, which can be increased, if necessary, to 90. The present strength is 19. This low number is one of the lowest in the country, proportionate to population. Prior to the war, the locality enjoyed a good reputation for the quota of recruits raised for the Territorial Force, and it has been commented upon that this reputation has not been revived since the war. With the advent of the new year the training schedule commences, and the present is the best time for the enlistment of recruits, as it enables the newly-joined to put in the requisite number of drills and carry out the musketry schedule, in time to qualify for all the benefits derived at the annual camp. It might be mentioned that the annual camp is this year being held at a leading South Coast resort, which will afford a splendid opportunity for every member to participate in a wonderfully healthy and enjoyable holiday, free from any expense. It is earnestly hoped that a number of candidates will present themselves for enlistment during the next few weeks to enable us to go ahead and show good form when our unit mingles with the Battalion in camp in August.
Yours faithfully,

LIEUTENANT R A YOUNG
OFFICER COMMANDING 13 PLATOON
4TH BATTALION, THE OXFORDSHIRE AND BUCKINGHAMSHIRE LIGHT INFANTRY
Letter to The Oxfordshire Weekly News, 27 January 1923.

"I am quite certain that neither the Government nor Parliament, nor, I may add, the Public will accept the abolition of the Territorial Force and they would think it astonishing that an Army Council which had so cordially endorsed all previous declarations on this subject should now stultify themselves by a complete reversal of policy."

WINSTON SPENCER CHURCHILL
2nd October 1919.

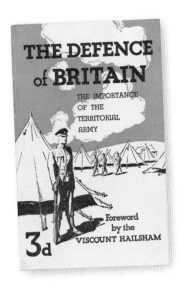

ABOVE *After the years of economic recession and reduced defence spending, the so-called deficiency programme was instituted in 1935. Although the Territorials were to receive far less than the amount recommended by the government's Defence Requirements Sub-committee, recognition of the need to rebuild the TA was illustrated by this pamphlet, with a foreword by the Secretary of State for War, the first Viscount Hailsham, who held the office from 1931 to 1935.*

COURTESY OF THE NATIONAL ARMY MUSEUM

had been called out by proclamation of imminent danger or great emergency, and only after Parliament had further legislated to authorise actual despatch of Territorials abroad. In addition, Churchill also promised that Territorial formations would retain their integrity in wartime in what became known as 'The Pledge'. Consequently, the general service obligation was so hedged with legislative qualifications as to prevent the War Office either from using Territorials in the very situation of medium-scale conflict, which was regarded by military opinion as their only likely employment, or from drafting Territorial manpower where it was most required. Nor, from the point of the War Office, did the new force come cheap, for Churchill also offered a £5 annual bounty for those completing a maximum of 50 drills, attending 15 days' camp and firing an annual musketry course. Recruits would receive up to £4.

In Churchill's view, the same kind of political necessity that had faced Haldane in 1906 and 1907 now demanded the reconstitution of what was now to be called from 1st October 1921 the Territorial Army given the goodly representation of the force in both the Commons and Lords. To some extent military opposition was assuaged by the proposal to revive the 74 battalions of the Special Reserve, which would now be renamed the Militia, hence the title of the enabling legislation for the new organisation of the Territorial Army and Militia Act. In the event, no effort was made to recruit the revived militia, and the Supplementary Reserve absorbed its function in August 1924. The purpose of the Supplementary Reserve was to provide the army with technical support in times of emergency, its favourable conditions and pecuniary rewards seriously denting recruitment for similar Territorial specialist units.

Churchill briefly contemplated a Territorial role in aid of the civil power, but there was understandable reluctance to employ part-time soldiers in potential strikebreaking. Thus, during the railway strike in October 1921, a 'Citizen Guard' was proposed, though not implemented. During the miners' strike in April 1921 a 'Defence Force' was raised. Territorial premises were utilised and Territorials were invited to enlist, but they were required to resign, although they would then be immediately readmitted after the expiry of the 90-day period of enlistment in the Defence Force, with service in it counted towards Territorial obligations. About half the Defence Force appear to have been Territorials. The War Office remained concerned that the connection between Territorials and Defence Force had been unwise and supported legislation in 1923 making permanent the arrangements adopted back in 1914 for a Special Constabulary to

be raised in similar circumstances. Thus, during the general strike in May 1926, a Civil Constabulary Reserve was so raised and Territorial premises again used, but the force was suspended after just two days when the strike collapsed. In May 1939 it was agreed that Territorials should not be enrolled in any future Civil Constabulary Reserve.

In reality, the terms offered the Territorials were not as generous as the War Office believed since immediate post-war wages were relatively high, while the commitment to 50 drills appeared excessive. It was reported that the delay in announcing government plans also had a detrimental effect in many cases, and it was by no means guaranteed that wartime servicemen would wish to find themselves back in uniform so soon, which was why a large number of associations chose not to go to camp in 1920. Indeed, almost half the recruits enlisted in the first eight months after reconstitution had not seen war service. In some areas, too, there was resentment at Churchill's other decision in January 1920 to reorganise the 56 yeomanry regiments in view of their perceived declining utility for modern war. Over the period 1920-21, therefore, 16 yeomanry regiments were disbanded (one voluntarily) while 26 converted to other roles, such as armoured car companies of The Tank Corps—they were the first cavalry units within the army as a whole to be mechanised—or brigades of The

ABOVE *Edward, Prince of Wales, wearing the uniform of the Welsh Guards, inspects the 1st (Rifle) Battalion, The Monmouthshire Regiment in the early 1920s at Newport.*

COURTESY OF THE ROYAL REGIMENT OF WALES MUSEUM, BRECON.

ABOVE *Marske Territorial camp, 3 July 1928. The image was taken by 26 (AC) Squadron. Seaside camps were always seen as an important recruiting draw, many men seeing it as the only opportunity to enjoy an annual break.*

COURTESY OF THE NORTHUMBERLAND FUSILIERS
MUSEUM, ALNWICK.

Royal Field Artillery (later Field Regiments of The Royal Artillery). It was said that one yeomanry officer, a well-known Master of Foxhounds, was determined to become a good battery commander and enlisted in mathematics evening classes. Confronted on the first evening with the 'Boot Rule' for calculating the angle of sight, he resigned his commission the following morning. Conversely, however, an eye for the ground was no handicap to the deployment of artillery. Only 14 regiments retained a mounted role, six with regular brigades and just eight allocated to the TA as such. In addition, the Lovat Scouts and Scottish Horse, both originally raised in 1901, were permitted to remain mounted as 'scouts'. Some 20 infantry battalions were also converted to other roles and 20 disbanded or amalgamated.

Churchill also failed to deliver on the recommendation by Milne's committee, endorsed by many associations, that employers be legally obliged to grant privileges to Territorials, such as allowing them to attend annual camp. This would have created difficulties for smaller employers and it was never implemented, not least because it would also have created friction with other employees and the unions. Similarly, periodic calls for a 'King's Roll' of co-operative employers to be favoured with preferential government contracts were impracticable and associations had to find other ways of encouraging support from business, especially once rising unemployment deterred men from risking their jobs by joining the Territorials, or encouraged absenteeism from camp. Associations established liaison committees but, just as before 1914, some

COURTESY OF IMPERIAL TOBACCO

firms co-operated and others did not. The response from local authorities was equally varied, with Labour-controlled councils particularly hostile even as late as 1938.

To some degree, socialist hostility—Labour governments cut funding support for the Territorial Cadet Force in both 1924 and 1930—reflected a wider anti-militarism in the inter-war years, though this can be exaggerated. Nonetheless, there was an undeniable image problem for the 'Saturday Night Soldiers' until the late 1930s. Lord Raglan was only partly correct when he remarked in July 1925 that the real enemies of the Territorials were 'women, trade unions and motor bicycles' though the GOC of the 42nd Division did claim that same year that mothers 'had an idea that if their boys went to the drill halls they would learn to drink'. Above all, there was the growing financial pressure, which increasingly threatened the TA's one great attraction, namely recreational facilities and opportunities. Although many larger employers rivalled the Territorials in providing sporting and other social activities, the annual camp was an enormous draw, especially if arranged at a seaside location. It was noticeable that recruitment always picked up immediately prior to such a camp. Men frequently arranged for their families to holiday nearby and it was also often the only opportunity for them to enjoy an annual break. Thus, there was considerable disquiet when the War Office appeared to counsel cancellation of the camps in 1921 on the grounds of transport difficulties and

BELOW *Territorials in the bar after a drill, 1938.* [IWM 18-4]

COURTESY OF THE IMPERIAL WAR MUSEUM

widespread opposition led by Staffordshire when many—but not all—camps were cancelled on similar grounds in 1926. The cancellation of all camps in 1932 was accepted with greater equanimity in view of the serious economic position but, in subsequent negotiations over the pledge that autumn, associations made it clear that any agreement was conditional upon restoration of camps.

Attending camp was not necessarily without cost to individuals despite the Regular Army rates of pay granted in 1920. It was not until March 1936 that married men under the age of 26 received separation allowances while in camp despite associations having pointed out two years earlier that extension of the concession would involve fewer than 7,000 men and cost only £8,395 even if every one eligible attended the full 15 days. Until the situation was corrected, however, there was the unfortunate spectacle of some Territorials' wives having

COURTESY OF IMPERIAL TOBACCO

PLAYER'S CIGARETTES

51ˢᵗ (WEST HIGHLAND)
ANTI-TANK REGT, R.A., 1939

BELOW *The trial mechanisation of 104 (Essex Yeomanry) Field Regiment RA involved replacing their beloved horses with mechanical tractors. 413 Battery are shown here towing their limbers behind Fordson tractors at Okehampton Camp in 1925.*

COURTESY OF THE ESSEX YEOMANRY COLLECTION, CHELMSFORD

to seek parish relief and being turned down by local authorities on the grounds that it was a government responsibility. Similarly, unemployed men were refused benefits in camp until May 1936 while their annual bounty or proficiency grant had only been exempted from means testing in 1934. The War Office evinced little sympathy for the increasing numbers of the unemployed enlisting in the Territorials, choosing in May 1934 to decline a request by 16 county associations for free issue of shirts and socks at camp in the belief that any man should be expected to provide his own. Yet, recruitment among the unemployed kept up remarkably well, Liddell Hart calculating after touring camps in 1935 and 1937 that more than half the Territorials in many northern, Welsh and Scottish units were unemployed.

Beyond camps, units had to rely on other means of attracting recruits. Providing military spectacle remained as much a routine part of recruiting as in the 19th century auxiliaries. The War Office also suggested in 1936 contrasting the civil and military life of a Territorial 'driving an out-of-date car or lorry in the day and an armoured car or Rolls-Royce in the evening'. The pull of friendship was often encouraged by 'bringing in' money offered by some associations. Unfortunately, Territorial premises were frequently in poor repair until new accommodation standards were agreed in 1937 and they compared unfavourably with many civilian clubs. Financial restrictions also continued to

ABOVE *Manning a No 10 Predictor Tracker of 471 HAA Regiment RA (TA), Dunfermline. Following the establishment of the Auxiliary Territorial Service (ATS) in 1938, women increasingly became integral to anti-aircraft units.*

COURTESY OF THE ROYAL ARTILLERY MUSEUM, WOOLWICH.

bite at Territorial grants, activities and equipment, with the Treasury and War Office alike consistently taking a cue from the perceived lack of purpose of the TA. In March 1922, as a result of the demands of the Geddes Committee for reductions, the abolition of some Territorial divisions was considered. In the event, Territorial establishments were cut at all levels, the bounty reduced to £3 for trained men and to £2.10s.0d for recruits and a range of officers' allowances also reduced with the effect of finding £1,175,000 of the total savings required of the army as a whole.

Overall, the Geddes cuts did so much damage to the army that the Cabinet accepted no more reductions could be contemplated for some time but, in February 1926, a further round of economies ensued. On this occasion, £160,000 was trimmed from Territorial training, building and clothing grants and five per cent of the surpluses accumulated from block grants yielded. The efforts of associations to husband resources had actually played into the hands of the Treasury, surpluses of some £360,000 being in hand. As already indicated, many camps were then cancelled that same year and another saving of £231,000 was demanded in February 1927; the suggestion being that establishments be reduced, the two London divisions amalgamated, travel grants cut, and bounties abolished for new recruits and those re-engaging. Associations were outraged—*The Times* accused the Army Council of not merely looking a gift horse in the mouth but 'extracting its teeth one by one'—and the War Office compromised by dropping the cuts to establishment and compensating for the

COURTESY OF IMPERIAL TOBACCO

PLAYER'S CIGARETTES

22ⁿᵈ BN. ROYAL TANK REGT.
(WESTMINSTER DRAGOONS), 1939

"...if the Territorial Army is to achieve the best results the Army must adapt itself to the complexities of the life of the nation, not expect the nation to adjust itself to the standards and requirements of the Army."

BREVET-COLONEL W E GREEN DFC TD
The Territorial in the Next War, 1939.

loss of the bounty by instituting a proficiency grant of £1.10s.0d. The Territorials were spared more cuts for a time but, in 1930, another £236,000 was trimmed from grants, with officers' allowances reduced in 1931 and a saving of £1 million announced that same year by limiting recruitment and, as again already indicated, cancelling camps for the following year.

Under such constant pressure, the Territorials fell consistently well short of even the reduced establishments. In 1922, when the establishment was 216,041 officers and men, the TA mustered only 136,600, although the strength did rise to 148,742 in 1926 at a time when the establishment had been reduced to 184,161. The nadir was a total of 128,757 officers and men in October 1932. Associations became obsessed with numbers to the extent that suspiciously high proportions of men attending camps registered by some units for the purposes of *The Daily Telegraph Cup* competition in 1934 revealed attendance being inflated by registering invalids, ex-soldiers and even civilian batmen temporarily as Territorials. One regular battery sergeant major from the north was even found to have gone to camp with a unit in the south as a lance corporal under an assumed name. Generally, associations were now prepared to accept any man willing to join, acknowledging, as the Cornwall Association noted in 1937, that 'not such a good type of man now joins'.

Although Liddell Hart claimed many Territorials were social climbers, recruitment of officers was especially problematic, with a deficiency of 1,055 in 1933. It was anticipated that the OTC would supply most of the TA's officers, OTC regulations being changed in 1933 to encourage the two to train together—OTC Section A being those already affiliated to TA units, Section B those ready for active service on mobilisation, and Section C those who would remain with OTC in the event of war. At the lowest ebb, however, the deteriorating international security situation began to offer new hope. The Ten Year Rule was abandoned and, in November 1933, the Cabinet agreed that a specially constituted Defence Requirements Sub-committee of the CID should make recommendations on deficiencies. The first DRC report in February 1934 recommended the provision of an expeditionary force, which

BELOW *Men of the 79th HAA Regiment about to board a Maidstone and District coach at Watford for the journey to their couverture station at Rochester, 25th June 1939*

COURTESY OF WATFORD CENTRAL LIBRARY

ABOVE *Training to use an anti-aircraft heightfinder, 1938.*

[IWM 18-13]

COURTESY OF THE IMPERIAL WAR MUSEUM

could only be reinforced by the Territorials, the committee proposing to spend £250,000 per annum for five years on modernising the TA. Its third report in November 1935 called for an expenditure of £26 million to enable the Territorials to reinforce the expeditionary force in four-division contingents at intervals of four, six and eight months after mobilisation.

Unfortunately, the DRC recommendations were not acceptable to the Treasury and the Chancellor of the Exchequer, Neville Chamberlain, was to prove a formidable obstacle to Territorial rearmament, although he was prepared to see an anti-aircraft role enhanced. Cabinet consideration of the first DRC report, therefore, resulted in just £50,000 per annum for the Territorials and there were only minor adjustments to grants and allowances. Even less survived from the third report, with agreement in February 1936 to spend only £250,000 per annum and to re-assess the situation after three years. Duff Cooper, who became Secretary of State for War in November 1935, did his best to improve matters, restoring the level of the 1920 bounty in March 1936 by increasing the proficiency grant and adding allowances for weapons training and extra drills.

In postponing consideration of the preparation of the Territorials as reinforcements for an expeditionary force, the Cabinet had not actually ruled it out altogether and Duff Cooper pressed for modernisation to begin in December 1936. As a compromise, the Minister for the Co-ordination of Defence, Sir Thomas Inskip, suggested spreading sufficient equipment across the TA to equip one or two divisions in an emergency, but Chamberlain would only accept modernisation of four Territorial divisions by April 1941. When Chamberlain

ABOVE *Officers and men of the 5th Battalion, The Green Howards (Alexandra, Princess of Wales's Own Yorkshire Regiment) inspect their new vehicles, 1939.*

COURTESY OF THE GREEN HOWARDS MUSEUM, RICHMOND.

became Prime Minister in May 1937, Duff Cooper was removed from the War Office and replaced by the flamboyant and controversial Leslie Hore-Belisha.

Initially, Hore-Belisha, perhaps best known to the public for the pedestrian crossing beacons named after him while he had been transport minister, suggested equipping four Territorial divisions to reinforce an expeditionary force. The Treasury rejected this. In the major policy review undertaken by Hore-Belisha and Inskip between December 1937 and February 1938, priority was accorded to anti-aircraft defence. During the course of the next few months, however, it emerged that those formations not required for this role, which would now also include three motorised divisions[1] and a new Territorial armoured division, would be earmarked for an expeditionary force designated for employment in an 'eastern theatre', essentially meaning Egypt. The new significance of the Territorials for home defence was also marked by bringing the Director-General on to the Army Council in October 1937 and by appointing the Northampton architect, Colonel Sir John Brown, Deputy Director-General with the rank of Major General. Brown had commanded 162 (East Midlands) Brigade between 1924 and 1928 and had then been recommended by his regular divisional commander as his successor, a request declined by the War Office. The appointment of Director-General itself had been abolished in 1935, but General Sir Walter Kirke, who had proved a firm friend of the Territorials at Western Command between 1933 and 1936, had campaigned for its revival. Funding was also restored for the Territorial Cadet Force.

Churchill, of course, had promised that Territorials would achieve higher commands but, as late as 1936, only eight out of 50 Territorial brigades were commanded by Territorials and the 'trade unionism' of the regulars survived, those regulars serving as adjutants to Territorial units receiving less pay than their counterparts in regular units and finding it more difficult to get into Staff

1.   50th, 55th and 1st London Divisions.

"The voluntary principle is one deeply rooted in the social structure of the British nation. But the possibility that any man should be financially handicapped as a result of voluntary service in its military forces is one which no self-respecting nation can face with equanimity."

The Times, 16th August 1934.

College. Under Hore-Belisha, however, some progress was made, with the number of Territorial brigade commanders rising to ten by mid 1938 with an acceptance that four more would be appointed by the end of the year. Moreover, in October 1937 Hore-Belisha announced that Colonel Claude Liardet, a Lloyds' insurance broker, then commanding the London Division's artillery, would become the first Territorial divisional commander, although considerable regular opposition—even Kirke claimed Territorials preferred to be commanded by regulars—meant that Liardet did not take up his post until early 1938. The Staff College was also opened to Territorial candidates, as the Imperial Defence College had been a year earlier.

The limited role for any expeditionary force and the absence of any continental liability envisaged by Hore-Belisha and Inskip was determined as much by financial considerations as strategy and this was not materially changed by the increasing pace of events in Europe. Nonetheless, the *Anschluß*—the German annexation of Austria—in March 1938 triggered a new interest in home defence and the Territorials. Anti-aircraft units did especially well, partly assisted by the Gaumont-British recruiting film, *The Gap*, released in April 1937, though it fell awkwardly between 'straight documentary and fiction with a moral'. It featured the 1st AA Division with technical advice given by Lieutenant Colonel J K Dunlop, the secretary to the TA Joint Publicity and Recruiting Committee and author of a well-known history of the British Army. Lord Nuffield also agreed to become Honorary Colonel of one of the brigades in 1st AA Division, signalling a new if partly fashionable interest in the Territorials. Local cinematic release of Alexander Korda's popular adventure film, *The Drum*, released in 1938 and set on the contemporary North West Frontier, was also used by the TA for local recruiting efforts.

There was also something of a rush of recruits generally, 77,000 new recruits in the course of 1938 boosting total strength to 200,190 albeit at the expense of disrupting manpower planning considerations, with the result that some 12,000 Territorials were to be returned to industry in the first three months of war in 1939. It was not until January 1939, however, that the government finally acted to try to give some direction to patriotically minded citizens with the so-called National Service Appeal, by which time the Territorials were competing with a deluge of recruits for the new Air Raid Protection Service. In September 1938 the Auxiliary Territorial Service (ATS) was also created to allow women to perform a non-combatant role in support of the armed forces. The original

PLAYER'S CIGARETTES

4TH/5TH BN. THE BUFFS (ROYAL EAST KENT REGT.) 1939

COURTESY OF IMPERIAL TOBACCO

"Whilst on a school trip to Germany in 1936, I was taken to see a Hitler Youth
training camp where the Gauleiter—a family friend—made me an honorary member.
Their advanced preparations frightened me and, on my return, I went straight down
to Portman Road Drill Hall in Ipswich and joined the 4th Suffolks as a private soldier.
I was underage but I felt I just had to do something."

JOHN TILLETT
2nd Battalion, The Oxfordshire and Buckinghamshire Light Infantry, 6th Air Landing Brigade.

title of Women's Auxiliary Defence Service (WADS) was quickly dropped when women objected to the acronym. County Territorial associations were invited to nominate women as County Commandants but, while conforming to the TA's structure and based at TA drill halls, the ATS was not strictly part of the TA, though affiliated to it. ATS personnel attended TA summer camps in 1939 as cooks, clerks and storekeepers and, ultimately, the ATS became an integral part of anti-aircraft defence. In April 1941 the ATS received full military status as part of the army, being succeeded by the Women's Royal Army Corps (WRAC) in February 1949.

The Munich Crisis in September 1938 further stimulated interest, the Treasury allowing units to recruit between 10 and 30 per cent over establishment, with anti-aircraft and coastal defence units being mobilised for a period of three weeks from 26th September to 14th October in what was called 'couverture'. However, no Territorial division had full equipment and none could be expected to take the field for at least eight months after any mobilisation. The Territorials had no tanks, no mortars, no proper mechanised transport and no gas masks. With the French now pressing strongly for a greater British commitment to an expeditionary force, limited liability was abandoned and, in December 1938, Hore-Belisha proposed that four Territorial divisions now be prepared to reinforce an expeditionary force between four and six months after mobilisation with the remainder properly equipped for training purposes. The Cabinet accepted the new policy in February 1939 but, by the time Hore-Belisha presented his annual estimates to the Commons on 8th March, he not only announced that the number of Territorial anti-aircraft divisions would be raised from five to seven but also that Territorials would eventually contribute nine infantry divisions, a motorised division, an armoured division and two cavalry brigades to the planned field force.

On 15th March 1939 the Germans occupied what was left of Czechoslovakia to set off a further surge of volunteering, more demands from the French, and a growing press campaign for the reintroduction of conscription. With the latter still anathema to the Labour Party and the union movement, Chamberlain was desperate for some gesture. With a meeting of the Conservative backbench 1922 Committee scheduled for the evening of 28th March, Chamberlain met Hore-Belisha that afternoon. Hore-Belisha suggested conscription but, when Chamberlain rejected it, he suggested on the spur of the moment doubling the TA. Hore-Belisha was immediately aware of the practical difficulties and, of

PLAYER'S CIGARETTES

7TH/9TH (HIGHLANDERS) BN.,
THE ROYAL SCOTS, 1939

COURTESY OF IMPERIAL TOBACCO

ABOVE *Pipers of the 7/9th (Highlanders) Battalion, The Royal Scots (The Royal Regiment) perform at the Regimental Depot, Glencorse on 24th June 1933.*

COURTESY OF THE NATIONAL WAR MUSEUM OF SCOTLAND, EDINBURGH.

course, no military advice had been sought, but Chamberlain eagerly took up the idea. On the following day, therefore, it was announced that the peacetime establishment of 130,000 would be made up to the wartime establishment of 170,000, then doubled. Two days later came another gesture in the form of a guarantee of support for Poland.

At least the crisis enabled the War Office finally to settle the matter of the pledge and the agreement already reached with regard to anti-aircraft and coastal defence units allowed them to be mobilised in an emergency before the rest of the Territorials were embodied. Chamberlain's apparent belief that Territorials could continue their civil employment by day and man anti-aircraft batteries by night for anything up to six months, even if manning by individual units was for no more than a month, was clearly unrealistic. Consequently, he was compelled to accept a limited measure of conscription so that Territorials and reservists could be relieved of the burden as conscripts became trained. Accordingly, on 26th April 1939 conscription was reintroduced with a Reserve and Auxiliary Forces Act enabling the government to call out Territorials and reservists without declaring a state of emergency. At the same time, a Military Training Act authorised the call up of 250,000 'militiamen' annually from among the nation's 20-year-olds for six months' training to be followed by a three-year Territorial liability. Of these 'militiamen', some 80,000 would be trained for anti-aircraft duties, the first batch of 35,000 being intended to arrive at units on 15th July. Since the legislation, which only came into effect

COURTESY OF IMPERIAL TOBACCO

BELOW *An ATS spotter on night duty, equipped with night glasses, reclining spotting chair, and warm clothing*

COURTESY OF THE ROYAL ARTILLERY MUSEUM, WOOLWICH.

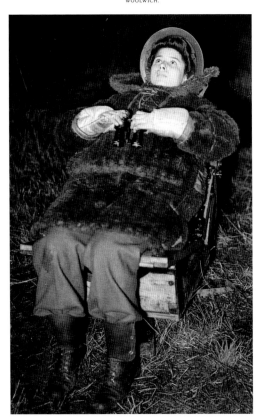

on 26th May, exempted men who had been enlisted or commissioned in any of the reserve forces before 27th April, many younger men had immediately joined the TA, preferring a voluntary part-time engagement to a full-time one or local voluntarily service with their friends now to being called up compulsorily later. This only compounded the TA's difficulties in dealing with the sudden expansion of numbers.

The greatest problem was the inevitable competition that ensued for equipment and instructors. Indeed, since government and War Office alike felt it necessary to conciliate public opinion after so suddenly reversing policy by bringing back conscription in peacetime, it was the 'militia' rather than the Territorials who were given priority. This caused some problems when the second period of 'couverture' began in late May 1939. Indeed, some employers dismissed Territorial employees, the then GOC of the AA Corps, Lieutenant-General Sir Alan Brooke, drawing attention in June 1939 to the plight of men 'being required to honour a liability for which they did not contract' when the government seemed more concerned for the 'financial well-being of the conscripted militia-men'.

There was not even any precise guidance on how the Territorials should be expanded, and individual associations and units followed their own whims in raising the so-called 'duplicate' units. In the case of the 99th (Bucks and Berks Yeomanry) Field Regiment, the division into 99th (Royal Bucks Yeomanry) Field Regiment and 145th (Berkshire Yeomanry) Field Regiment resulted in the commanding officers cutting cards for which received most of the guns and equipment since there was only sufficient for one regiment.

Although the Territorials had again failed to become the principal means of expanding the army, however, there was not the same level of resentment of the Great War due to the fact that militiamen would pass into the Territorials and because Territorials themselves were attracting plenty of recruits. The newly raised 2nd Queen's Westminsters, for example, recruited a company from among journalists and actors, including journalists Lord Killanin and William (later Lord) Deedes, and actors Frank Lawton, Hugh Williams, Guy Middleton and Nigel Patrick. It also included the male chorus from Ivor Novello's *The*

Dancing Years, whose drill was said to be especially impressive. Some 80,000 recruits had already signed up by the end of April 1939 and there was also a rush of older men who were directed towards the National Defence Corps (later Home Defence Battalions), formed in 1936 to utilise men between 45 and 55 to provide guards for vulnerable points.

Before any of these problems could be resolved, the approach to war quickened. Anti-aircraft and coastal units were called out on 21st August, the National Defence Corps on 25th and 26th August, reservists on 31st August and the remainder of the TA on 1st September 1939. In one sense, the TA effectively ceased to exist as a separate entity within weeks. The Armed Forces (Conditions of Service) Act of September 1939 suspended Territorial status for the duration as well as removing all remaining restrictions on liability to general service and transfer between units. The Military and Air Forces (Prolongation of Service) Act then also extended all terms of service for the duration. But although Territorials were now an integral part of a single national army, distinctions were to remain.

ABOVE *ATS women attached to the Royal Electrical and Mechanical Engineers, itself a new wartime creation in 1942.*

COURTESY OF THE ROYAL ELECTRICAL AND MECHANICAL ENGINEERS MUSEUM

THE PLEDGE

ABOVE *Conscripts for the 'militia' are welcomed by a member of the Medical Board. The legislation for the calling up of 250,000 'militiamen' under the Military Training Act came into force in May 1939.* [IWM 28-1]

COURTESY OF THE IMPERIAL WAR MUSEUM

WITH THE TA at a very low point in 1932, associations came reluctantly to acknowledge that a fundamental revision of Churchill's 'Pledge' back in February 1920 to maintain the integrity of Territorial units in wartime was necessary to justify their continued existence. Although the pledge had been reiterated in 1928, the Stephens Committee had recommended in May 1931 that it be abolished in order to enable the Territorials to provide and maintain an immediate reinforcement of eight infantry divisions and one cavalry division for any expeditionary force outside Europe. The long-time president of the West Lancashire Association, the Earl of Derby, offered some support, but opposition was led in the Council of County Territorial Associations in May 1932 by another long-standing Territorial, the Earl of Scarbrough, who had been Director-General of the Territorial Force and remained chairman of the West Riding Association. The moment to negotiate was hardly auspicious from the point of view of the War Office in view of the cancellation of the 1932 summer camps and it became increasingly clear that no agreement could be

> "From my experience of the Military Members of the Army Council I have little doubt that they would welcome abolition and if thereby they can save something substantial for the Regular Army they will probably press for it, and if successful, destroy the one thing that keeps the voluntary spirit alive in the Country."

THE EARL OF SCARBROUGH
17th January 1922.

reached unless camps were restored in 1933. The War Office could give no such guarantee when financial decisions were not within its control.

When improved financial conditions enabled a decision on restoring camps to be made, the War Office tried again in February 1933, suggesting the pledge be withdrawn only from new recruits and that the rights of those already serving or subsequently re-engaging would not be affected. Associations found this more acceptable and all but five within the Council of County Territorial Associations voted for abolition for all Territorials on 24th May 1933. The War Office decided only to withdraw it from new recruits with effect from 1st May 1934, but then foolishly communicated with an association not represented on the Council, giving it an assurance that men would only proceed overseas in their own units. Consequently, the War Office had to give the same guarantee to all and, rather than again submit to complicated negotiations, settled for a general service obligation and dropped the matter of unit integrity for another five years.

In June 1938 the Council of County Territorial Associations agreed on total abolition of the pledge provided serving pre-1933 Territorials were allowed to re-engage on the old terms and if the War Office promised not to use Territorials merely as drafts unless absolutely unavoidable. There was confusion, however, on whether abolition could be achieved without a full consultation process extending to individuals. The War Office was prepared to allow a discharge to those not accepting general service terms and, on 29th March 1939, a specially convened meeting of the Council of County Territorial Associations finally swept away the pledge. The same meeting also agreed that all Territorials be asked to sign their assent to an agreement already put to anti-aircraft and coast defence units to come out in an emergency before the Territorials were formally embodied.

BELOW *'Militia' recruits being taken to their new quarters by a Lance Corporal of the 7th (Southwark) Battalion, The Queen's Royal Regiment (West Surrey). Until 1937 the battalion had been 24th London Regiment (The Queen's).* [IWM 28-7A]

COURTESY OF THE IMPERIAL WAR MUSEUM

ANTI-AIRCRAFT DEFENCE

ABOVE *A victory salvo of 21 3.7 inch guns fired by 60 HAA Regiment RA (TA) by order of 21 Army Group at HQ Germany in 1945 to celebrate VE Day.*

COURTESY OF THE ROYAL ARTILLERY MUSEUM, WOOLWICH.

IN 1921 THE Geddes Committee had recommended a new Territorial role in anti-aircraft defence and the War Office had itself resolved to establish two Territorial anti-aircraft divisions. Lack of funding meant that only a low priority was accorded at the time, with only four air defence brigades[1] established for London. The Steel-Bartholomew Plan of 1923 suggested all anti-aircraft defence being vested in the Territorials, but little more was done until two additional brigades were raised by conversion for the air defence of Plymouth and Portsmouth in 1932, the London defences also reaching a total of six brigades by this time. In December 1935 eight London infantry battalions from 47th (2nd London) and 56th (1st London) Divisions were also converted into anti-aircraft brigades within a Southern AA Division, the remaining battalions being merged into a single London Division. In 1937 The London Regiment disappeared, those remaining battalions becoming once more single battalions affiliated to regular regiments, as they had been before 1908. Technically they had been so since 1916, though the name had continued and battalions had not changed their titles. On the doubling of the TA in 1938 a second London Division was again formed, and the 47th (2nd London) and 56th (1st London) revived as titles in November 1940.

1.   51 to 54 AA Brigades, Royal Garrison Artillery.

Invasion, meanwhile, had become even less of a fear with the CID reducing the likely scale of attack in 1929 to no more than 2,000 men. Thus, although the role of coastal defence was handed to the Territorials in 1932, it had been decided to reduce this to the minimum commensurate with security. With the merger of The Royal Field Artillery and The Royal Garrison Artillery in 1924, the former Territorial Coast Brigades, RGA had been redesignated as Heavy Brigades, RA. In 1934 a reorganisation resulted in 30 coastal defence batteries in 14 brigades, the number rising to 40 batteries by 1939.

Neville Chamberlain, a former chancellor and now Prime Minister, had little interest in re-equipping the Territorials, but he became increasingly worried by the state of anti-aircraft defences. Thus, in 1937 it was decided to convert another Territorial division to an anti-aircraft role—the 46th (North Midland) became the 2nd (Northern) AA Division while the existing Southern Division was renamed 1st (Southern) AA Division. As in the case of the Southern Division, infantry battalions were converted to Royal Artillery if manning guns and to Royal Engineers if manning searchlights. It was not always a smooth process. In the case of the 4th Leicesters, more than 75 per cent of the other ranks took the free discharge offered upon conversion into the 44th (Leicestershire Regiment) AA (Searchlight) Battalion, RE.

By 1938 the 3-inch anti-aircraft gun in service since the Great War was being replaced by the 3.7-inch gun. The policy review undertaken by Hore-Belisha and Inskip between December 1937 and February 1938 proposed to convert three more divisions into anti-aircraft formations and to use others to maintain public order in the aftermath of air attack. In April 1939 it was decided to expand the number of anti-aircraft divisions to seven and by the outbreak of war, a total of 32 anti-aircraft brigades (later regiments) existed, though the 6th and 7th AA Divisions had hardly begun to form. Five Light AA Regiments armed with Bofors guns were also formed for vulnerable points, such as key factories, in the summer of 1938—half the manpower being raised from the workforces, who

"With very slight assistance from the Regular Army, the Territorial Army now carries the entire burden of the defence of our fortified ports against attack from the sea, and of the whole island against attacks from the air."

LT COL J K DUNLOP MC TD
The Problems and Responsibilities of the Territorial Army, 1935

ABOVE *A 3.7-inch AA gun of 97th Heavy Anti-Aircraft Regiment (London Scottish) bombarding enemy positions on the Gothic Line, 2nd September 1944. Like the Germans with their 88-mm anti-aircraft gun, the British realised the usefulness of the 3.7-inch in both general artillery and anti-tank roles.*

[IWM NA 18197]

COURTESY OF THE IMPERIAL WAR MUSEUM

OPPOSITE *A company of Territorial Royal Engineers leave Liverpool Street Station on 18th July 1928, en route for their annual camp on Salisbury Plain.*

COURTESY OF GETTY IMAGES

became members of the TA Reserve, and half from Territorials. By September 1939 a further 25 LAA Regiments had been formed.

Anti-aircraft units proved popular as international tensions grew and there was something of an echo of the old volunteers in the way firms, sporting clubs and old boys' associations formed new batteries. These new Territorials, however, often demanded better facilities, better equipment and better instruction, with friction between old and new Territorials being marked by the circulation by the War Office in June 1938 of a memorandum submitted by new recruits in one London anti-aircraft battery critical of instructional standards. One complaint from a searchlight battery was that a special NCOs course of 37 hours' duration had spent just two hours on the technicalities of searchlight equipment and the remainder on either very elementary theories of electricity or the correct placement of battery latrines. There were clearly problems for, as one officer of the 79th (Herts Yeomanry) AA Regiment at Watford put it, not only was training restricted to two evenings a week, but also the only instructional texts issued were *Field Service Regulations* and the *Manual of Military Law*: these had 'their uses as paper-weights, bedside reading, etc,' but 'are of little assistance in instructing a squad on predictor numbers'. Understandably, many existing Territorials keenly resented the criticism of newcomers who had not been there to keep the Territorial spirit alive in the years of neglect.

On 26th September 1938 the first of some 58,000 Territorial anti-aircraft personnel were mobilised, as were coastal defence units, though all were stood down on 14th October. The lack of equipment, however, was acute and it transpired that the 1st AA Division had been able to deploy only 126 guns out of a supposed establishment of 216. The Territorials had also taken between 12 and 48 hours to become operational. Hore-Belisha was compelled to find two regular anti-aircraft regiments to give London immediate protection in the event of hostilities and pressed to explain the deficiencies. This was especially difficult for, earlier in 1938, the dubious nature of some of Hore-Belisha's claims concerning modernisation of Territorial anti-aircraft equipment had been exposed by Churchill's son-in-law, Duncan Sandys MP, who also happened to be a second lieutenant in one of the London anti-aircraft batteries.

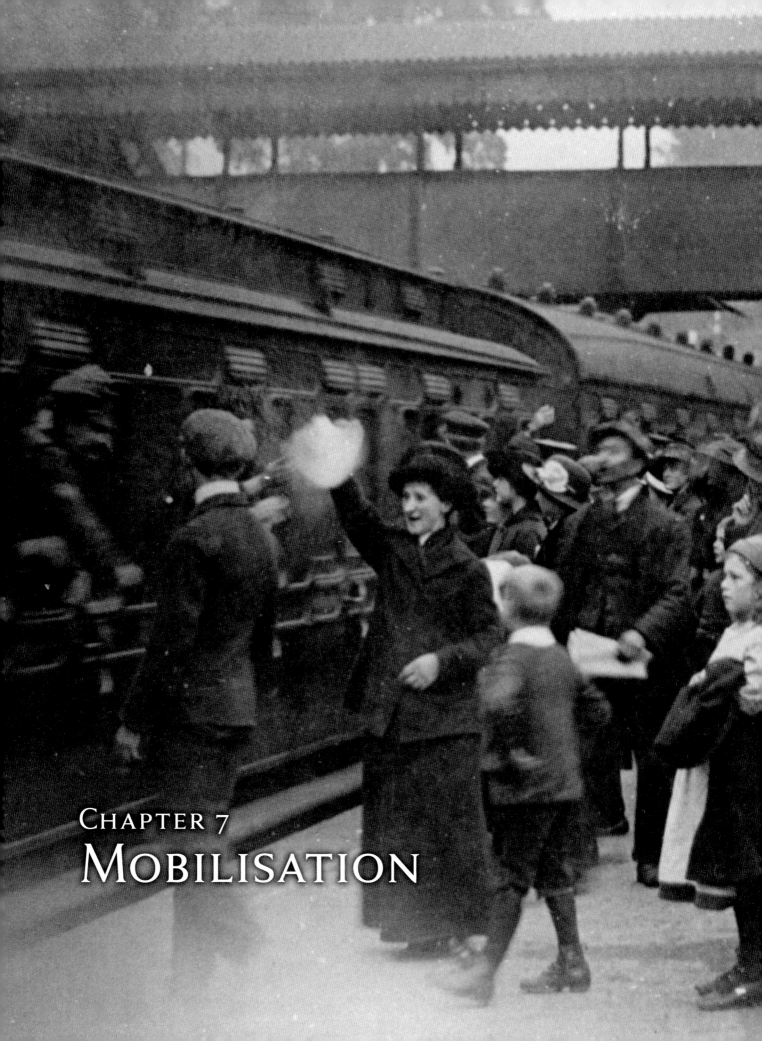

CHAPTER 7
MOBILISATION

"Between supper and breakfast in the normal routine of the nation's life the AA units of her citizen army had changed their lounge suits for khaki, factory hands and office workers had become soldiers."

HOWARD N COLE—EDITOR OF 'DEFENCE'
Commenting on the call-out of the TA Anti-Aircraft Divisions on 26th September 1938, during the Munich crisis.

O N 5TH AUGUST 1914 one officer of the 1/15th London (Civil Service Rifles) strode out into The Strand from regimental headquarters in Somerset House, drew his sword to wave down a bus, ejected the passengers, and commandeered it to collect a million rounds of small arms ammunition from the magazine in Hyde Park. A colleague similarly commandeered a taxi to take the battalion's bayonets for sharpening at a cutler's workshop. Such was the nature of mobilisation in many units, although others had made rather more comprehensive preparations in advance, which worked well despite the short time between men arriving back from summer camp and the notification of call up over a bank holiday weekend. Formal notification was by Adjutant's postcard accompanied by TF embodiment form E365 ordering men to report to headquarters while a proclamation announcing embodiment was also widely distributed and posted on public buildings. There was then the complications of applying the Imperial Service Obligation and recruiting up to war establishment at the same time as successively recruiting second and third line units in competition with Kitchener's appeal for his 'New Army'. Finding sufficient equipment was often a problem while there was an astonishing variety of vehicles. In the case of 1/1st City of London Yeomanry (Rough Riders), these included a two-storey mineral water van complete with its advertisements driven by a trooper garbed in a lounge suit, a straw boater and puttees. Similarly, 1/13th London (Princess Louise's Kensington Regiment) acquired a number of Idris mineral water delivery vans that were not exchanged for army GS (General Service) wagons until they embarked for France in November 1914.

In 1939, as in 1914, some units were mobilised earlier than others and many units also had two categories of men, key individuals being called out earlier than others. As in 1914 many units were not long back from camp and the doubling of the TA in the previous year again complicated finding sufficient equipment. One young TA infantry subaltern took a careful note of any item he was either required to carry, or thought it necessary to do so, on his person upon mobilisation. Apart from his actual uniform (15 separate items) and equipment

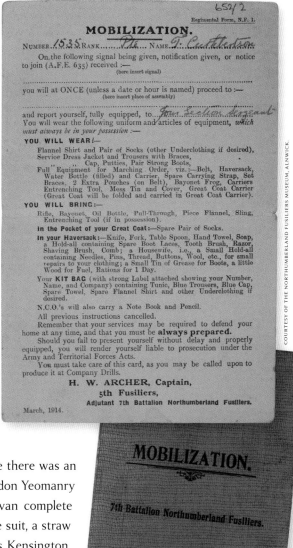

OPPOSITE *One of the original four companies of The Royal Monmouthshire Regiment leaves Troy station in 1914.*

COURTESY OF THE CASTLE AND REGIMENTAL MUSEUM, MONMOUTH/MARK DAVEY

COURTESY OF THE NORTHUMBERLAND FUSILIERS MUSEUM, ALNWICK

COURTESY OF THE NORTHUMBERLAND FUSILIERS MUSEUM, ALNWICK

> "...to call out the 20,000 odd officers and men of the Supplementary Reserve would not appear to the nation to indicate any severe crisis. But to embody the Territorial Army would, in the popular mind, mean that affairs were taking a serious turn."

LIEUTENANT COLONEL J K DUNLOP MC TD
The Problems and Responsibilities of the Territorial Army, 1935.

BELOW *Captain Louise Clark of The Royal Monmouthshire Regiment, Royal Engineers commanded the first formed body of TA soldiers to be mobilised under the Reserve Forces Act 1996, when her troop deployed to the Balkans with 21 Engineer Regiment in 1997.*

COURTESY OF THE CASTLE AND REGIMENTAL MUSEUM, MONMOUTH.

(21 items), he had 30 separate items in his pockets including a bottle of aspirin, a whistle and a pack of field dressings; seven items in his respirator haversack including a tin of ointment and a bundle of cotton waste; 20 items in his small pack, including two separate ration packs each containing 15 biscuits, two tea packs, two bars of chocolate, a pack of porridge, a packet of meat, a packet of chewing gum, four meat stock cubes, three lumps of sugar, and 15 boiled sweets; 16 items carried outside his large pack, including a ground sheet and six yards of white whipcord; and 33 items inside his large pack, including a copy of *War and Peace*, a tin of dubbin and a torch.

In the 1980s, when the Soviets posed the main threat, mobilisation would have been at drill halls before deployment at the order of the chain of command by civilian aircraft or ferries, with much of the equipment to be drawn from pre-positioned stocks in Germany before units reported to combat positions. In exercises in both 1980 and 1982, for example, The Royal Monmouthshire Royal Engineers (Militia) took 500 or so soldiers to Germany by air, picking up the pre-stocked unit equipment (PUE), including vehicles, at Recklinghausen and Dulmen before deploying to prepare bridges over the Weser for demolition, laying trackways, preparing defensive positions and, in the final phase, acting as infantry. In April 1999, however, the centralised Reserves Training and Mobilisation Centre (RTMC) was opened at Chilwell, near Nottingham, with a staff of 85, designed for an annual throughput of 3,600 soldiers with a maximum capacity of 200 at any one time. There were undoubted problems in the mobilisation process through Chilwell when Territorials began to serve in the Balkans, with too long a period between individuals volunteering and notification of selection being received, and then often too short a period between receiving such notification and the date at which to report to the mobilisation centre. In the first case, it might be as much as three months and, in the second, as little as three days. Some soldiers were called out and then stood down, and there were irregularities in pay.

In 2003, too, more than 200 call out notices were sent on less than a week's notice and some soldiers informed before their units. By Operation TELIC 2, it was said that 98 per cent of those mobilised had received 21 days' notice or more and matters have continued to improve with a smoother process of 'intelligent selection', the issue of call out notices, reporting to Chilwell for two days of the customary paperwork, as well as medical and dental inspections, collection of equipment and then mobilisation plus an eight-day pre-deployment training package (comprising administration, refresher training, collective training, specific training for theatre and function), pre-deployment leave and, on occasions, further training with a regular unit if the latter itself is newly deploying to area. Initial

training will usually be at Chilwell and subsequently at other training locations such as Stanford Training Area in Norfolk, the Lydd and Hythe ranges in Kent, or even overseas locations such as the French military training area at La Courtine. Upon arrival in theatre, there are mandatory briefings as part of the Reception, Staging and Onward Integration (RSOI) package.

As indicated by the National Audit Office in March 2006 and the Public Accounts Committee in June 2007, there is room for further improvement at Chilwell, notably in terms of medical and dental inspection tests. The 'pay as you dine' arrangements have also aroused some criticism. Nonetheless, the system is clearly superior to the temporary mobilisation centres envisaged in the 1980s and the often ad hoc arrangements of the past.

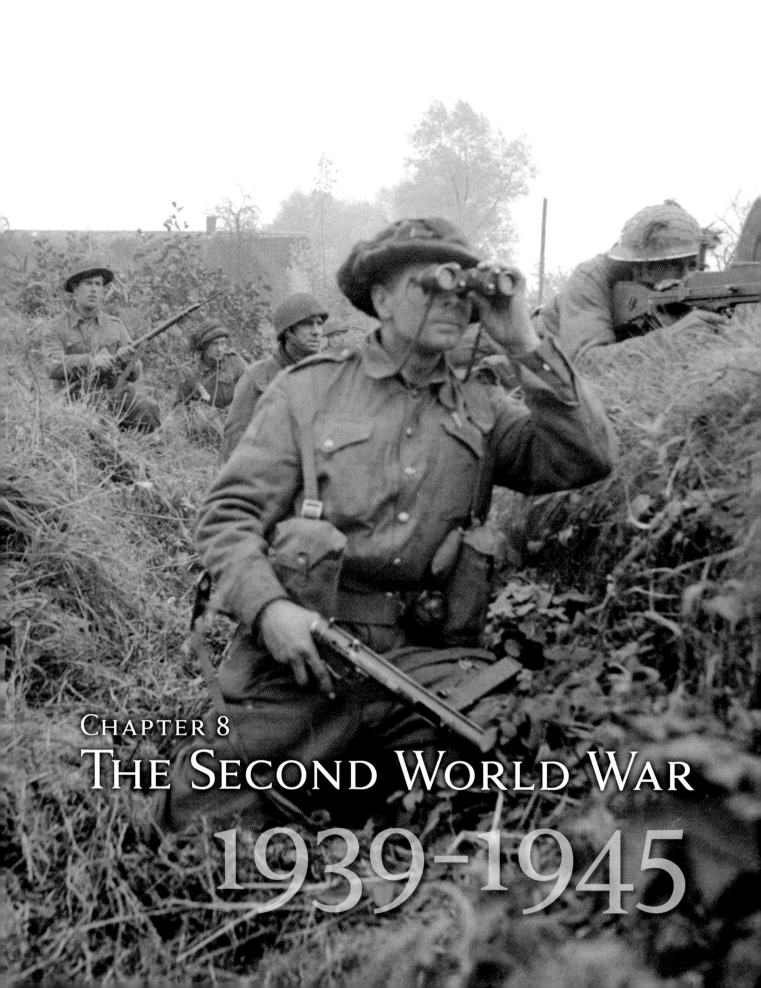

CHAPTER 8
THE SECOND WORLD WAR
1939-1945

"The nation must deal fairly with the
Territorial Army, and the Territorial Army
must fulfil its responsibilities to the nation."

LIEUTENANT COLONEL J K DUNLOP MC TD
The Problems and Responsibilities of the Territorial Army, 1935.

THERE WAS NOTHING logically to determine that a Territorial should not be as good a soldier as a regular after an appropriate period of wartime training, however deficient regulars deemed TA pre-war training to have been. It was unfortunate, therefore, that regulars had so often misunderstood the limitations placed upon Territorials by the nature of their civilian employment and had given far too little consideration to Territorials' susceptibilities. In turn, Territorials had failed to recognise that their jealously-preserved safeguards of integrity were a luxury in modern total war and that, even in peacetime, an exceptionally difficult financial position compelling the War Office to give priority to regulars might legitimately imperil such safeguards.

Now, in theory, there was a single integrated national army. Thus, in September 1939, there came an order for Territorial officers to remove the 'Ts' from their shoulder straps. Many resented the move—in one unit they responded to the regular adjutant's congratulations that they were now spared a stigma by continuing to wear them under their pocket flaps—though others equally did regard the removal of the 'T' as dispensing with a mark of inferiority. Just as in the Great War, there were tensions. Colonel E J King of the Middlesex Association, for example, recorded in 1943 that he felt the attitude of regulars in the first few months of the war was even worse than he had experienced in the Great War: 'The less intelligent type of staff officer, in the sacred name of discipline, lost no opportunity of shewing his contempt in the most offensive and provocative manner for the TA and all its ways.' As King also recalled: 'In at least one case a large body of commanding officers was informed that the TA had ceased to exist, and the sooner they forgot its traditions, and the fact they had ever belonged to it, the better.'

The Armed Forces (Conditions of Service) Act had suspended commissions in the TA, with wartime officers simply receiving 'emergency' commissions in the army as a whole rather than in specific units, as was the case in the Great War. As in the latter stages of the Great War, after the immediate commissioning of those qualified through OTC or TA qualification certificates, service in the ranks was a necessary prerequisite, OTC being effectively replaced by wartime Officer Cadet Training Units (OCTU) and renamed simply Training Corps in September 1940 so as not to preempt the role of OCTU.

Territorials had been selected previously for substantive promotion as vacancies occurred, but all wartime promotion would be temporary, with no opportunity for substantive advancement and reversion to the pre-war rank at

OPPOSITE *Troops of 2nd
Derbyshire Yeomanry take cover
in a ditch during an attack on
St Michielsgestel, Holland on
24th October 1944. The yeomen
acted as the divisional armoured
reconnaissance regiment for the
51st (Highland) Division but have
here discarded their vehicles.*
[IWM B 112220].

COURTESY OF THE IMPERIAL WAR MUSEUM.

ABOVE *Men of the 4th Lincolns resting at Skagge watch a Norwegian soldier examine one of their Short Magazine Lee Enfield rifles. Their 200-strong party had just carried out a 56-mile forced march under the command of Captain WRJ Craig [below] across snow and mountains to avoid being cut off by the Germans. Although they ditched their helmets to avoid recognition, not one soldier or weapon was lost.*

[IWM N 82]

COURTESY OF THE IMPERIAL WAR MUSEUM.

the war's end, whereas regulars would retain their wartime rank. Following continued representation, the Army Council agreed to examine the problem in June 1944. By this time 17,213 pre-war TA officers remained in the army, of whom 1,394 were now prisoners of war (POWs) and 752 unemployed. Currently, 90 Territorial substantive lieutenant colonels and 17 substantive colonels held higher acting or temporary rank, with 195 lieutenant colonels, 38 colonels and one major general holding appointments in their actual rank. Despite concern that Supplementary Reserve officers might claim the same privilege, it was resolved in October 1944 to introduce 'time' promotion for Territorial lieutenants after three years' service, captains after eight years' service, majors after 17 years' service and lieutenant colonels after 22 years provided there had been 12 months' successful performance in a temporary or acting higher rank. Colonels and general officers would still require special selection for time promotion, the latter after three years' service in an appointment carrying the higher rank. The concession only took effect in May 1945.

It was noticeable that, in October 1944, in addition to the single substantive major general, of the 15,067 Territorial officers employed, only 1,554 had risen above the rank of major. A total of just 36 Territorials[1] held the rank of brigadier, seven[2] that of major general and only one—a substantive colonel—that of lieutenant general. Indeed, of the 160 major generals who commanded field force divisions in North Africa, Italy and North-West Europe between 1940 and 1945, only three were Territorials. Throughout the war as a whole, nine out of ten officers holding the rank of brigadier or above were regulars or regular reservists. Indeed, the Army Council had decided in March 1940 to begin to replace Territorial commanding officers with regulars, having concluded that 55 per cent were too inexperienced or unfit to hold their commands. By October 1941, therefore, a total of 253 Territorial commanding officers had been removed compared to just 72 regulars. In April 1941 it was also indicated that every TA battalion should have at least five regular officers in addition to the commanding officer and quartermaster.

1. Eleven of them substantive colonels and 25 lieutenant colonels.
2. Five colonels and one lieutenant colonel.

ABOVE *A Bren Gun Carrier of one of the Territorial battalions of The Highland Light Infantry (City of Glasgow Regiment) on exercise, 1939.* [IWM H 1019]

COURTESY OF THE IMPERIAL WAR MUSEUM.

As in the Great War, complaints were raised that Territorials were being passed over, with Colonel Greenwell MP telling the Commons in 1944 that 'it may be said that it would be easier for a cable to go through the eye of a needle than for a Territorial Army officer to aspire to a rank higher than that of major, and certainly the command of formations such as brigade and higher seems to be almost exclusively though not entirely, reserved for Regular officers'. Similarly, Frederick Bellenger MP argued that, while TA officers had received promotion as Territorials before the war, once it broke out 'the regular officers did their best to displace them on every possible occasion'. Passed over in favour of a junior regular for command of his battalion despite his own nomination by Montgomery, one Wiltshire Territorial noted: 'by this time we Territorials had learnt that they always had the priority over us'. Others had similar experiences, the one surviving Territorial commanding officer in 48th Division noting in April 1941 that 'there is a very definite set against Territorial officers... I have sensed a feeling of hostility for some weeks on the part of the higher command'. Another Territorial, acting commander of 26 Armoured Brigade, doubted in May 1944 whether he would even continue to command his own regiment: 'I still have the ever-present spectre of some suitable Lt Col arriving from way back, either a loathsome little tick from the Tank Corps or else an equally horrible cast-off from some cavalry regiment—we've had plenty of experience of them this war.'

In part, regulars' suspicion of the TA reflected perceptions of the value of pre-war training. Major General Sir John Kennedy, a former GOC of 46th Division, had written in August 1938 that Territorial training was 'largely a veneer—which the rough usage of war destroys almost at once—unless it is carefully preserved until war experience gradually produces the real fighting soldier'. Pre-war training had been hampered by the turnover in personnel, the difficulty of concentrating men from even the same section on a particular evening, especially if a unit was scattered through a rural area, and the concomitant unevenness in military knowledge. Often both weekend and annual camps had been devoted to unit and sub-unit training so that Territorials had even less experience of combined arms practices than regulars. Indeed, unlike regulars theoretically trained to undertake appointments two ranks above their current

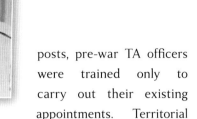

Changi Prisoner of War Camp,

SINGAPORE

16th June, 1942.

My dear Mrs Clarke,

    I am sure you would like to know a little more of the circumstances of your husband's death. May I first say how sorry I am, and I realise how dreadful the blow is for you, because your married life has been so short, you have the very deep sympathy of us all who knew and valued your husband very greatly.

    In his death the Battalion suffered the first casualty of the Battle of Singapore. Jimmy had been out for several days working hard driving military trucks, there was so much to do as we had only been on the island a few days, and the Japanese had made a successful landing. Jimmy was sent out with a sargeant to collect petrol from a supply depot, while he was there there was heavy shelling and a shell burst near his trunk, and he was hit by a piece

posts, pre-war TA officers were trained only to carry out their existing appointments. Territorial officers had been able to attend short courses at Sandhurst, but battalion commanders had not been required to attend a Senior Officers School before appointment. Doubling the TA in 1938 meant that there had not been enough instructors to establish a training cadre in order to raise a duplicate unit as well as maintain the original unit's own efficiency when it, in turn, had been required to absorb new recruits in order to reach wartime establishments. Thereafter, Territorials had as much or as little training as the rest of the army, but beginning from a weaker position, not least in terms of equipment. It can be noted, however, that Territorials often proved innovative. General (later Field Marshal) Sir Claude Auchinleck, who commanded in the Middle East from June 1941 to August 1942, believed Territorials to be 'more enterprising' and 'less hidebound' than regulars.

One highly effective trainer of infantry was Captain (later Major) Lionel Wigram, a Territorial in The Royal Fusiliers, who established the first divisional battle school to accustom men to live firing conditions in 47th (2nd London) Division in July 1941, using a former holiday camp at Chelwood Gate, West Sussex. Successively attached as chief instructor to the GHQ Home Forces Central Battle School at Barnard Castle, in County Durham, and the new School of Infantry, Wigram was co-author of the GHQ Home Forces infantry instructors' manual in October 1942, having also published a tract on infantry training, *Battle School*, at his own personal expense in July 1942. Some within the War Office criticised what they regarded as 'standardised rules for standardised tactical problems' but Wigram countered that, if an individual lacked natural initiative, it was preferable that he be taught something specific. There was also criticism of 'blood and hate' methods used to induce hatred of the enemy, which were dropped in May 1942. Generally, however, it was recognised that hard, realistic training improved morale and military knowledge. Wigram himself

"He was given a Christian burial in a special grave in a garden of a large plantation on the North East corner of the island of Singapore. I mention this because in the later stages of the battle we did not always get the opportunity of giving so much time to burials."

REV. E W B CORDINGLY,
9TH BN NORTHUMBERLAND
FUSILIERS

ABOVE *Men from D Company,
1st London Irish Rifles training
with a PIAT at Forli, Italy, 1st
February 1945. The PIAT was
based on a prototype developed
by a Territorial officer, Stewart
Blacker.* [IWM NA 22007]

COURTESY OF THE IMPERIAL WAR MUSEUM

went overseas in May 1943 and was killed in Italy in February 1944.

Less successfully, the Blacker Bombard, later known as the Spigot Mortar and introduced to the Home Guard in 1941, was the invention of Lieutenant Colonel Stewart Blacker, an eccentric former commander of 58th (Sussex) Field Brigade, RA (TA) who, when an Indian army soldier, had once been part of the 1933 Houston-Mt Everest Expedition and became one of the first men to fly over the great peak. While claimed as a combination of an anti-tank and bombardment weapon capable of firing 14lb anti-personnel and 20lb anti-tank bombs, the Bombard had a mixed reputation. Its inaccuracy almost killed Charles de Gaulle at its first demonstration for Churchill at Chequers in August 1940. Another idea proved more fruitful, with Millis Jefferis developing the PIAT (Projector Infantry Anti-Tank) from one of Blacker's experimental prototypes. At least five Second World War VCs were won by infantrymen disabling German tanks or artillery with PIATs, the only D-Day VC, Sergeant Major Stanley Hollis, a Territorial company sergeant major with the 6th Green Howards, engaging a German gun with one. The most prolific inventor of trench warfare munitions in the Great War had also been a Territorial: Captain Henry Newton of the 1/5th Sherwood Foresters.

In an attempt to bolster TA formations, there was much cross-posting to even-out strengths in 1939, with some 'first line' formations[3] posting back younger men to the 'second line' in the manner of August 1914 although there was no official authority to do so. At least 11,000 'immatures' were sent to AA Command in October 1939 from those TA divisions intended for the BEF. Units were also interchanged, with most Territorial divisions receiving one regular battalion per brigade and regular divisions receiving between one and three Territorial battalions in return. Artillery regiments and engineer field companies were also switched. Thus, 7th Worcesters, 1/8th Lancashire Fusiliers and 99th (Royal Bucks Yeomanry) Field Regiment RA replaced 2nd Royal Warwicks, 1st Border Regiment and 18th Field Regiment RA in 2nd Division, ultimately serving through the Burma campaign. Another exchange between artillery formations took place after the fall of France so that those who had experienced action

---

3. Those regarded as senior at the time of the doubling of the TA in 1938.

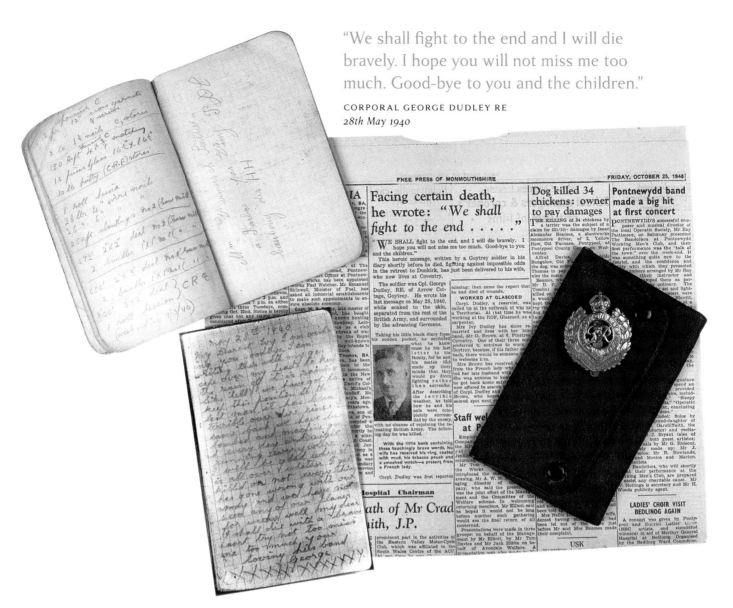

"We shall fight to the end and I will die bravely. I hope you will not miss me too much. Good-bye to you and the children."

CORPORAL GEORGE DUDLEY RE
28th May 1940

ABOVE The tobacco pouch, cap badge and notebook belonging to Corporal George Dudley—a Territorial Royal Engineer from Goytrey. It contains the scribbled story [photocopied leaf] of his final desperate hours during the Battle of France but it did not reach his widow until 1946.

In spite of receiving official notification that George had died of wounds, one of his three sons had refused to leave Goytrey in case his father ever returned.

COURTESY OF THE CASTLE AND REGIMENTAL
MUSEUM, MONMOUTH

could pass on lessons to home units. There was also the constant turnover of personnel through drafting, posting and volunteering so that the proportion of pre-war Territorials in any unit was steadily eroded. Some Territorial HAA regiments serving in Italy and the Middle East even received 'dilutees' from the African Auxiliary Pioneer Corps (later the African Pioneer Corps)[4] from June 1944 onwards.

Yet, whatever perceived shortcomings, Territorials were still expected to be ready for overseas service in advance of any pre-war calculations. The assumption in 1938 was that no fully equipped Territorial division could take the field for eight months after mobilisation. By April 1939 it had been anticipated that ten TA divisions could be sent abroad after six months, with the remainder by 12 months. In the event, three Territorial divisions[5] arrived in France in January and February 1940, the time between the dispatch of the initial regular

4. Mainly Basutos.
5. The 48th (South Midland), 50th (Northumbrian) and 51st (Highland) Divisions.

field force and their arrival having been cut to four months. Government, however, had resolved to avoid alienating public opinion by giving priority to the first batches of conscripts, and instructors were thin on the ground. By the time the German offensive in France and the Low Countries opened on 10th May 1940, there were 13 divisions in the BEF, of which eight were Territorial—the 12th (Eastern), 23rd (2nd Northumbrian), 42nd (East Lancashire), 44th (Home Counties) and 46th (North Midlands) Divisions having all arrived in April 1940, though the 12th, 23rd and 46th were intended merely as line of communications troops. Of the remaining TA divisions, the 43rd (Wessex), 45th (2nd Wessex) and 52nd (Lowland), all regarded as training formations, formed the nucleus of Southern Command, while the 38th (2nd Welsh), 47th (2nd London), 59th (Staffordshire) and 61st (2nd South Midland) Divisions were allocated to provide aid to the civil power in London, South Wales, Lancashire and the Midlands respectively. The 9th (2nd Highland) Division was spread all over Scotland.

It was in Norway in April 1940, however, that Territorials first saw action, the main burden of providing a hastily improvised expeditionary force to counter German invasion falling on 49th (West Riding) Division, 146 Brigade (MAURICEFORCE) landing at Namsos on 16th April and 148 Brigade (SICKLEFORCE) at Aandalsnes on 18th April. Without motor transport, radios or

COURTESY OF IMPERIAL TOBACCO

LEFT *A 4.2-inch mortar of the 1st Battalion, Princess Louise's Kensington Regiment in action near Adrano, Italy, 6th August 1943.* [IWM NA 5666]

COURTESY OF THE IMPERIAL WAR MUSEUM.

LEFT *Members of the LDV being instructed in simple German phrases including 'Halt' and 'Hands Up'.* [IWM HU 50154]

COURTESY OF THE IMPERIAL WAR MUSEUM

sufficient ammunition, and with little artillery, no anti-aircraft defence and only anti-tank rifles, the attempt to save Norway was doomed, the TA brigades being withdrawn between 1st and 3rd May. Losses were heavy with, for example, only six officers and 150 men returning from the 1/5th Leicesters.

The 1940 campaign in France and Belgium was much more finely balanced than popularly supposed. Just ten out of 141 German divisions used were armoured and the Panzers soon outstripped their infantry support, 80 per cent of the army still being dependent upon horse-drawn transport. The French actually had more and better tanks than the Germans but the allied command structure was ill coordinated. Orders passed down the tortuous command chain bore little reality once they had reached formations. By comparison to the French, the British benefiting from their more pragmatic approach and the ability to muddle through despite the shortage of manpower, the lack of air support, poor communications, and the shortages of food, water and fuel. Despite the manifold disadvantages, Territorials offered stubborn defence, with

BELOW *A sergeant instructor explains the workings of a rifle to two LDV members at Bisley Ranges, 1940.* [IWM H 1917]

COURTESY OF THE IMPERIAL WAR MUSEUM

the 48th Division fighting first on the Dendre, and 42nd and 44th Divisions on the Escaut. Initially held in reserve, 50th Division was committed to the celebrated counter-attack at Arras on 26th May 1940. Though never intended as fighting formations, the 12th, 23rd and 46th Divisions were all thrown into the attempt to hold back the German threat to the BEF's southern flank on 19th May while 1st Queen Victoria's Rifles landed to defend Calais on 22nd May. Detached to gain experience with the French back in April, 51st Division became the nucleus of the 'Second BEF' following the end of

the Dunkirk evacuation on 3rd June, its efforts to hold a new line south of the Somme assisted by the arrival of elements of 1st Armoured Division and 52nd Division. The 51st Division was compelled to surrender at St Valéry-en-Caux on 9th June while the remaining armour and 52nd Division, of which only 157 Brigade had been seriously engaged, was withdrawn through Cherbourg on 17th June.

Defeat raised the prospect of invasion and brought new responsibilities for county associations that had been left with no real function beyond the welfare of their units, for they were tasked with administering a new auxiliary force similar to the VTC in the Great War. It was, of course, the Local Defence Volunteers (LDV), which was raised in response to the radio appeal on the evening of 14th May 1940 by Anthony Eden, the Secretary of State for War in the new Churchill coalition government. Administration of the LDV[6] was placed in the hands of the CTAs on 30th June 1940. Associations were permitted to authorise the appointment of administrative assistants for battalion strength formations with a grant of £300 per annum for such purposes, while the same instruction also provided for a capitation grant for the associations of £1 per man per annum.

ABOVE *A parade of 'Old Contemptibles' who had enlisted in the Local Defence Volunteers in May 1940. All have only LDV arm bands by way of uniform—a measure intended to prevent them being treated as 'franc tireurs' and therefore shot out of hand on capture—and none appear to have weapons.* [IWM H 2005]

COURTESY OF THE IMPERIAL WAR MUSEUM

The task of administering the LDV was not easy. As the chairman of Gloucestershire's finance sub-committee put it, compared to the well understood TA peacetime regulations running to 500 pages, associations were expected to administer the LDV 'on instructions contained in one Army Council Instruction of 29 paragraphs together with a few non-committal letters from the War Office'. A total of 24 association secretaries had been recalled to the forces in 1939, the increased amount of work resulting in 11 returning in response to requests from the associations in September 1940. It was pointed out that they would suffer financially, but the Treasury refused compensation on the grounds that they had returned to associations voluntarily. In February 1941 Sir John Brown, who remained DGTA until, significantly, the post was redesignated that of Director General of the Home Guard and TA in May 1941, requested some reward for

6. Renamed the Home Guard on 23rd July 1940.

ABOVE *Sergeant McPherson*
tries to convince Gunner Willcox
that he is getting 'the best in the
shop' as the 156th Lanarkshire
Yeomanry) Field Regiment RA
refit with tropical uniforms in the
Anzio bridgehead, 2nd May, 1944.

[IWM NA 14448]

COURTESY OF THE IMPERIAL WAR MUSEUM

BELOW *Humber armoured cars*
of the Inns of Court Regiment,
9th Armoured Division, on
parade at Guisborough in
Yorkshire, 19th August 1941.

[IWM H 12981]

COURTESY OF THE IMPERIAL WAR MUSEUM

association staffs struggling with Home Guard administration and welfare after having already presided over the doubling of the TA and its mobilisation. He suggested civil OBEs but this was rejected, as there was no provision for awarding civil OBEs to those working for defence departments. Associations also remained responsible for cadets, a new expanded Army Cadet Force being established in April 1942, with cadet units affiliated to TA units and officers initially commissioned by lords lieutenant before being given the sovereign's commission in the TA Reserve of Officers.

The initial LDV role was a limited, static one with an emphasis upon observation, hence the early epithet of 'Look, Duck and Vanish', but also entailing blocking roads and guarding vulnerable points. General Sir Walter Kirke, appointed Commander-in-Chief of Home Forces in September 1939, had envisaged regulars providing a mobile defence but, on 25th June 1940, Kirke's successor, General Sir Edmund Ironside, declared in favour of a coastal 'crust' of mostly second line Territorial divisions backed by what became known as the GHQ Line of some 2,500 pillboxes, many to be manned by the LDV. There was doubt as to the wisdom of placing mobile reserves well to the rear of the GHQ Line. General Sir Alan Brooke, who replaced Ironside on 20th July 1940, placed emphasis instead on holding the coast in greater strength with mobile reserves closer to the beaches. The return of the BEF materially improved the manpower situation but while, in theory, 1.3 million men were available, only approximately half were sufficiently trained to act as a field army and the losses of equipment

in France had been considerable. As a result, the first reduction of Territorial and other divisions occurred—the 12th, 23rd and 66th (2nd East Lancashire) Divisions being broken up in June and July 1940.

As is now known, Hitler only issued a directive establishing the necessary pre-conditions for Operation SEALION on 16th July. Those preconditions, not least the elimination of the RAF, were not achieved and the initial decision to attempt an invasion on 15th September 1940 was first postponed to 21st September and then, on 12th October, until the spring of 1941. There is some evidence that a SEALION II was contemplated in July 1941 but

planning notice was set at eight months in September 1941 and at 12 months in March 1942. In Britain itself only armed sabotage was being contemplated as a risk by November 1943 though, with the approach of D-Day, plans were updated against possible suicidal spoiling raids. Most local invasion committees ceased to function by the summer of 1943 and the Home Guard was stood down on 31st December 1944. Its strength had reached around 1.7 million by March 1941.

Some 145,000 men from the Home Guard served in 93 rocket and 27 HAA batteries and a further 7,000 in coastal artillery batteries from 1942 onwards, thus supplementing Territorials tasked with home defence. ATS personnel also joined anti-aircraft units from April 1941 onwards, the first mixed battery being formed four months later. In 1939 AA Command's seven divisions comprised 51 HAA, 30 LAA and nine Searchlight Regiments, to which could be added 41 Searchlight Regiments found by the Royal Engineers and by some infantry units. Anti-aircraft and coastal artillery units together comprised more than 40 per cent of the TA's overall strength in 1939. All searchlight regiments were then transferred from the RE to the RA in August 1940. Initially comprising 17 heavy artillery regiments, Territorial coastal artillery was also reorganised in September 1940 into 35 (later 39) Coast Regiments. Subsequently, more infantry battalions were converted while other new anti-aircraft and searchlight units were also formed around cadres taken from within existing Territorial units in AA Command. Expansion to 12 divisions in three corps was authorised in

ABOVE *410 Coast Regiment RA (TA), Fan Bay, Dover manning a BL 9.2in/47 Mark X coastal defence gun. Designed in the late 1890s for pre-Dreadnought battleships and armoured cruisers, these guns were capable of firing a 380lb shell out to 18 nautical miles at a rate of one per minute.*

COURTESY OF THE ROYAL ARTILLERY MUSEUM, WOOLWICH.

ABOVE *Lieutenant Colonel G D Fanshawe, OBE [left] commanding 86th Field Regiment (Hertfordshire Yeomanry) together with his Adjutant Captain R R Thornton [writing at table], and RSM T Lightfoot at camp near Romney in the New Forest in May 1944. A pen and wash drawing by Anthony Gross. The Regiment was attached to 69 Infantry Brigade (50th Division) for the assault landing on* GOLD *Beach.* [IWM ART LD 3942]

COURTESY OF THE IMPERIAL WAR MUSEUM.

November 1941, this structure being replaced by seven 'groups' in October 1942.

There were shortages of ammunition and of both target and towing aircraft. Over the harsh winter of 1939-4, many isolated anti-aircraft and searchlight batteries, such as those on the Norfolk and Lincolnshire coasts, the Derbyshire peaks and the Shetlands, suffered extraordinarily difficult service conditions, sometimes under canvas. Southern airfield defence batteries in 6th AA Division were among the first to become engaged in August 1940 although there were also aerial attacks on a number of cities in the North and Midlands including Birmingham and Liverpool, both the responsibility of 4th AA Division. The first bombing raid on London occurred on 6th/7th September 1940, its anti-aircraft defences being the responsibility of 1st AA Division. Other towns and cities were also targeted through 1940 and 1941 and, though the London 'Blitz' ended on 10th May 1941, the provinces suffered the 'Baedeker'[7] raids in 1942 and

7. Following the bombing of Lübeck in 1942, the Luftwaffe launched a series of retaliatory raids against strategically unimportant but picturesque British cities. The cities were reputedly selected from the German Baedeker Tourist Guide to Britain.

OPPOSITE *Infantry of 17 Platoon, 'H' Company, 2nd London Irish Rifles hurl hand grenades during an attack on a German strongpoint on the southern bank of the River Senio, 22nd March 1945. The sergeant at left is holding a Devry cine camera which was on standard issue to the Army Film and Photographic Unit.* [IWM NA 23243]

COURTESY OF THE IMPERIAL WAR MUSEUM.

The Sherman was alarmingly flammable, hence the German epithet of 'Tommy Cookers' and the British of 'Ronsons', after a cigarette lighter which 'lit every time'.

1943. The 'Baby Blitz' of January to May 1944 was then followed by the V1 and V2 offensive, at its height between June and September 1944. In all, AA Command accounted for 822 enemy aircraft, probably destroyed a further 237 and damaged an estimated 422. It also accounted for just over 2,000 V-1s.

It should not be thought, however, that anti-aircraft units remained in Britain throughout the war since many proceeded overseas to act in base and airfield defence, or in mobile grounds roles. Thus, 44th (Leicestershire Regiment) AA (Searchlight) Battalion, RE became 121st LAA Regiment, RA in 1942, armed with Bofors guns, and was subsequently deployed to Normandy in 1944. The infantry shortage eventually led to the conversion of 38 Territorial anti-aircraft and coastal artillery units back to infantry as garrison regiments, and to the combing out of fitter personnel to be transferred to the field army.

Manpower generally was a crucial problem since a consequence of manpower policies far better ordered than during the Great War was an increasing shortage of men for the army as sustaining economic production took priority. The problem, which became acute by 1944, underpinned the increasing unwillingness of British commanders to risk unnecessary casualties. Compared to the 56 infantry divisions present on the Western Front in 1917, the largest commitment of British forces to any theatre between 1939 and 1945 was 10 infantry and five armoured divisions in North-West Europe in 1944. Even this required considerable effort and, inevitably, TA divisions suffered further reduction. Indeed, of the 24 Territorial infantry divisions existing during the war, ten were broken up, the three disposed of in 1940 being followed by the 44th and 54th in 1943; and the 38th, 45th, 47th and 59th in 1944. The 42nd was converted to an armoured division in November 1941 but was then also disbanded without seeing action as a division. The 54th (East Anglian), 55th (West Lancashire) and 61st Divisions remained in Britain throughout the war. After its experiences in France in May 1940, the 48th Division also ceased to be regarded as a first line division in 1942 with many of its units transferred: 143rd, 145th and 147th Field Ambulances together with 22nd and 23rd Field Dressing Stations, for example, were all sent to 15th Division. While 51st Division was reconstituted after its loss in June 1940 by renaming the 9th Division, one entire

ABOVE *A 25-pounder of 152nd Field Regiment (Ayrshire Yeomanry) in action on the Gustav Line in Italy, 13th May 1944. The gun is fitted with a flash eliminator. The regiment had been stationed in Orkney and Shetland before arriving in North Africa in 1942, then served throughout the Italian campaign.*
[IWM NA 14783]
COURTESY OF THE IMPERIAL WAR MUSEUM.

OPPOSITE *A Sherman crew from the 2nd County of London Yeomanry (Westminster Dragoons) repair damage to one of the tank's suspension units caused by a German 88-mm shell, Normandy, 7th June 1944.*
[IWM B 5423]
COURTESY OF THE IMPERIAL WAR MUSEUM.

ABOVE *Major H S Flower, acting CO of the 9th Battalion, The Northumberland Fusiliers, went forward under cover of a white flag at 4pm on the 15th February 1942 to parley with the commander of the Japanese 11th Infantry Regiment (first on left, facing) in Singapore.*

COURTESY OF THE NORTHUMBERLAND FUSILIERS MUSEUM, ALNWICK

THE SELARANG BARRACKS INCIDENT

On 30th August 1942, the Japanese demanded that all PoWs in Changi sign a 'no escape' promise. The Allied PoWs refused to do so on the grounds that it was their duty to escape. Over 15,000 PoWs — Regulars and Territorials alike — were herded into the 800-man Selarang Barracks [top]. After four days, when dysentery took hold and men began to die, Allied commanders ordered their men to sign [left].

BELOW *Preparing a goat in the Selarang Barracks cookhouse.*

COURTESY OF THE ROYAL ARTILLERY MUSEUM, WOOLWICH.

RIGHT *The Crusader tanks of the Northamptonshire Yeomanry make their way along a three-mile battle practice run on the Linney Head AFV ranges in Pembrokeshire on 17th December 1942. The targetry consisted of mobile dummy tanks and dummy anti-tank guns that could simulate opening fire.* [IWM H 26380]

COURTESY OF THE IMPERIAL WAR MUSEUM.

BELOW *The crew of a Sexton Self-propelled Gun of 147th Field Regiment (Essex Yeomanry) preparing to fire on 21st November 1944. The unit was the first to fire its guns inside German territory.* [IWM B12023]

COURTESY OF THE IMPERIAL WAR MUSEUM.

division was lost in tragic circumstances. Intended as a reinforcement for the Middle East, 18th (2nd East Anglian) Division was diverted towards India while still at sea in December 1941. Early Japanese success then prompted its further diversion to Singapore—53 Brigade arriving on 13th January 1942 and the remainder of the division on 5th February. 53 Brigade was immediately thrown into the fighting, but the rest hardly had time to fire a shot before Singapore was surrendered on 15th February 1942 and they passed into a brutal captivity.

There was occasionally some resentment at the disappearance or substantial restructuring of units. In February 1941, for example, the West Riding Association opposed the Director General's plan to turn over funds collected privately in 1939 for the benefit of the staff of 49th Division to the division itself, now serving in Northern Ireland. It was said that the division had been effectively reconstituted after the Norwegian campaign to the extent that it had no direct connection with the original. No pre-war unit was actually disbanded but went into suspended animation, retaining the unit identity with no posted strength until it could be reconstituted. In the case of artillery units, however, the War Office made a distinction in December 1943 between batteries and regiments, enabling batteries to be disbanded but regiments to be retained, albeit in suspended animation.

As in the Great War there was also a shift in the perceived need for different kinds of troops. Between 1914 and 1918 not only had the ratio between what might be termed 'teeth' arms and support arms changed from 8.3:1.6 to 6.4:3.5 with the growth of the Army Service Corps and the Labour Corps but, within the 'teeth'

arms, the proportion of men in the infantry had declined from 53 per cent to 31 per cent, with the appearance of new kinds of units such as The Machine Gun Corps and The Tank Corps. In the Second World War, there was a shift towards more artillery, armoured and mechanised units as well as entirely new specialists such as paratroops, commandos and glider-borne troops. In 1939 the TA had 232 infantry battalions. In many cases, they were chosen for conversion to new roles. 1st Princess Louise's Kensingstons of The Middlesex Regiment, for example, became a specialised infantry support regiment; their mortars, machine guns and 20mm anti-aircraft cannon intended to provide close fire support and fire protection at brigade level. Infantry battalions that converted to an armoured car or tank role included the 4th Manchesters, 6th Royal

ABOVE *A gun crew from The Shropshire Yeomanry brew up in Italy, 1943. The yeomen formed both 75th and 76th Medium Regiments, RA when converted to the artillery role in 1940, both serving in the Middle East and Italy.* [IWM TR 1404]

COURTESY OF THE IMPERIAL WAR MUSEUM

ABOVE *The 5th Battalion, The Royal Berkshire Regiment were the Beach Battalion on* JUNO. *The battalion intelligence officer, standing beside the DUKW, oversees the embarkation of two groups of German prisoners on to landing craft on the evening of 6th June 1944.*

COURTESY OF THE RIFLES (BERKSHIRE AND WILTSHIRE) MUSEUM, SALISBURY.

Northumberland Fusiliers, and 6th Gloucesters. 159 (Welsh Border) Brigade, comprising the 1st Herefordshires, 4th King's Shropshire Light Infantry (KSLI) and 3rd Monmouths, with the remainder of 53rd Division, had been stationed in Northern Ireland since April 1940 when it was selected in May 1942 to be the Lorried Infantry Brigade in 11th Armoured Division, subsequently taking part in the North West Europe campaign. Three infantry battalions converted to paratroops, the 10th Royal Welch, 10th Green Howards and 2/4th South Lancashires becoming respectively the 6th (Royal Welch), 12th (Yorkshire) and 13th (Lancashire) Parachute Battalions. Some battalions also became the infantry component of Beach Groups; a brigade-sized formation responsible for facilitating the landing of men, vehicles and supplies across open beaches as well as clearing, organising and defending beach sectors. Thus, 2/4th Hampshires provided the defence component for Nos. 20 and 21 Beach Groups at Salerno, in Italy, in September 1943, and 5th (Hackney) Battalion, Royal Berks for No. 8 Beach Group on JUNO Beach on D-Day, 6th June 1944. Whole divisions could also be given new roles. Thus, the 52nd was trained as a 'mountain' division' but, as one historian put it, 'was then selected by some War Office humorist for the invasion of Walcheren' in the Netherlands in 1944.

Of the TA's 29 yeomanry regiments in 1939, eight went to Palestine as part of 1st Cavalry Division. In January 1941, the CIGS, Sir John Dill, wanted only three retained mounted. The CinC in the Middle East, Wavell, concurred. However,

while Dill suggested the three senior yeomanry regiments[8] remain horsed, Wavell suggested retaining one of the two regular regiments in the division—The Royal Scots Greys—and two different yeomanry regiments—the North Somerset Yeomanry and the Yorkshire Dragoons. The Army Council went largely with Wavell, though substituting the Cheshire Yeomanry for the Greys, with the Wiltshires and Warwickshires initially becoming lorried infantry[9] and the Yorkshire Hussars an armoured regiment. Subsequently, the Cheshires saw mounted action against the Vichy French in Syria before converting to Royal Signals in 1942. The North Somerset Yeomanry became 4th (later 14th) Air Formation Signals, tasked with providing communications for army-RAF liaison, while the Yorkshire Dragoons became a motor battalion before being redesignated as 9th King's Own Yorkshire Light Infantry (KOYLI).

The remainder of 1st Cavalry Division became 10th Armoured Division, serving in North Africa until broken up in June 1944. If this was the only true

ABOVE *A man of 63rd Anti-Tank Regiment (The Queen's Own Worcestershire Hussars) views a road sign at Stonehenge Camp on the Imphal to Kohima Road in Burma, November 1944.* [IWM SE 2955]

COURTESY OF THE IMPERIAL WAR MUSEUM.

8.   The Royal Wiltshire Yeomanry, the Warwickshire Yeomanry and the Yorkshire Hussars.

9.   Both were later armoured.

LEFT *Men of the 5th Battalion, The Wiltshire Regiment scramble aboard their storm boat at Vernon in order to force a crossing over the mist-laden River Seine. Five minutes after this photograph was taken, this boat was raked by enemy machine-gun fire. There were no survivors.*

COURTESY OF THE RIFLES (BERKSHIRE AND WILTSHIRE) MUSEUM, SALISBURY.

1ST HEREFORDSHIRES ADVANCE INTO GERMANY *Private Ward from Birmingham, shortly before going on leave [opposite top left]. Privates Hargest and Lewis examine a pair of Panzerfaust anti-tank weapons near Peterslager, 7th April 1945 [opposite top right]. Private Sinar on sentry duty near Sonsbeck, 6th March 1945 [top]. Men of the 1st Herefordshires sprint into action during a contact near Sonsbeck, 6th March 1945 [above]. Brewing up before moving to Lübeck, 2nd May 1945 [opposite bottom].*

COURTESY OF THE HEREFORDSHIRE LIGHT INFANTRY MUSEUM, HEREFORD.

RIGHT *Having manned their 25-pdr guns throughout three days and nights of thunder, lightning and torrential rain, Sergeant Hamilton and Gunner Tennant of 156th (Lanarkshire Yeomanry) Regiment RA, rescue what remains of their bivouac from the Italian mud on 5th December, 1943. Not a single man a managed to keep his kit dry.*

[IWM NA 9444]

COURTESY OF THE IMPERIAL WAR MUSEUM

OPPOSITE *Troops of the 5/7th Gordon Highlanders advance through the Reichswald 24 hours in to Operation* VERITABLE, *9th February, 1945. The attack on the Reichswald, which the German Army had been given five months to fortify, was preceded by the most concentrated artillery barrage of the war in the West. Half a million shells were fired in five and a half hours against a single German division on a seven-mile front.* [IWM B 14413]

COURTESY OF THE IMPERIAL WAR MUSEUM

Territorial armoured division, the number of units converted to the armoured role, in addition to the 12 tank battalions that had existed in 1939, meant that there was a Territorial presence in several armoured divisions and not just armoured units. The lorried infantry of 7th Armoured Division, for example, was provided by 131 Brigade drawn from The Queen's Royal Regiment (West Surrey). At Salerno in September 1943 it found itself serving alongside three more Territorial battalions from the same regiment serving in 169 Brigade with 56th Division. It was the only occasion when a brigade entirely composed of battalions from a single regiment was relieved in the line by another brigade drawn from the same regiment.

Britain had lost the early lead in medium tank design it had enjoyed in the early 1920s and entered the war with models that were well armoured but lightly armed and mechanically unreliable, though far better tanks such as the Churchill and Crusader were eventually available. American models such as the Sherman made good deficiencies of production in terms of numbers but the Sherman was alarmingly flammable, hence the German epithet of 'Tommy Cookers' and the British of 'Ronsons', after a cigarette lighter which 'lit every time'. The experience of armoured warfare in North Africa, Italy and North-West Europe was often a difficult one and remains a matter of historical controversy.

British armoured doctrine was uneven in its development and far from uniform in its application although cooperation between infantry and armour markedly improved in Normandy. In Operation EPSOM, which was part of the

RIGHT *A Cromwell tank crew from 4th County of London Yeomanry (Sharpshooters) preparing a meal in a Normandy field, 17th June 1944. From left to right: Trooper Arthur Nelson, Trooper William Leonard and Sergeant A Gordon. Following heavy losses, the 3rd and 4th County of London Yeomanry were amalgamated in August 1944.* [IWM B 5681]

COURTESY OF THE IMPERIAL WAR MUSEUM.

BELOW *Infantrymen of the 3rd Monmouthshire Regiment atop Sherman tanks of the 2nd Fife and Forfar Yeomanry awaiting orders to advance. Taken near Argentan in Normandy on 21st August 1944.* [IWM B 9528]

COURTESY OF THE IMPERIAL WAR MUSEUM.

attempt to break out of the Normandy bridgehead between 26th and 28th June 1944, 15th and 43rd Divisions and 11th Armoured Divisions combined reasonably well to force a way across the Odon River, albeit at heavy cost since the armour was committed prematurely. Indeed, most problems arose from inappropriate use of armour on narrow fronts amid *bocage*[10] country that did not lend itself to mobility. Operation GOODWOOD from 18th to 21st July 1944 saw 7th, 11th and Guards Armoured Divisions committed without sufficient artillery or infantry support, resulting in the loss of more than 400 tanks. Among those hardest hit was the 2nd Fife and Forfar Yeomanry in 11th Armoured Division, which lost virtually all its tanks. The Sherwood Rangers Yeomanry lost 40 tank commanders between 6th June and 11th July alone. Shortcomings were also manifest in the misfortunes of 4th County of London Yeomanry (Sharpshooters) of 7th Armoured Division at Villers-Bocage on 13th June 1944, when it lost 15 tanks, a half track and three scout cars to six German Tiger Tanks commanded by the redoubtable Michael Wittman. Again, the regiment had lacked both infantry and artillery support.

10. Small fields enclosed by hedgerows which typically consist of an earth bank three or four feet in height, with a ditch either side and topped by a line of thorny bushes whose roots bind the earth into a wall tough enough to render them impenetrable even to armoured vehicles.

The largest wartime expansion was that of the Royal Artillery, firepower being increasingly seen as a substitute for manpower, and heavy bombardment as a prerequisite for all set piece attacks. There had been 222 Territorial artillery units in 1939, with 100 field and medium regiments, 20 anti-tank regiments, eight Light Anti-Aircraft (LAA) regiments, and four survey regiments in the field force component. Six yeomanry regiments were newly converted to artillery, and artillery regiments themselves were also converted in many cases to a new specialism: when 86th (Hertfordshire Yeomanry) Field Regiment received its new Bishop self-propelled guns in March 1943 only one subaltern had ever driven a tank and it reputedly took two days to move all 24 guns the few miles from the railway station to the unit's camp. As in the Great War, artillery techniques were constantly refined. Thus, the gallant action fought by 107th Regiment RHA (South Notts Hussars Yeomanry) at KNIGHTSBRIDGE in the Western Desert against the German 15th and 21st Panzer and 90th Light Divisions from 27th May to 6th June 1942 reflected an initial tendency to use dispersed artillery in a forward role in line-of-sight engagements, with concomitant heavy losses. Subsequently, concentrated artillery fire became an integral element in the limited and carefully controlled set piece operations Montgomery favoured in North Africa and North-West Europe.

Other support units were equally redesignated, the plethora of the workshops and recovery sections maintained separately by the Royal Engineers (RE), Royal Army Ordnance Corps (RAOC), and the Royal Army Service Corps (RASC) being rationalised in August 1942 by establishing the Royal Electrical and Mechanical Engineers (REME) to detach tank maintenance and repair from the overworked RAOC and vehicle maintenance and repair from the equally stretched RASC. Thus, Tyne Electrical Company, RE became the 128th Electrical and Mechanical Company. Unchanged, however, were the 35 field ambulances, four hygiene companies and 15 general hospitals in the TA's establishment in 1939.

ABOVE *Lieutenant General W G Holmes, GOC 9th Army, stands on a Sherman tank of the Royal Wiltshire Yeomanry (Prince of Wales's Own) to watch a gunnery display in North Africa, 5th April 1943. Retained as horsed cavalry until 1940, the regiment converted to lorried infantry in 1941 and to armour in 1942.* [IWM E 23451]

COURTESY OF THE IMPERIAL WAR MUSEUM.

COURTESY OF IMPERIAL TOBACCO

503 FIELD COMPANY RE AT WAR

TOP *The Gennep Bailey Bridge built across the flooded Maas by 503 Field Company RE. At just over a mile long, it was the longest Bailey Bridge in the world and was strafed several times by German jet aircraft.*

ABOVE *Construction of the Venlo Bailey Bridge was hampered by dead bodies continually fouling the pontoons; nothing could be done except freeing them to float away.*

LEFT *The Bayeux bypass. The present day bypass follows the same route.*

COURTESY OF MR T MCCORKINDALE/THE ROYAL ENGINEERS MUSEUM, CHATHAM.

NORTHUMBRIAN BRIDGES OVER THE RHINE
The Tyne and Tees bridges were built by both Regular and Territorial Royal Engineers including 505 Field Company RE. [Top to Bottom] Wooden piles being driven in on the west bank of the Rhine. The work site with stores clearly visible. Engineers fixing the Bailey Bridge to the bulk timbers. Corporal Jimmy Belford ferrying stores across the Rhine at Rees. The concrete approach roads on the east bank of the Rhine.

COURTESY OF THE ROYAL ENGINEERS MUSEUM, CHATHAM.

RIGHT *An advance patrol of The 2nd Derbyshire Yeomanry, part of 6th Armoured Division, greeting Corporal Race [left] of the SAS Regiment.* [IWM NA 684]

COURTESY OF THE IMPERIAL WAR MUSEUM.

COURTESY OF IMPERIAL TOBACCO

OPPOSITE *Grand Admiral Doenitz, Hitler's designated successor as Führer, after surrendering to British forces at Flensburg on 23rd May 1945. The two pennants from his staff car were 'removed for safe custody' by the 1st Herefordshire Regiment. They are still very safe.*

COURTESY OF THE HEREFORDSHIRE LIGHT INFANTRY MUSEUM, HEREFORD.

By the war's end, Territorials had fought in every theatre and won 17 VCs and three GCs. Nine divisions had served in the 1940 campaign[11]; one had served in Norway (49th); five had served in the Middle East[12]; four had served in Sicily[13], and two in Italy[14]; eight had served in North-West Europe[15] and one had been lost in Malaya and Singapore (18th). As indicated earlier, however, Territorial units had also served with regular or even Dominion formations. The critical early defence of Kohima in Burma against the Japanese 31st Division, for example, between 5th and 19th April 1944, was led by the 4th Queen's Own Royal West Kents attached to 161 Indian Brigade of 5th Indian Division until the arrival of the first units of 2nd Division. The battalion had already served with 2nd New Zealand Division in North Africa before reaching India where it took part in operations in the Arakan.

The war, however, did not end for all with the defeat even of Japan in August 1945. The 2/7th Middlesex came under fire in the clash between French and Syrian nationalist forces in May 1945 and from Jewish terrorists in Palestine in September 1945. The 145th (Berkshire Yeomanry) Field Regiment only went overseas in September 1945, taking part in the reoccupation of Malaya. It was then attached to 5th Indian Division in Java until April 1946 to assist the restoration of order and fight against Indonesian nationalists, who were resisting the return of Dutch colonial authorities. Such unexpected conflicts suggested that the post-war world would not be free of problems.

11. 12th, 23rd, 42nd, 44th, 46th, 48th, 50th, 51st, and 52nd Divisions.
12. 44th, 46th, 50th, 51st and 56th (1st London) Divisions.
13. 46th, 50th, 51st and 56th Divisions.
14. 46th and 56th Divisions.
15. 15th, 43rd, 49th, 50th, 51st, 52nd, 53rd (Welsh) and 59th Divisions.

TERRITORIALS AND THE BATTLE FOR FRANCE

ABOVE *The defenders of*
Calais. The image was taken by
a Wehrmacht photographer who
entered the town on 27th May
1940, the day after it fell.

COURTESY OF THE ROYAL GREEN JACKETS MUSEUM,
WINCHESTER.

"We were so tired,
we didn't care if
they'd mowed us
down. We'd reached
the end of the line."

PRIVATE R MATTHEWS,
THE BUCKINGHAMSHIRE
BATTALION

GERMAN ACCOUNTS IN 1940 often praised the efforts of poorly equipped Territorial units to win precious time for the BEF to escape to the coast. When landed at Calais on 22nd May, 1st Queen Victoria's Rifles, ostensibly a motorcycle battalion, had no transportation and a third were armed only with revolvers, with which they had had no chance to practice. There were no bombs for their 2-inch mortars and only five rounds for each Boys anti-tank rifle, which few had actually fired. Riflemen had only fired a maximum of 50 rounds with their .303 Lee Enfields in practice and the battalion as a whole had only once conducted a Bren Gun course. The Territorial 1st and 2nd Searchlight Batteries, also involved in the gallant defence of Calais between 22nd and 26th May, had no infantry training, had never fired an anti-tank rifle and only rarely fired a Bren. One of the searchlight officers captured at Calais was Airey Neave, the first Briton to escape from Colditz and, later, as a Conservative MP murdered by the IRA in 1979.

Similarly, when detached to defend Hazebrouck between 26th and 28th May, the 1st Bucks Battalion of 48th Division had been mostly employed in digging defences and repairing roads since arriving in France in January and had had to absorb a large draft in April with only six months' training. There was little practice ammunition available, and both officers and men were inexperienced.

"We must recognise that the British fighters were magnificent. We must assume that these were their crack regiments. Each soldier was of marvellous physique and full of fighting spirit. At Hazebrouck our soldiers had to storm each house separately."

GERMAN RADIO BROADCAST OF 2ND JUNE DESCRIBING THEIR ENCOUNTER WITH TERRITORIALS IN MAY, 1940.

Yet, their resistance to the 8th Panzer and 29th Motorised Divisions was described by a German broadcast as 'truly worthy of the highest traditions of the British army'. Less than a third of the battalion escaped.

One of the more remarkable performances was that of the 12th and 23rd Divisions. As second line formations, they were only supposed to be employed as labour. They had only 15 field guns and two 4.7-inch howitzers between them and were without maps, air support, or any means of communication other than dispatch riders. Committed to the support of the French south of the perimeter forming around Dunkirk, they faced seven German Panzer divisions and were virtually destroyed on 19th May. In marked contrast to the French involved, they were given full credit by German war diaries for their efforts. Even the few hours' delay that they helped impose on the Germans was vital to the security of the Dunkirk perimeter. A report by the German IV Corps concluded that, while less well trained than regulars, Territorials had proved their equal in morale.

ABOVE *The original cartoon that appeared in The Daily Mail on 5th June 1940.*

COURTESY OF THE ROYAL GREEN JACKETS MUSEUM, WINCHESTER.

LEFT *Officers and men of The Buckinghamshire Battalion marching into captivity after the fall of Hazebrouck on 28th May 1940.*

COURTESY OF M. DOMINIQUE FAIVRE.

Territorials and the Desert War

ABOVE *Men of the 98th Field Regiment (Surrey and Sussex Yeomanry), lighting up their Italian cigars in Tobruk, 10th November 1941. Originally taken from the Italians in the first major British offensive of the Second World War, Tobruk successfully withstood siege by the Germans from April to December 1941 though it was to fall quickly to a second German assault in June 1942. [IWM E 6509]*

COURTESY OF THE IMPERIAL WAR MUSEUM

FOR ALMOST TWO years after Italy's entry into the war in June 1940, four regular British divisions[1] supplemented by ten Empire and Dominion divisions, fought the war in the Western Desert. 50th Division's North African baptism of fire came only in May 1942 when 150 Brigade was overwhelmed in the battles around Gazala as Rommel launched his second major offensive. The second Territorial division to arrive was the 44th, which was brought up to the front by Montgomery as soon as he assumed command of Eighth Army in August 1942. It was followed by 51st Division, which arrived on the eve of the second battle of El Alamein, as did the Territorial 10th Armoured Division. Curiously, following its reconstitution in June 1940, the Highlanders had been commanded successively by two future Eighth Army commanders, Sir Alan Cunningham, who commanded in the desert from September to November 1941, and Neil Ritchie, who commanded from November 1941 to June 1942.

Allocated to XXX Corps, the 51st was led by Major General Douglas 'Lang Tam' Wimberley, who insisted on maintaining its distinctive Scottish identity: 7th Middlesex, the divisional machine gun battalion, were classed as 'mascots to the Jocks'. Allowed two months to acclimatise after landing in Egypt in August,

1.   1st, 2nd and 7th Armoured Divisions and 70th Division.

the 51st undertook four full-scale divisional exercises prior to Second Alamein. Tasked with spearheading Montgomery's main offensive in the north—Operation LIGHTFOOT—XXX Corps would advance on 23rd October with massed artillery support to fight through the German defences and minefields in order to enable the armoured units of X Corps, including 10th Armoured Division, to pass through in turn. In the south, XIII Corps, including 50th Division and 132 Brigade of 44th Division—the other two brigades had become motorised brigades for 7th and 10th Armoured Divisions—would hold German reserves. An attritional battle would then be fought within the German defensive zone before a breakout was launched.

In the event, progress through the minefields was slower than anticipated as the engineers[2] worked painstakingly to find and lift anti-personnel and anti-tank mines: each infantry division needed to cut at least three 16-yard lanes to a depth of 6,000 yards and each armoured division three 40-yard lanes. It was not until 1st November, therefore, that Operation SUPERCHARGE was mounted in the north, one of Wimberley's brigades being put under command of the New Zealand Division for the occasion. With its armour severely depleted and supplies running low, the Afrika Korps began to retreat on the following day. The cost to the 51st was a high one. So was the subsequent fighting in Tunisia as the Eighth Army pursued the Afrika Korps and linked with the allied forces that had landed in French North Africa in November. The frontal assault on the Wadi Akarit in Tunisia, in which the 50th and 51st took part on 5th April 1943, was described by Montgomery as 'the heaviest and most savage fighting we have seen since I have commanded the Eighth Army'.

ABOVE *Captain David Lloyd Owen with Private 'Tich' Cave on the back of the 30 cwt truck behind, outside the Farouk Hotel in Siwa. Lloyd Owen joined the 'Y'(Yeomanry) Patrol of the Long Range Desert Group in mid-1941 and went on to lead it after the original Commanding Officer was wounded.* [IWM HU 25299]

COURTESY OF THE IMPERIAL WAR MUSEUM

2. 274th, 275th and 276th Field Companies, RE in the case of 51st Division.

RIGHT *A 25-pdr field gun of 153rd Field Regiment (Leicestershire Yeomanry) during a practice shoot in the mountains near Tripoli in the Lebanon, 7th June 1943.* [IWM E 25017]

COURTESY OF THE IMPERIAL WAR MUSEUM

THE 43RD WESSEX DIVISION
IN NORTH-WEST EUROPE

TOP *Troops of 130 Brigade,*
43rd (Wessex) Division take cover
from mortar fire, 10th July 1944.

[IWM B 6852]

COURTESY OF THE IMPERIAL WAR MUSEUM

In support of the
Rhine crossing in
March, the 43rd
subsequently helped
take Bremen, with
the 4th Wiltshires
capturing a
lieutenant general, a
vice admiral and, for
good measure, the
local Nazi bishop.

VETERAN EIGHTH ARMY formations brought back to Britain to participate in the North-West Europe campaign sometimes proved less effective than anticipated in the breakout battle from the Normandy bridgehead in June and July 1944. Montgomery, indeed, despite criticising the home army in the past for supposed failures to learn appropriate lessons, began to show a preference for using fresh formations, such as 15th and 43rd Divisions, that had not experienced the campaigns in North Africa and Sicily. Firepower was meant to offset limited manpower but, in the *bocage* country, did not always have the influence expected. Infantry comprised only 15 per cent of 21st Army Group but took 70 per cent of the casualties. In Operation EPSOM, 15th Division took 2,331 casualties or 50 per cent of its rifle company strength.

Major General Gwilym Ivo Thomas, who commanded the 43rd from March 1942 to September 1945, was a tough, uncompromising figure. The division consisted of 129, 130 and 214 Brigades, and had a full supporting cast of a machine gun battalion, an armoured car reconnaissance regiment, three artillery field regiments, an anti-tank regiment, LAA regiment, divisional signals, four RASC companies, three RE field companies and a bridging platoon, a RAOC field park and a mobile laundry and bath unit, three REME brigade workshops, a provost

company, a field security section, a postal unit, as well as three RAMC field ambulances, two dressing stations, and a hygiene section. Chosen as the divisional emblem in 1933, the Wyvern was intended to reflect Wessex's Anglo-Saxon heritage: some, however, referred to it as the 'Pregnant Prawn'.

The 43rd soon perfected 'pepper pot' artillery tactics of firing off all their weapons in a bombardment—including anti-aircraft and anti-tank guns and medium machine guns—in order to demoralise a defence. It also practiced the 'sandwich' method of using infantry between, rather than behind, two echelons of tanks, providing better infantry-tank cooperation. This did not mean, however, that the division was spared hard fighting. The struggle for Hill 112 and nearby Maltot between 10th and 13th July 1944 proved particularly bloody, earning Thomas the nickname 'Butcher' in some quarters. The division suffered 2,000 casualties in just 36 hours, the 5th Duke of Cornwall's Light Infantry (DCLI) taking 320 in 11 hours while trying to hold 'Cornwall Wood'. There was a welcome period of rest once the 43rd got across the Seine in August 1944 and small groups were allowed into Paris. One quick-thinking padre, who reached the city unofficially and whom Thomas spotted in the Champs-Elysées, claimed he was there to buy communion wine. Next, the 43rd were part of the abortive attempt to reach the beleaguered 1st Airborne Division at Arnhem. There followed the difficult advance to the Siegfried Line around Geilenkirchen in atrocious winter weather in November 1944 and the clearing of the Reichswald Forest around Cleve and Goch in February 1945. In support of the Rhine crossing in March, the 43rd subsequently helped take Bremen, with the 4th Wiltshires capturing a lieutenant general, a vice admiral and, for good measure, the local Nazi bishop. Between 24th June 1944 and 5th May 1945, the 43rd had 12,484 casualties, of whom 1,587 were killed in action, including a brigadier and 12 battalion or regimental commanders.

ABOVE *Infantrymen from 43rd Wessex Division sheltering in a slit trench between Hills 112 and 13 in the Odon valley, 16th July 1944.* [IWM B 7441]
COURTESY OF THE IMPERIAL WAR MUSEUM

BELOW *A soldier of the 5th Duke of Cornwall's Light Infantry from 43rd Division armed with a PIAT, 18th November 1944.* [IWM B 11928]
COURTESY OF THE IMPERIAL WAR MUSEUM

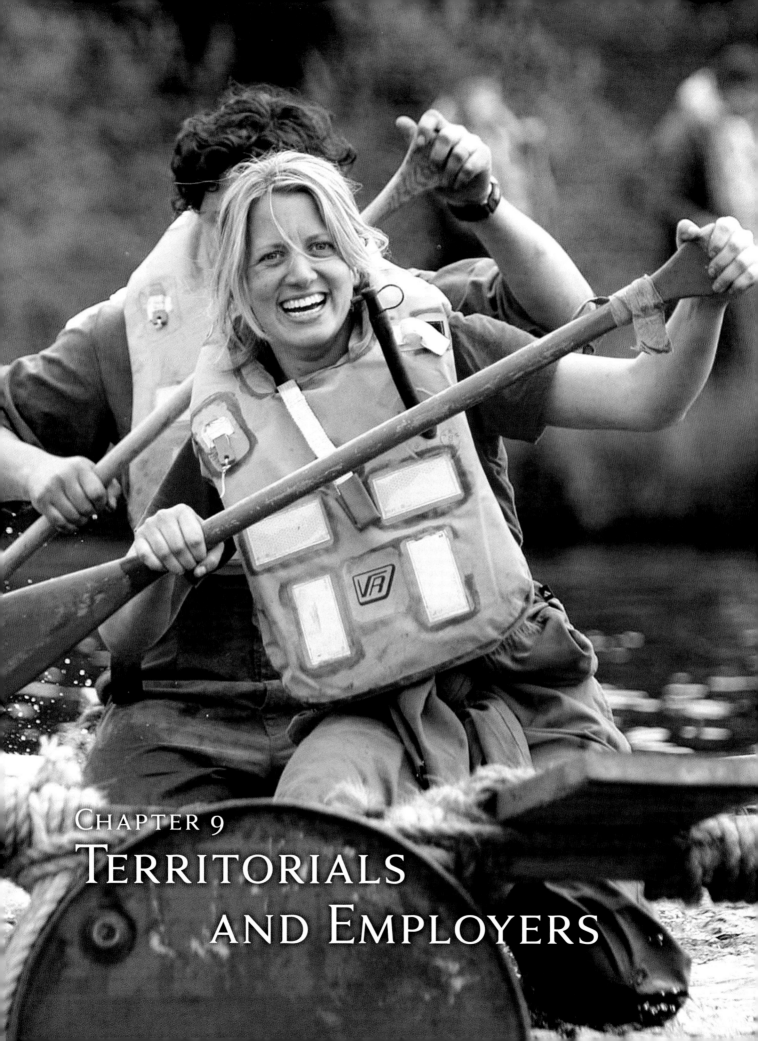

CHAPTER 9
TERRITORIALS AND EMPLOYERS

"Not infrequently the employer may represent himself as out to help, but on investigation it is found that it is the foreman or charge hand who is the stumbling block."

COLONEL G R CODRINGTON CB DSO OBE TD
The Territorial Army, 1938.

THE TERRITORIAL AND his predecessors in auxiliary forces have always been civilians first and foremost and, therefore, the ability to meet training and other commitments has always rested on the nature of an individual's employment and the co-operation of an individual's employer. In the past it was not unusual for some employers, in the manner of some landlords, to insist upon participation in local forces. In the 1790s, for example, the East India Company threatened to dismiss any of its employees who did not join its London volunteer battalions while, in the 1860s, a volunteer dismissed from his corps would face instant dismissal with employers such as the London and North Western Railway Company, Cunard and Tetley. Equally, from the beginning, other employers refused to support the auxiliaries. There was particular opposition from northern spinning manufacturers and mill owners in the 1860s. Cook, Son & Co of Manchester, for example, ordered their warehousemen to leave the volunteer force in August 1861. In 1924 refusal of leave to attend annual camp was fairly widespread in Leicestershire, and there were instances of men attending camp finding they had no job to go back to in West Lancashire in 1922 and Derbyshire in 1924.

Not surprisingly, therefore, Territorials and their predecessors have frequently emphasised the value of auxiliaries as employees though the *Volunteer Service Gazette* may have taken this a little far in suggesting that 'the toils of the countinghouse, the warehouse and the shop would be undertaken in a new spirit of dutiful delight'. Little changes in the essential nature of this appeal. In 2006, in co-operation with the government agency Jobcentre Plus, 51 (Scottish) Brigade ran a seven-week course, SUMMER CHALLENGE, to recruit youngsters and train them to basic soldier standard in order to encourage recruitment to both army and TA. Significantly, however, it was advertised as an opportunity to gain skills required by employers, such as team-working, initiative, reliability and communication skills. More than 2,000 applications were received for the 250 places available, with 210 passing the course.

Historically, some units have enjoyed a particularly close relationship with employers, such as the Postal and Courier Service (TA), contemporary successor to the 49th (later 24th) Middlesex (Post Office) Rifle Volunteer Corps (RVC) of 1868, most of whose officers and soldiers have always worked for the Post Office. Colonel William Cockburn, for example, commanded the Postal and Courier Service from 1986 to 1992 before becoming managing director of Royal Mail from 1992 to 1995. Similarly, The Engineer and Logistic Staff Corps,

OPPOSITE *Junior executives battle their way over Hawley Lake on an improvised raft during Exercise Executive Stretch.*

COURTESY OF STEWART TURKINGTON/SERFCA

ABOVE *The Employers Abroad
Scheme, an initiative run by
SaBRE, allows employers to
see their reservist employees
on active service. A Territorial
from 4 PARA demonstrates the
SA80 A2 to his employer.*

COURTESY OF SABRE

RE (V)—contemporary successor to the Engineer and Railway Volunteer Staff
Corps of 1865—though theoretically now separate from the TA, enjoys a close
relationship with the engineering profession. In 1982 its new commanding
officer, Colonel I M Campbell, was deputy chairman of British Rail.

Whereas in the past it was left to individual Territorial county associations
to liaise with their local business community, from 1986 onwards the National
Employers' Liaison Council (NELC), now the National Employer Advisory Board
(NEAB), became responsible to the Secretary of State through the MoD for
advising on all employment issues relating to reservists.

Moreover, under the auspices of NEAB, SaBRE (Supporting Britain's Reserves
and Employers), which has its own regional co-ordinators within Reserve Forces
and Cadets Associations (RFCAs), was established in September 2002 under the
chairmanship of Lord Glenarthur to engage employers and promote the benefits
of employees belonging to the reserves and acquiring transferable skills such as
leadership, self-confidence and initiative. More than 100 companies including
the RAC, Stagecoach Group, RWE nPower, Thomas Cook, Asda Stores, Comet,
Barclays, Jaguar Cars, Marks and Spencer, and Motorola have pledged support
for the campaign. SaBRE has also produced model personnel policies. To give
an example of its advisory role, the MoD in 2007 applied for exemption from
parts of new EU legislation on vocational drivers. This effectively requires
those who are also members of the TA to record the hours spent driving during
evening or weekend training as part of their overall driving commitment, and

some employers might well take the view that they cannot afford to allow their drivers to remain in the TA in such circumstances.

In a further effort to engage the business community, NELC initiated the Exercise EXECUTIVE STRETCH programme funded by RFCAs to bring TA and business together by providing weekend adventure training for business people and this has continued. With the current high level of deployment, the adoption of the Operational Commitments Plot (OCP) is also intended to give due notice of mobilisation so that Territorials, as well as employers can be prepared. In theory, OCP gives a warning of the requirement for mobilised units five years in advance, a warning order to units and an estimate for individuals two years in advance, and a mobilisation plan for the year in question.

BELOW *Simon Barnes, an HAC officer on Full Time Reserve Service, escorting the Director of Nursing Services and Quality, NHS Fife on a visit to reservists serving with 205 (Scottish) Field Hospital (Volunteers) in Iraq, July 2005.*

COURTESY OF SABRE

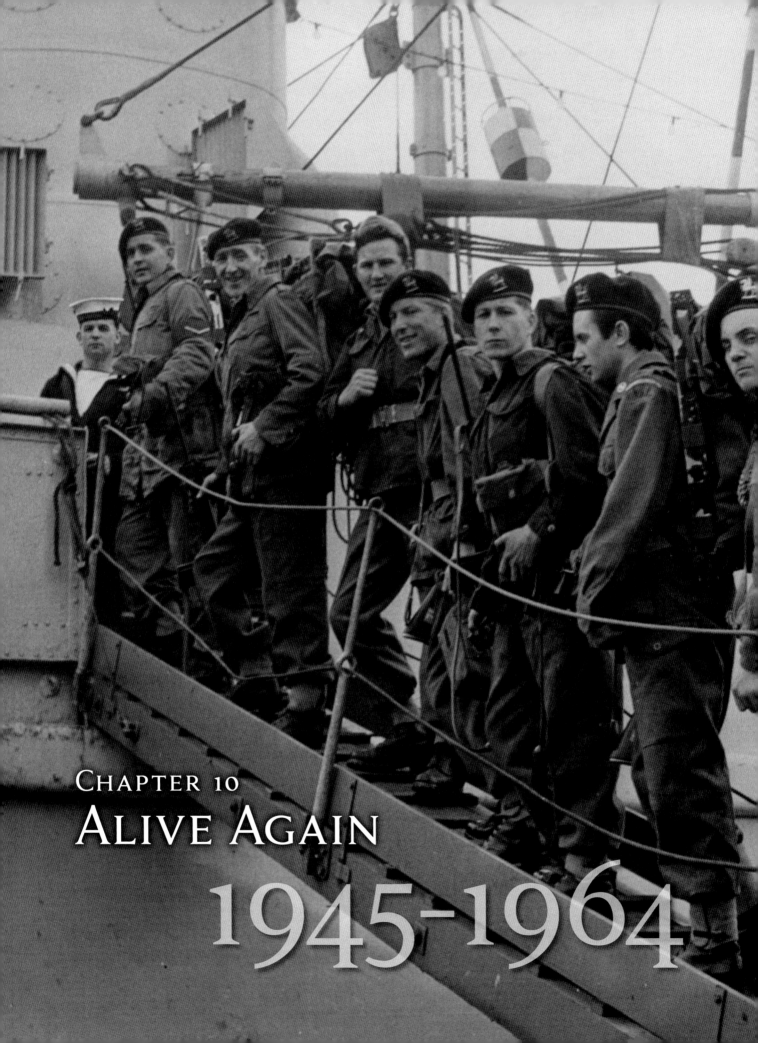

CHAPTER 10
ALIVE AGAIN
1945-1964

"The whole question boils down to this—how much can we knock the Territorial Army about and still keep it as a useful instrument or, indeed, at all? Any successful volunteer movement must believe that its services are wanted. There is a limit beyond which I cannot go without general disintegration setting in."

CHRISTOPHER SOAMES MP
23rd May 1960.

I N OCTOBER 1948 there was a Royal Review by King George VI in Hyde Park, in which some 8,000 men of the reconstituted TA participated. It was, however, also the last major parade of the TA as an entirely volunteer organisation[1] for ten years, illustrating the almost constant state of readjustment required of the Territorials in terms of role and organisation in the post-war years. The post-war story of the TA partly reflects constant change driven by frequently shifting perceptions of strategic need through the 'Cold War' years and subsequent conflicts of the 'New World Order', but also the often-uncertain state of the British economy. Anthony Eden wrote in his memoirs of the situation when he became Prime Minister in 1955 that the UK 'had attempted too much in too many spheres of defence, which had contributed to the economic crisis which every administration had suffered since 1945'. What was true of 1955 could equally be said of many other occasions thereafter. Certainly, the TA's post-war experience could not be divorced from the continuing retrenchment that affected the army as a whole but, initially at least, the lesson of the 1930s appeared to be that a large army with large reserves was necessary until global stability was assured.

The most immediate threat to Britain in 1946-47 was not initially seen as deriving from the Soviet Union's presence in central and eastern Europe, since it was assumed that the Soviets would not be ready to wage a large-scale conventional war until about 1957. More significant were not only the immediate post-war occupation responsibilities in Germany, Austria, Italy and the former Italian colony of Libya—200,000 out of the 476,000 army personnel stationed overseas were in Germany alone in April 1947—but also wider security concerns. While Britain left the Indian subcontinent and Palestine in 1947, the Middle East remained a vital strategic area, and a presence in the Far East appeared essential for the security of the Commonwealth. A decision to continue wartime conscription had been taken in October 1944, but it was felt necessary to demobilise actual wartime service personnel as soon as possible. Men continued to be conscripted under wartime legislation until 31st December 1946; the final batch being demobilised in March 1949. Clearly, therefore, the substantial manpower demands would have to be satisfied, alongside increasing financial difficulty exacerbated by the withdrawal of US wartime economic support, fluctuating share prices and balance of payments crises coinciding

OPPOSITE *Territorials from The Monmouthshire Regiment board HMS St David at Cardiff docks in preparation for an anti-terrorist exercise on the island of Lundy.*

COURTESY OF THE ROYAL REGIMENT OF WALES MUSEUM, BRECON.

----

1. From 1950 until it ended, the National Service commitment included a period of service in the Territorial Army.

COURTESY OF IMPERIAL TOBACCO

PLAYER'S CIGARETTES

22ND (CENTRAL LONDON RANGERS) THE KING'S R.R.C., 1882

BELOW *Members of 16th Airborne Division undergo instruction on the 3-inch mortar at Stanford Training Area in Norfolk, September 1953.*

COURTESY OF THE IMPERIAL WAR MUSEUM

in July 1947. Retention of conscription in the form of national service, while unpopular with the public, appeared a relatively cheap, if not always efficient, means of attempting to meet the manpower challenge. The decision to bring in new national service legislation, therefore, was announced in November 1946. Subsequently, the beginning of the Berlin Blockade in June 1948 heralded the deterioration of relations with the Soviet Union and suggested a major conflict potentially sooner than previously envisaged, hastening British participation in what became the North Atlantic Treaty Organisation (NATO) in April 1949. The outbreak of the Malayan Emergency in June 1948 also signified the growing threat of (usually communist-inspired) nationalist insurgency in colonial and dependent territories.

The question of a reconstituted TA, therefore, became bound up in the issue of national service and, through integration into it, the TA remained within the single national army concept. Under the National Service Act of 1947, national servicemen were initially to serve one year with the regulars and six years in the TA, though it was not intended to commence national service until 1st January 1949, with the first national servicemen not reaching TA units until the summer camps in 1950. Conscription itself was initially intended to endure only until 1954 with the assumption that, by then, greater stability and a reduction of commitments elsewhere would enable an all-volunteer army to be revived.

Under pressure from the Army Council and in the context of the increased threat perception, the National Service (Amendment) Act of 1948 changed this to 18 months with the regulars and five and a half years in the TA, with the National Service (Military Forces) (Amendment) Regulations of 1950, issued against the background of the Korean War, then amending this to two years with the army and three and a half years in the TA.

So far as the TA was concerned, the Council of Territorial Associations raised the future of the force with the Army Council in November 1945 but, at

that stage, no firm decisions had been taken beyond continuing associations in their present form. The DGHG&TA suggested that, in the interim, units be kept together as clubs or voluntary associations until matters were decided. In fact, work on the outline of the post-war TA had begun within the War Office in May 1945 with a preliminary survey of the current status of pre-war units, whether active or in suspended animation. On 14th June 1945, in concluding that the post-war TA must be a properly balanced force and meet the needs of the active field force, the Army Council had also decided that it must ascertain the extent to which disbanding units might be acceptable. On 20th March 1946 it was intimated to associations that post-war needs were still unclear but, on 19th August, that plans would soon be forthcoming. In reality, the Inter-Service Working Party on the Future of the TA and Air Force Associations had been established on 3rd April 1946 and the Auxiliary Army Sub-committee of the Standing Committee on Army Post-war Problems on 2nd May 1946. Indeed, on 26th June 1946 the Army Council had accepted that a reconstituted TA should be responsible for home defence, making good deficiencies in the field force and providing the 'second line' as a basis for wartime expansion.

Although it would have a substantial anti-aircraft component, the post-war TA would have new kinds of 'teeth' and support units that had not existed prior to 1939. The TA must also have a far higher state of readiness than previously. It was envisaged that 250,000 Territorials would be needed for anti-aircraft units, 50,000 to complete field force formations, and possibly 320,000 as a nucleus for

ABOVE *Members of the Green Howards undergo basic radio telephony training at Selly Hill in 1948. They are using No 38 Mk2 Wireless Sets which were developed in 1942 and had an effective range of about one mile.*

COURTESY OF THE GREEN HOWARDS MUSEUM, RICHMOND.

The acquiescence of women in TA commitments remained especially important...therefore, consideration was given as to whether standing camps might be set up close to commercial holiday camps to facilitate easy contact between soldiers and their families.

wartime expansion on the assumption that there would be eight TA divisions in peace, expanding to 24 in the event of war. Upwards of 620,000 Territorials, of course, was almost three times the size of the TA at any time since 1908, hence the need for a substantial component of national servicemen although the War Office had examined options for reconstituting the TA as an entirely voluntary body. Accordingly, since the first national servicemen would not be available to the TA until 1950 it was decided initially to try to obtain 175,000 volunteers: 75,000 would be allocated to anti-aircraft units, 10,000 allocated for completing the active field force, and the remainder providing skeleton units for eight divisions. In effect, the TA would be in a state of limbo for some three years until the full impact of conscription was felt.

ABOVE *Members of 264 Beach Brigade aboard a DUKW, September 1949. Intended to compensate for the lack of Scottish infantry battalions in the revived TA, the Beach Brigade was allocated to Scotland despite the combined operations school being at Barnstaple.*

COURTESY OF SOLDIER MAGAZINE.

On 7th August 1946 the Army Council agreed on a provisional framework for two armoured divisions, six infantry divisions, three independent armoured brigades, three independent infantry brigades, a 'beach brigade', and a brigade group for Northern Ireland. The whole would be organised in three regional corps. It was decided to reopen recruiting for volunteers aged between 18 and 40 for a four-year term of engagement on the assumption that 15-day camps could be held in 1947, with the other liabilities set at 34 compulsory training periods (12 of which could take the form of weekend camps) and up to 50 voluntary training periods. There was subsequent concern that too few Scottish infantry battalions had been allowed for and, therefore, it was decided to allocate the 'beach brigade' to Scotland even though this was hardly conducive to administrative efficiency given that the combined operations school was at Barnstaple in Devon. The Admiralty also queried whether the 60 per cent share of national servicemen being claimed by the army was intended primarily to sustain the reconstituted TA, but the War Office responded that its demands were related solely to Regular Army commitments. In many respects, the policy to bring in national service had preceded any actual strategic decisions as to the deployment of the TA. Initially, since the main priority was the Middle East rather than Europe, four TA divisions were intended to be ready for that theatre within three months of any

LEFT *Chief of The Imperial General Staff, Field Marshal Sir John Harding* GCB CBE DSO MC—*a former Territorial—presents new Colours to The 4th (TA) Battalion, The Oxfordshire and Buckinghamshire Light Infantry on 28th August 1954.*

COURTESY OF THE OXFORDSHIRE AND BUCKINGHAMSHIRE LIGHT INFANTRY MUSEUM, OXFORD.

mobilisation. Among other recommendations, the Harwood Report in February 1949 suggested five TA divisions for home defence and five for overseas service, of which two would be allocated to the Middle East, but this largely Treasury-driven exercise was quickly shelved. By November 1949, the Chiefs of Staff had concluded that two of the four TA divisions to be made available after mobilisation should be allocated to the defence of Europe. Interestingly, in an echo of the distrust of Territorial artillery prior to 1914, the Territorial armoured division was not intended to be among the first four mobilised.

On 20th August 1946 it was agreed that the new Director of the TA and Army Cadet Force (DTA&ACF) should be responsible to the Parliamentary Under Secretary of State for War. In September it was decided that the DTA&ACF would no longer have responsibility for all TA administration, which would be divided between War Office directorates as appropriate. He would retain control over only organisation of county associations, honours and awards, and the disposal of unit funds. The ACF would be entirely under War Office control. As a result, the TA Advisory Committee, which had previously existed between 1935 and 1939, was revived in 1948 to inform War Office policy and advise the Army Council on TA matters. Whereas, however, the Under Secretary had presided in the inter-war years, the Deputy CIGS would now replace him as chairman. This illogical arrangement was reversed in 1956. In November 1946 it was settled that, alongside selection for vacancies, TA officers would be eligible for substantive promotion to captain on the basis of six years' service or upon attaining the age of 27, and for promotion to major after 13 years or upon reaching the age of 34.

The formal announcement of reconstitution was made to the Commons on 19th November 1946. Those units in suspended animation were reactivated on

COURTESY OF IMPERIAL TOBACCO

...the emphasis was upon recruiting older men than had been the case before 1939. The preference now was for those with wartime experience who could act as leaders and instructors for national servicemen.

1st January 1947, though no personnel were assigned until commanding officers and permanent staff had been appointed in March and April 1947. A new War Office TA Committee had its first meeting on 20th March to ensure a smooth transition to the reconstituted force, recruiting for which opened on 1st May 1947 under the slogan, 'The TA is alive again'. There had been some concern in February that the original deadline of 1st April could not be met since only 29 associations had expressed the ability to be ready—the supply of recruiting forms and posters being delayed by the consequences of the fuel crisis.

Welsh associations had also demanded that only Welshmen be appointed to command units in the principality, which had further complicated matters. Subsequently, Welsh nationalists complained that there were English units in the reconstituted 53rd (Welsh) Division and also objected to proposed training areas. Given that farmers had raised no objections and that it would be impracticable to raise an entirely Welsh division unless six English battalions were reduced and replaced by six new Welsh battalions, it was decided that no change could or should be made. Another older grievance also resurfaced in January 1947 with a demand from some quarters that Territorial officers be once more allowed to wear the pre-war 'T'. The Army Council felt strongly that 'emphasis should now be laid on the existence of a national army, of which the active army and the TA formed integral parts, from which it should follow that distinguishing marks of the types suggested were an anachronism'. There was also concern at potential differentiation between volunteers and national

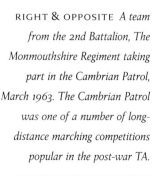

RIGHT & OPPOSITE *A team from the 2nd Battalion, The Monmouthshire Regiment taking part in the Cambrian Patrol, March 1963. The Cambrian Patrol was one of a number of long-distance marching competitions popular in the post-war TA.*

COURTESY OF THE ROYAL REGIMENT OF WALES MUSEUM, BRECON.

servicemen within the TA, and a War Office circular on 26th March 1947 made it clear that the 'T' would not return. The policy was reiterated in March 1948 and again in May 1958, the Council of Territorial Associations having twice decided not to press the matter in November 1956 and November 1957.

Given the nature of the TA upon reconstitution, the emphasis was upon recruiting older men than had been the case before 1939. The preference now was for those with wartime experience who could act as leaders and instructors for national servicemen. Among inducements offered was a bounty free of income tax. Understandably, perhaps, many wartime servicemen had no wish to come forward when they had so recently re-established themselves in civilian life and had experienced long separation from homes and families. Moreover, conditions were very different from those of the inter-war years since employment was fuller, wages better, and most families could now afford a summer holiday. The acquiescence of women in TA commitments remained especially important. Many single Territorials left once they were married. With recruiting slow in the summer of 1947, therefore, consideration was given as to whether standing camps might be set up close to commercial holiday camps to facilitate easy contact between soldiers and their families. Some questioned, indeed, whether the whole idea of the summer camp was now out of date and might be replaced by more weekend camps. In June 1947, however, it was decided there could be no encouragement of 'Butlins' for the TA since this would erode

Understandably, perhaps, many wartime servicemen had no wish to come forward when they had so recently re-established themselves in civilian life and had experienced long separation from homes and families.

ABOVE *Minister for War, John
Profumo, watches Corporal
Hammett become one the first
'Ever Readies' to sign up at Duke
of York's Barracks in June 1962.*

COURTESY OF SOLDIER MAGAZINE.

'On parade and lets
all march together,
March together,
March together,
March together,
Let the whole world
see the people on
parade.'

CHORUS, OFFICIAL TA SONG
May 1949

proper training and, in February 1948, it was also decided that dispensing with summer camp altogether would have no training benefits.

It became increasingly difficult to find sufficient volunteers and a major recruiting campaign was launched in October 1948. On occasions, the efforts were lamentable. Thus, an official TA song and march, *People on Parade*, composed by Lieutenant Colonel David Heneker, was adopted in May 1949. Its chorus ran: 'On parade and lets all march together, March together, March together, March together, Let the whole world see the people on parade.' Perhaps wisely, Gracie Fields declined the invitation to record it on the grounds that 'it was not right for her' while the BBC, feeling the chorus was actually better than the verses, declined to give it any special broadcast prominence. Other recruiting drives throughout the late 1940s and 1950s tended to emphasise 'challenge and adventure' in training though, at local level, there was more of an emphasis, as in the case of the 4th Royal Norfolks, on 'the idea of the Territorial Army as a sort of club rather than a fighting force'. Interestingly, a survey carried out in 1965 for consultants Colman, Prentis and Varley suggested social activities certainly promoted comradeship, but found that derived from 'good, hard, interesting training is far more important'. Unfortunately, it concluded that what deterred men most was repetitive and uninteresting training on outdated equipment.

One particular problem appeared to be that officers and soldiers might be out of pocket as a result of camp expenses. In January 1950, the Council of Territorial Associations commissioned a report from Brigadier R Ashton Hamlyn, a chartered accountant, on possible remedies. Hamlyn concluded that,

ABOVE *Men of 44 Independent
Parachute Brigade gather their
equipment and make for the
forming-up area during an
exercise in November 1957.*

COURTESY OF SOLDIER MAGAZINE.

on average, soldiers were £8.18s.6d out of pocket at camp and recommended that an additional £4 be paid for each week's attendance so that an individual would receive £12 for one week and £16 for two weeks. Reviewing officers' allowances for messing, uniform and training, he also suggested that they should receive a similar bounty for camp attendance. Having mislaid the report for six months, the War Office was uncomfortable with 'awkward suggestions in regard to the recognition of loss of earnings', and the calculation that such concessions would cost £240,000 in 1950-51 rising to £425,000 by 1954 if one in four national servicemen chose to join the TA. In the event a working party reporting in October 1950 found there was no case for offering any more money to soldiers, but it did recommend offering an additional £5 to cover subalterns' expenses, as this would only cost £25,000 in 1951-52. By 1953 there was serious concern at the 'maldistribution' of officers between the north and south of England and, in 1954, by the relatively low response in the build up of the volunteer component in the Scottish Highlands, Northumberland and Durham, Devon and Cornwall, and Wales.

The primary difficulty was that Territorials were deprived of the 17-20 age group, while national servicemen were only liable to 60 days' training in their three and a half years (inclusive of the 15-day annual camp). Fines could be levied for non-attendance but, if days were missed, a national serviceman could opt to undertake four one-hour training periods in lieu. True volunteers were liable to 30 hours a year in addition to camp, with a £12 bounty offered for an additional

30 hours' training. Liability for part-time training for national servicemen, however, effectively ceased in 1956 since it was reduced to just 20 days over three years, not much more than one camp in three and a half years, though men continued to be posted to TA units. In April 1957 the training liability for national servicemen ceased altogether—the smaller numbers attending camps immediately apparent. The April 1957 Defence White Paper of the Minister of Defence and former Territorial, Duncan Sandys, issued in the wake of Suez and in the belief that too large a share of GDP was being devoted to defence, placed the emphasis upon nuclear deterrence with a concomitant reduction in conventional forces. It signalled the end of national service as a whole; this being phased out from 1960, with the last national serviceman leaving the army in May 1963 and, in theory, the TA in 1966. Since national servicemen represented more than 60 per cent of the TA by 1960, this posed a significant new challenge.

LEFT *Signallers from 16th Airborne Divisional Signals, Royal Corps of Signals (Middlesex Yeomanry) pictured in 1953. The Middlesex Yeomanry had acted as a signals unit to both the 1st Cavalry Division and the 2nd Armoured Division during the Second World War.*

COURTESY OF THE ROYAL SIGNALS MUSEUM, BLANDFORD.

As already mentioned, at the time of reconstitution in 1947 it was decided to form one airborne division[2], two armoured divisions[3] and six infantry divisions[4]. In addition to 107 (Northern Ireland) Independent Infantry Brigade Group, there was an additional independent brigade group formed as 162 (Beds, Herts, Hunts and Northants) Independent Infantry Brigade Group, while the three other originally intended independent infantry brigades comprised 26 (Scottish), 155 (Lowland) and 161 (East Anglia) Independent Infantry Brigades. The three independent armoured brigades were 9 (South Midlands), 23 (Lancashire) and 30 (Lowland) Independent Armoured Brigades, while the beach brigade was 264 (Scottish) Beach Brigade. There remained, too, a substantial artillery component outside of the divisional and 'Army Groups, RA' intended for the field force. There were still 20 coastal artillery regiments, but the majority of artillery units were organised into anti-aircraft brigades within AA Command or within army groups as anti-aircraft defence for the field force. A mixture of HAA and LAA regiments, searchlight regiments and a new hybrid of LAA/Searchlight regiments were required. As a result, all pre-war TA artillery and searchlight units were reactivated while 29 reactivated

ABOVE *Men of the 4th Battalion, The Oxfordshire and Buckinghamshire Light Infantry set up a listening post to intercept and record enemy radio messages.*

COURTESY OF SOLDIER MAGAZINE.

infantry battalions were converted to artillery and a further 15 entirely new artillery units raised. In all, artillery now accounted for about 40 per cent of the Territorial Army.

Although the wartime Special Air Service (SAS), originally formed in 1941, had been disbanded in October 1945, a Territorial SAS was also established in September 1947, having been agreed in June 1947. It was effected by the conversion of the Artists Rifles, which had remained an officer-training unit throughout the Second World War, as 21st Battalion, The Special Air Service Regiment (Artists Rifles), TA. The Artists were transferred nominally to the Army Air Corps (AAC) and included within the new 16th Airborne Division.

2. 16th Airborne Division.

3. 49th (West Riding and North Midland) and 56th (London) Divisions.

4. 42nd (Lancashire), 43rd (Wessex), 44th (South Eastern), 50th (Northumbrian), 51st (Scottish), and 53rd (Welsh) Divisions.

The idea appears to have originated with two wartime commanders of the SAS Brigade, Brigadiers Roderick McLeod and Michael 'Mad Mike' Calvert, who wanted to preserve the regiment's *esprit de corps* and a nucleus for future wartime expansion. They lobbied hard but it is not entirely clear why the War Office acceded to the request, though the Directorate of Tactical Investigation favoured retaining a 'behind the lines' capability. Similarly, there was lobbying for continuing the wartime GHQ Liaison Regiment (Phantom), which was preserved as Army Phantom Signals Section (Princess Louise's Kensington Regiment), TA. It was not until May 1950 that the SAS became a separate corps and the regular Malayan Scouts officially established to fight communist insurgents in Malaya under the corps' warrant in January 1951. The Scouts were renamed 22 SAS in 1952. Subsequently, a second reserve TA unit, 23 SAS, was established, and a Territorial SAS signals unit, 63 (SAS) Signal Squadron.

Reference has been made to the establishment of a Northern Ireland Brigade Group in 1947, which requires some explanation. An Irish militia had existed at various times in the 17th and 18th centuries before it was revived between 1793 and 1816. Prior to this, there had been an Irish volunteer movement in the 1770s and 1780s, which had become increasingly politicised and had been outlawed in 1793. An overwhelmingly Protestant yeomanry then existed between 1796 and 1834. While the Irish militia was revived in 1852, British governments feared that authorising new volunteer corps on the British model would run too many political and military risks. Ireland was also excluded from raising Territorial Force units in 1908, though Special Reserve units were permitted. Thus, two yeomanry regiments—The North Irish Horse and The South Irish Horse—raised in 1902 from Irish contingents that had served in the South African War were included within the Special Reserve. Of course, the two rival communities

ABOVE *A Territorial Royal Signal line-laying team, Bradford 1963.*

COURTESY OF THE ROYAL SIGNALS MUSEUM, BLANDFORD.

COURTESY OF IMPERIAL TOBACCO

ABOVE *In March 1958, the 4th
Battalion, The Oxfordshire and
Buckinghamshire Light Infantry
became the first Territorials to
use helicopters on exercise.*

COURTESY OF SOLDIER MAGAZINE.

raised their own paramilitary volunteers—the loyalist Ulster Volunteer Force
and the nationalist Irish National Volunteers—immediately prior to the Great
War. Many members of both organisations enlisted in the army in 1914, but a
diehard rump of the Irish National Volunteers, now calling themselves National
Volunteers, were involved in the Easter Rising in Dublin in April 1916. In the
Great War, Irish VTC units were authorised, some in Dublin becoming victims
of the Easter Rising, but there was no change of policy with the division of
Ireland in 1921. Indeed, when the matter was raised in May 1929 the Northern
Ireland government felt it unwise 'to afford training activities to men—more
especially in bomb throwing and machine gun practice—who might use the
knowledge which they had acquired for subversive purposes'.

In 1937, however, a heavy artillery coastal battery and a fortress engineer
squadron were established in County Antrim together with an Antrim County
Association. By 1939 three anti-aircraft units and a RASC unit had been added.
A Home Guard was also established during the Second World War but, in
the absence of county associations, affiliated to the Special Constabulary. As
it happened, there was some Territorial representation in the army's 'Irish
Brigade' established in January 1942. The 38 (Irish) Brigade comprised regular
battalions of The Royal Irish Fusiliers and The Royal Inniskilling Fusiliers and
the 2nd London Irish Rifles, which was associated with The Royal Ulster Rifles.
In 1960, indeed, the Prime Minister of Northern Ireland specifically urged the
British government to retain the London Irish as the only 'Irish' TA unit on the
mainland, pointing out that it recruited men from all over Ireland.

In 1947 there were still some fears that 'unreliable elements' might gain
admission to associations 'and misuse the information obtained there' but it

was resolved to establish the TA throughout the province. In the event, with some 7,000 members by 1954, and about 6,000 thereafter, the TA in Northern Ireland was far closer to establishment than many TA units on the mainland. By 1969, following a reduction of the establishment to 4,063, there were 3,277 Territorials serving in the province, the largest single contingent of 357 serving with 74 Engineer Regiment.

Within a short time of reconstitution, it was concluded that anti-aircraft guns were of little utility in a missile age and, in 1950, a total of 43 of the 76 units removed from the TA order of battle were artillery though, in most cases, units reverted to previous roles rather than being disbanded. A tenth 'mixed' division[5] was reconstituted in March 1950 with some of the army groups' artillery being allocated to it but, on 1st December 1954, it was announced that AA Command would be disbanded with effect from 10th March 1955. Conventional anti-aircraft units would only be retained for the defence of the field force, ports, bases and

5. 52nd Division.

BELOW *Civil defence exercises, such as the one shown involving the Monmouthshire Regiment, became part of the Territorial role as a result of the 1960 Defence White Paper. One camp in three was to be devoted to training for response to nuclear incidents.*

COURTESY OF THE ROYAL REGIMENT OF WALES MUSEUM, BRECON

vital targets. In all, more than 90 units formerly part of AA Command or within the army groups were reduced by amalgamation—sometimes by multiple amalgamation—leaving four anti-aircraft brigades for home defence and three Army Groups, RA for support of the field force. The end of the coast artillery followed with effect from 31st October 1956, with the removal of another 28 major TA units through disbandment, amalgamation or conversion, leaving just 89 field, light and LAA units for the field force. Some attempt was made to persuade TA officers from the disbanding anti-aircraft and coastal units to join the so-called Mobile Defence Corps (MDC), nominally part of the Army Emergency Reserve (as the Supplementary Reserve had been renamed in 1952) intended to support civil agencies. The MDC itself, however, was then abolished in December 1958 since it was felt that the TA could assist Civil Defence without the need for any additional special organisation.

One curious anomaly was the revival of the Home Guard during the Korean War under the provisions of the Home Guard Act of April 1951. It was intended to raise 170,000 men in approximately 1,000 cadre units on the basis of a two-year term of enlistment and a liability of 15 hours' training every three months. However, only 300 cadres of 100 men each were raised in November 1952 and these were first reduced in 1955, and then disbanded in August 1957. The Korean War also saw the government selectively recall up to 235,000 so-called 'Z Reservists', mostly former wartime servicemen, for 15 days' training, some 80,000 attending TA annual camps in 1951 and 1952. Few, however, could be induced to join the TA.

Upon reconstitution, the TA's role had been defined as providing a field force component for the army in either Europe or the Middle East, which implied being fully prepared to fight overseas in an emergency; providing anti-aircraft and coast defence for the UK; and supporting the Civil Defence organisation in the event of enemy air or nuclear attack. With the RAF now tasked with air defence and the Royal Navy and RAF jointly tasked with repelling any seaborne threat, a new appraisal was required. Moreover, by this time, it could be argued that reliance upon a manpower-heavy defence policy squeezed the resources available for new technologically advanced equipment. The army queried the prevailing assumption that a future war would be a nuclear one by raising the threat still posed by communism outside Europe and the possibility of 'broken-backed warfare', in which there would still be a period of conventional conflict even after an initial limited nuclear exchange. The TA role appeared

COURTESY OF IMPERIAL TOBACCO

PLAYER'S CIGARETTES

NOTTINGHAMSHIRE YEOMANRY (SHERWOOD RANGERS), 1897

ABOVE *A command group from the 2nd Battalion, The Monmouthshire Regiment in Sennybridge, 1962.*

COURTESY OF THE ROYAL REGIMENT OF WALES MUSEUM, BRECON

inappropriate for both these circumstances, however, as well as any limited-war scenarios short of nuclear confrontation. It was not just strategic concerns, however, that informed the mood, for the Chancellor of the Exchequer, R A Butler, had warned the Cabinet, amid mounting inflation and a deterioration in the balance of payments in 1955, that the defence budget would rise from £1,527 million to £1,929 million by 1959-60 unless cuts were made. The political and financial consequences of the Suez crisis of October 1956 then provided the strategic and economic impetus for substantial cuts; the Sandys White Paper heralding not only the end of national service but also the reduction of the Regular Army itself to 180,000, with the loss of 17 infantry battalions, seven armoured regiments and 21 artillery units. Inevitably, therefore, the TA faced reductions.

It was announced in December 1955 that only two infantry divisions,[6] two armoured brigades and a parachute brigade would be maintained at full-scale as a field force reinforcement for NATO in defence of Western Europe. As a result, 16th Airborne Division was reduced to 44 Independent Parachute Brigade Group. The eight other divisions and an independent infantry brigade would be reduced in establishment for home defence only. The Army Emergency Reserve also now had only a home defence role. It implied reduced equipment scales for the majority of the TA at a time when the availability of national servicemen was increasingly problematic, and an uncertain role seemed unlikely to attract volunteers. Nonetheless, there was evidence of some increase in volunteer

6. 43rd (Wessex) and 53rd (Welsh) Divisions.

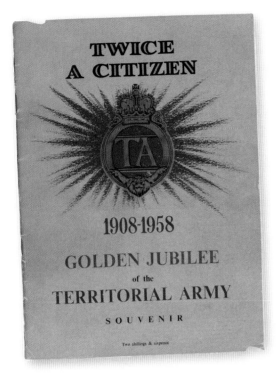

TWICE
A CITIZEN

1908-1958

GOLDEN JUBILEE
of the
TERRITORIAL ARMY
SOUVENIR

Two shillings & sixpence

BELOW *Territorial paras from
16th Airborne Division armed
with No 4 Lee Enfields execute
a mock charge at Stanford in
Norfolk. A smiling civilian—
probably a journalist—can be
seen through the smoke at the left
hand edge of the picture.*

[IWM D 68507]

COURTESY OF THE IMPERIAL WAR MUSEUM

numbers—the number of Territorials with no previous military experience doubling from 7,000 in 1956 to 14,000 in 1957.

It was in these uncertain circumstances that the TA's Golden Jubilee was celebrated in 1958 with a Royal Review by the Queen Mother in Belfast on 10th May, followed by thanksgiving services in Westminster Abbey and Westminster Cathedral on 21st June, and two further Royal Reviews by the Queen in Hyde Park on 22nd June and at Edinburgh on 5th July. The CIGS, Sir Gerald Templer, released a letter to the national and provincial press in May praising the TA, and a locomotive was named *The Territorial Army 1908-58* at Euston Station on 23rd July. A whole series of events was held nationwide, such as a church parade in Kinross on 8th June, a 'mechanised march' through Leicester on 5th July, and a march past in Truro on 6th July. Both the *Glasgow Herald* and *Birmingham Post* published special TA supplements. The Lord Mayor's Show then rounded off the celebrations on 10th November 1958 with a pageant involving a series of 18 tableaux tracing the history of the TA and its antecedents. The Lord Mayor, Sir Harold Gillett, had served with the 1/7th Middlesex in the Great War, winning the Military Cross.

The public praise for the TA at the time of the Jubilee, not least by Prime Minister Harold Macmillan, was to prove embarrassing to the government as more reductions were contemplated. Following consideration by the Army

Council and recommendations by a committee chaired by the Under Secretary of State for War, Hugh Fraser MP, on the implications of the end of national service, the TA's role was further redefined with an announcement to the Commons on 20th July 1960. The War Office had concluded in 1959 that there was no limited-war role for the TA, but it was deemed politically unacceptable to allow the TA to wither. Meeting for the first time on 10th December 1959, Fraser's committee reported on 17th March 1960. Using farming analogies, Fraser argued: 'The bull may never fight, but for it to survive it must be allowed to exercise in the training ring. To castrate and dehorn would not produce a Home Office sacred cow but a corpse.' The bill for the 'bull' would be large at perhaps £24 million a year, with £10-15

ABOVE *Gunners from the Oxfordshire Yeomanry prepare ammunition before firing their 25 pounder on Salisbury Plain in 1964. Two types of shell are being used: those on the groundsheet are standard Mk1D HE shells fitted with Mk117 double-action fuzes. The two shells being worked on are being fitted with VT time fuzes.*

COURTESY OF THE OXFORDSHIRE YEOMANRY TRUST

million for new equipment and £3.5 million for rehousing the TA, but Fraser assumed savings in the longer term. He also argued that the TA remained a national institution that was both 'touchy' and politically entrenched. Indeed, in May 1960 the Secretary of State for War, Christopher Soames, resolved that 'it was not practical politics' to consider disbanding the TA altogether. When the Minister of Defence, Harold Watkinson, demanded an absolute limit on TA expenditure of £75 million over five years, Soames replied on 23rd May that: 'The whole question boils down to this—how much can we knock the Territorial Army about and still keep it as a useful instrument or, indeed, at all? Any successful volunteer movement must believe that its services are wanted. There is a limit beyond which I cannot go without general disintegration setting in.' Soames also pointed out that significant reductions would be politically embarrassing in the wake of the Jubilee celebrations and his successor, John Profumo, promised the TA Advisory Council on 10th November 1960 that the TA would get 'as large a slice [of the cake] as we can afford'.

The TA's first task as outlined to the Commons was now 'to fight the battle for survival' in the home base by assisting army and the civil power in the UK; secondly, to reinforce British Army of the Rhine (BAOR); and, lastly, provide a

ABOVE *A Welsh Territorial Anti-Tank Platoon train on the 120mm MOBAT recoilless anti-tank rifle.*

COURTESY OF THE ROYAL REGIMENT OF WALES
MUSEUM, BRECON

framework 'on which, in a period of rising tension, general preparations for war can be built up'. It was assumed that 6,000 Territorials would be required for UK air defence, 85,500 for support of the UK civil authorities, 40,000 for supporting the army in the UK, and only 18,500 for the reinforcement of BAOR. In line with the emphasis upon assisting Civil Defence, one annual camp in three would be devoted to training in the detection of and protection against radiation, and rescue work in the event of nuclear attack. At one camp[7] of the 4th/6th Royal Berkshires, the Sappers managed 'commendable imitations' of atomic bombs from 40-gallon drums stuffed with assorted combustibles. The TA would be re-equipped over five years with the 7.62mm (FAL/FN) Self-Loading Rifle (though not the General Purpose Machine Gun), modern wireless sets, modern Scout cars, Saladin armoured cars and quarter-ton trucks. This, however, would come at the cost of an establishment reduced from 300,000 to 190,000. Moreover, notwithstanding the assumptions of Fraser's committee of the need for a force of 150,000 Territorials, only 123,000 (65 per cent of the new ceiling) would be actively recruited, with the balance made up on mobilisation from the TA Reserve of men who had completed their term of engagement. The actual strength of the TA's volunteers in July 1960 was some 120,000—a substantial increase from the 70,000 three years earlier.

Amalgamations followed as the new organisation came into effect on 1st May 1961, the Army Council having met for more than nine hours in three different meetings to consider the 731 suggested changes to the new scheme received from associations and units. Thus, it was decided, after representation,

7. Officially named after Assandune, Edmund Ironside's battle against the Danes in 1016, the exercise soon became 'Effing Down' to those involved.

G George   U Uncle
H How   V Victor
I Item   W William
J Jig   X X-ray
K King   Y Yoke
L Love   Z Zebra
...ke

ABOVE *Voice procedure training
for WRAC cadets and student
officers, 1952.*

COURTESY OF OXFORD UNIVERSITY OFFICERS'
TRAINING CORPS.

to retain the London Irish as an 'under implemented' reconnaissance unit for 56 Infantry Brigade when amalgamation proposals foundered. Similarly, it was decided that, as senior yeomanry regiment, the Royal Wiltshire Yeomanry could remain as an armoured car regiment, as it had been since 1941, but with a new reconnaissance role. However, there could be no second TA battalion for the King's Own Scottish Borderers.

Overall, the ten TA divisional headquarters were merged with Regular Army districts, which were matched to Civil Defence Regions since it was intended to achieve 'continuity' between peace and war. The number of infantry brigades was reduced from 31 to 23, while the two armoured brigade headquarters were disbanded. Eighteen infantry battalions were reduced by means of amalgamation, but there was no reduction in the four parachute battalions or the two SAS units. In the case of artillery, only 26 field and 18 anti-aircraft regiments were retained, with the addition of three independent batteries. The HAC now combined a role in officer training with its previous functions, being organised into a field artillery regiment and an infantry battalion. Former AER engineering field and works regiments were combined into one large formation, 111 Engineer Regiment, while other functions such as bomb disposal, survey, movement control and postal communications remained within separate engineer units. The Royal Signals lost four major units. No RAC regiments were reduced, but one armoured regiment and three armoured car regiments were converted to reconnaissance regiments. The changes were often complex. Thus, the

Hallamshire Battalion of the York and Lancaster Regiment amalgamated with part of 271 (Sheffield) Field Regiment and 865 Anti-Aircraft Reporting Battery as the Hallamshire Battalion, The York and Lancaster Regiment while, within Fife, Perth, Stirling, Clackmannan and Kinross, 433 LAA Regiment was reorganised as a Headquarters Transport Column, RASC and two heavy general transport companies RASC. Matching TA strength in peace and war even meant reducing the number of TA chaplains to 256.

A further measure under the provisions of the Army Reserve Act of April 1962 was to call out for up to six months in any 12 those volunteering to be immediately available for overseas service without recourse to proclamation in a new TA Emergency Reserve (TAER). Profumo suggested the TAER was for 'the young man who is fit and adventure-minded, the man who is prepared to offer his service and training to help the British Army keep the peace in the world'. The so-called 'Ever Readies' received in return an additional annual £150 bounty and £50 upon call out. The intended strength of 15,000 was never attained; some 4,262 men having joined by October 1963 but the number dropped to 2,400

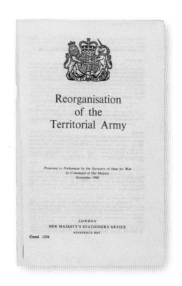

ABOVE *Following from the recommendations of the Fraser Committee, the government's White Paper on the reorganisation of the TA, published by the Secretary of State for War, John Profumo, in November 1960, reduced establishment from 300,000 to 190,000 but with actual recruitment limited to 123,000. It involved the loss of 13 infantry battalions and major units in both the Royal Engineers and Royal Corps of Signals, conversion of armoured and armoured car regiments to reconnaissance regiments, and substantial amalgamation of units within the Royal Artillery.*

COURTESY OF THE ROYAL ENGINEERS MUSEUM, CHATHAM.

LEFT *A permanent staff instructor from the Highland Light Infantry teaches officer cadets the intricacies of the LMG.*

COURTESY OF OXFORD UNIVERSITY OFFICERS' TRAINING CORPS.

ABOVE *A band practise for the musicians of the 16th Airborne Division (TA) at camp during Exercise King's Joker at Stanford Training Area, 1953.*

[IWM D 68537]

COURTESY OF THE IMPERIAL WAR MUSEUM

against a reduced establishment of 7,800 by 1968. The TAER would be able to train abroad, the first members to do so going to Libya in March 1963, with 200 men going to the Far East later in the year.

The TAER bounty was thought inadequate and there was also employer resistance to the six months' liability. With the Regular Army stretched by its commitments, a total of 175 reservists were then called up on 14th April 1965 for service in the Middle East, Far East or Cyprus. Of these, 123 Ever Readies went to Aden, reinforcing a battalion required for the Radfan campaign that preceded the more general outbreak of insurgency in Aden itself. A total of 25 reservists were subsequently called up for service on Cyprus and 21 for the Indonesian Confrontation in Borneo. Twelve of these 36 reservists were Ever Readies. The TAER was also utilised to retain the expertise of 59 former TA Travel Control Security specialists, for whom there appeared no actual role, but whose techniques it was felt should be retained within the institutional memory.

Reorganisation in 1960 assumed a future cost of £135 million over five years, including £22 million for re-equipment, a total questioned by the Treasury, which was not persuaded that the force had any real role. It was clear to most observers, however, that the TA was under-manned, underfunded and under-equipped. The lowest point of post-war TA fortunes was now at hand.

OPPOSITE *A paratrooper, armed with a Lee Enfield No 4 Rifle, of the 16th Airborne Division pictured during Exercise King's Joker at Stanford, 1953.*

[IWM D 68515]

COURTESY OF THE IMPERIAL WAR MUSEUM

❖

EVER READIES IN ADEN

ABOVE *Ever Readies in an*
observation post in Aden, 1965.

COURTESY OF SOLDIER MAGAZINE.

WHEN THE 175 Ever Readies were expectedly called up in April 1965, a total of 14 appealed against the decision, ten arguing that their employers objected, with the others claiming financial, domestic or health reasons. By contrast, some men had neglected to inform either their employers or their families of their liability since there was no actual legal obligation to notify an employer. The first Ever Ready to proceed overseas was Lieutenant J M Campbell of 299 Field Regiment, RA (TA), who joined 4 Field Regiment, RA in the Far East. Most attention was drawn, however, to the three officers and 120 men of the Ever Readies who served with 1st Royal Sussex

Regiment, which had been sent to Aden for a six-month emergency tour but had only two rifle companies. The Ever Readies provided the manpower for a third company, the battalion forming three small companies and dispersing the Ever Readies evenly through these and the headquarters company. The 123 included 30 soldiers from the 3rd and 4th Queen's Surreys and 40 from the 5th (Cinque Ports) Battalion of the Royal Sussex, the contingent as a whole coming from the Home Counties Brigade.

The whole group arrived in Aden on 27th May, immediately joining the Royal Sussex at Radfan Camp—a tented affair with few amenities or services—in the height of the hot season. Complaints about the conditions were aired in the press, though most Ever Readies took the view that they were fulfilling their duty. More significantly, others complained that the rigorous active service conditions prevented them from taking their 12 days' leave entitlement in theatre as the MoD insisted they should, and that this should be granted at the end of the engagement before they returned to civilian employment. The MoD declined to meet this complaint but it did relent on another, ensuring that those with less than 12 months' service received the annual bounty upon return from Aden rather than having to wait until 12 months elapsed.

After three days' acclimatisation and five days' skills training, it was a routine of static guard duties, mobile internal security patrols and counter-insurgency operations against hostile tribesmen. The men returned home in October 1965. It had been a considerable success, the commanding officer of The Royal Sussex writing that their 'steadiness, reliability and ever-present sense of humour have been noteworthy'. Moreover, one of the Ever Readies, Lieutenant Mike Smith, became the first Territorial to win the Military Cross since the Second World War.

It has also been claimed that 18 Ever Readies from Norfolk served in Aden earlier from 29th May to 12th June 1964 though there appears no official record of this. However, when 131 Airborne Engineer Regiment (TA) went to Aden for its summer camp in 1964, two squadrons were attacked on the Dhala Road near the Yemen border. Two men were killed and the regimental medical officer was awarded the MBE for gallantry for rescuing two others badly injured. It was not possible to award any other decoration as the unit was not embodied for active service.

CHAPTER 11
TRAINING

The highest and most difficult task for the Territorial Army is to train fighting leaders in time of peace.

LIEUTENANT COLONEL J K DUNLOP MC TD
The Problems and Responsibilities of the Territorial Army, 1935

FOLLOWING ON NATURALLY from the character of part-time Territorial commitment, it was inevitable that additional training would always be required in the event of wartime mobilisation. Territorials have been essentially reactive forces, frequently poorly equipped and resourced and, therefore, unready for war. As the Director General, Lieutenant General Sir Edward Bethune, suggested in July 1912: 'The whole system of training the Territorial Force is one of compromise, and we have to evolve the system which will best meet all requirements.'

Training, of course, has always been part of the obligation of auxiliaries. Muster Oak at Codsheath in Kent, for example, and innumerable places named 'The Butts' throughout the country testify to the longevity of the activity. Mile End in London was a traditional location for militia musters in the 16th century and the then open fields north of Bloomsbury and firing ranges at Chalk Farm equally popular for military exercises during the Napoleonic Wars. In December 1803 Charles Kirkpatrick Sharpe of Annandale in Dumfries, Scotland, complained that 'a sober-minded Christian' could get no peace when 'Gentlemen and clowns are at it from morning till night' and 'the very cows and hogs at the approach of a hostile cur draw up in battle array, in imitation of the two-legged bumpkins who are spoiling the exercise under every hedge'. Training also had an undeniable social aspect in the past such as the skills at arms competitions and speed trials customarily held by yeomanry regiments in the 1820s and 1830s, which invariably attracted spectators. From the 1860s onwards, however, the principal training activity became the annual summer camp. This remained a purely voluntary component of training until 1901, when it became compulsory for yeomanry and volunteers, and was simply carried on into the Territorials. Overseas training has also become an increasing feature since 1956 though, at one point, only Ever Readies could be trained overseas and even then it could not be made compulsory and individuals were required to volunteer for it in lieu of annual camp at home. By the 1970s there was usually an overseas camp every third year, then once every other year in the 1980s before reverting to the previous pattern of one-in-three thereafter. In the case of 131 Independent Commando Squadron, RE (V), annual camp in the 1980s might involve exercises in Norway or Schleswig-Holstein in Germany in support of 3 Commando Brigade, Royal Marines, with opportunities to participate in smaller exercises in Canada, Cyprus, Kenya and the US. In 1997, with the deployment of Royal Marines to provide an offshore presence during the final handover of Hong

OPPOSITE *10 Para on exercise at Stanford Training Area, Norfolk in November 1957. The presence of the 2-inch mortar and the Wireless Set No 88—the first British-developed VHF-FM tactical transceiver—would suggest that this is a platoon headquarters.*

COURTESY OF SOLDIER MAGAZINE.

ABOVE *Watched by their TA*
officers, potential junior NCOs
are instructed on the finer points
of model-making and formal
orders delivery by the Regular
staff of the Infantry Training
Centre, Catterick, March 2007.

COURTESY OF 7 RIFLES.

Kong to China as part of a seven-month Exercise OPEN WAVE, exercises took place in Brunei, Egypt, Malaysia, Singapore and South Africa. Two years later, the squadron supported exercises in Romania. There are also opportunities for participation in national and international military competitions and other activities through the tri-service UK Reserve Forces Association, which has links to other reserve forces in NATO and the 'Partnership for Peace' initiative with former members of the Soviet bloc.

Responsibility for training activities was vested at an early stage in permanent staff who were invariably ex-regulars, attached to militia, yeomanry or volunteers. From 1873 onwards the inspection and training of militia, yeomanry and volunteers was vested in regulars commanding brigade depots, with remaining auxiliary adjutants progressively replaced by regulars on attachment though, in the case of yeomanry, regimental adjutants were withdrawn in 1893 and replaced by brigade adjutants. Among those who served as regular adjutants with auxiliaries were Field Marshals Sir John French (later Earl of Ypres) and Sir Henry Maitland 'Jumbo' (later Lord) Wilson; Lieutenant General Sir Adrian Carton de Wiart; and Major Generals Orde Wingate and J F C Fuller. Regular staffs remain the 'battery' of the TA.

As long as they can prove themselves efficient, Territorials are paid a tax-free bounty every year, thus the certificate of efficiency which qualifies them is central to the annual training goal of the volunteer soldier. In addition to meeting the minimum attendance levels laid down in TA Regulations, from 1st

"...the men who join the Territorial Army are choosing the hobby which they enjoy and to which they are anxious and prepared to devote as much of their spare time as they can. This factor, coupled with a real thirst for knowledge, brings it about that the Territorial is as a rule far more readily teachable than the Regular, and he will assimilate in a few lessons what it may often take weeks of instruction to get into the head of a Regular."

COLONEL G R CODRINGTON CB DSO OBE TD
The Territorial Army, 1938.

April 2006 the volunteer must also pass the Military Annual Training Test (MATT). MATT replaced the Individual Training Directives (ITD) which, though similar in principle, were less stringent and did not meet the emerging need for a higher state of readiness prior to deployment.

The MATT—like the old ITD—is the mechanism by which a pan-army standard is maintained. They cover shooting, fitness, battlefield casualty drills (BCD), chemical, biological, radiological and nuclear (CBRN) protective measures, map reading, and values and standards. All except the latter have three levels that are tailored for individuals deployed on operations—trained soldiers not warned for deployment and non-deployable personnel (e.g. careers information staff and recruits). MATTs training takes longer to achieve than its ITD predecessor and the eternal problem of getting an entire TA unit in the same place at the same time means that MATTs training occupies a greater part of the training calendar than it would for a regular unit. With sub-units often scattered in location, unit collective training can usually only be accomplished at weekends or at camp.

The penalty for failing to earn the Commanding Officer's certificate is now largely financial but this has not always been the case. From 1863 the War Office paid the princely sum of £1 for every volunteer soldier rated as efficient plus a further ten shillings for proficiency on the rifle range, this capitation grant being raised to £1.15s.0d in 1870. Being judged inefficient meant that the hapless

BELOW *Route march with a difference, ca 1938.*

COURTESY OF THE RIFLES (BERKSHIRE AND WILTSHIRE) MUSEUM, SALISBURY.

volunteer was immediately struck off strength and—in some corps—dragged before a magistrate and fined for lack of diligence.

Experience in Iraq and Afghanistan has led to a new recruit training system being introduced in October 2006 to increase the emphasis on individual training excellence in order to boost retention. Recruits undergo two phases of training. Phase 1 is conducted at regional training centres manned by TA personnel and covers the Common Military Training syllabus. The recruit has the choice of doing this either over six[1] non-contiguous training weekends or on a two-week block. Phase 2 is considered special-to-arm training so infantry recruits spend two weeks on the Combat Infantryman's Course run by the Regular Army Infantry Training Centre in Catterick, North Yorkshire. A third option called Exercise SUMMER CHALLENGE is a recent addition to the basic training suite. Held annually and based on Regional Recruiting Centre areas, SUMMER CHALLENGE is a seven-week, fast-track course designed to turn newly attested recruits[2] into fully trained soldiers. By reason of its length, the exercise can never replace the two-phase system, but trials have produced positive results and it is becoming a regular feature of the training calendar. Potential officers who complete the course emerge ready to go to RMA Sandhurst.

Although the training foundation—the level below which the common skill set must not drop—of the TA is not expected to be as high as that of the Regular Army, more emphasis is now placed in all TA training on physical fitness, with military annual training tests that must be passed.

ABOVE *The Royal Rifle Volunteers composite company during live firing tactical training on the Pyla range complex in Cyprus, June 2006.*
COURTESY OF JOHN SKLIROS.

OPPOSITE *Regular Army instructors teach TA Phase 2 recruits to control their aggression on the bayonet fighting stand during a Combat Infantryman's Course at the Infantry Training Centre, Catterick in March 2007.*
COURTESY OF JOHN SKLIROS.

1. TA infantry must complete a further three bringing the Phase 1 total to nine weekends.
2. Current capacity is 30 infanteers, 30 non-inf and 30 potential officers.

TERRITORIALS IN THE PROPAGANDA WAR *This sequence of images was taken during the filming of a Movietone News feature at Coleraine, Northern Ireland in October 1941. The movie, which shows Territorials from The Royal Berkshire Regiment training to defeat German 'blitzkrieg' tactics, was shown in cinemas all over the UK and at the Chicago Exhibition. Still photographs were used in the American 'Life' magazine and were also dropped over Germany by the RAF. The German 'tank' — christened 'Old Faithful' — was constructed from petrol tins by the Pioneer Platoon.*

COURTESY OF THE RIFLES (BERKSHIRE AND WILTSHIRE) MUSEUM, SALISBURY.

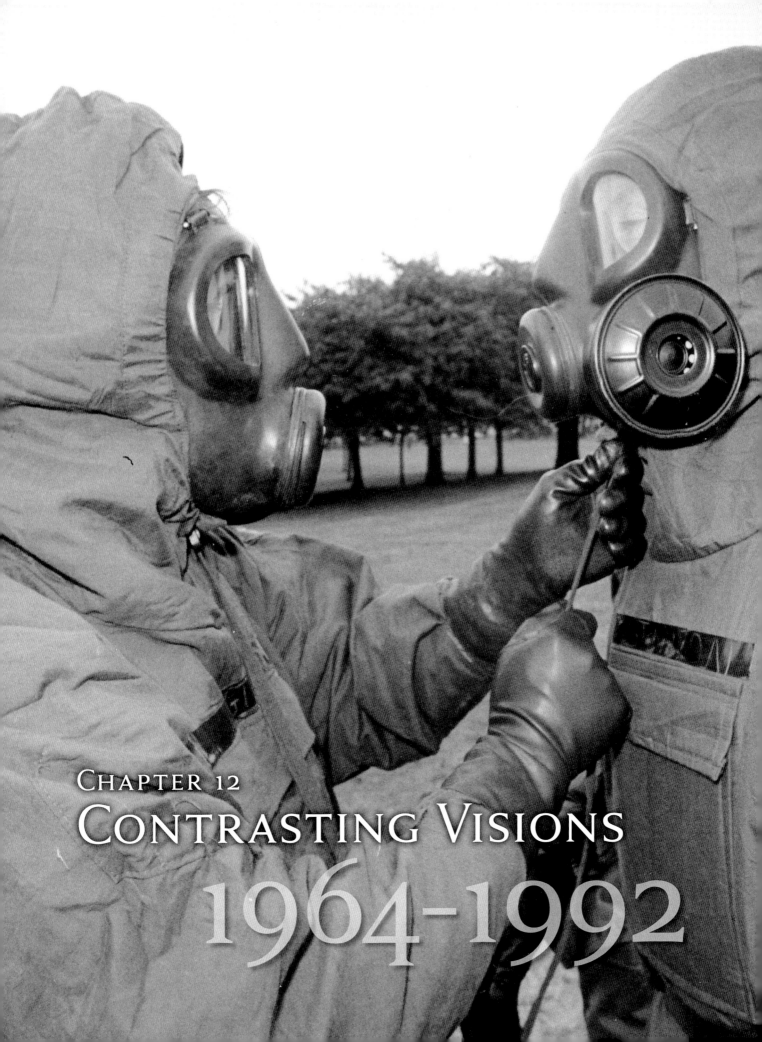

CHAPTER 12
CONTRASTING VISIONS
1964-1992

The TA role would now be to provide key individuals and a few units for immediate reinforcement of the army in a 'come as you are' limited war, which would offer no opportunities for large-scale reinforcement.

COURTESY OF IMPERIAL TOBACCO

A S A NEW Labour government took office in 1964, the strategic certainties of the Cold War remained constant, but the pace of technological change had accelerated markedly with new weapons, new materials, new control systems and new methods of weapon delivery all contributing to a demand for new equipment and posing new managerial problems at the heart of defence. Labour had committed itself in the election campaign 'to put our defences on a sound basis and to ensure that the nation gets value for money'. In practice, this meant pegging defence spending at £2,000 million at 1964 prices, with the new Minister of Defence, Denis Healey, remarking in the Commons in November 1964 that Britain was 'spending more on defence than any other country of her size and wealth' in trying to sustain three major roles in maintaining an independent nuclear deterrent, contributing to NATO and deploying a significant military capacity overseas. As so often before, wider defence cuts augured ill for the TA and, though there were to be subsequent brief revivals in its fortunes over the next 28 years, the overall pattern was one of reduction.

On 29th July 1965, in the belief that it was difficult to envisage any conflict requiring large numbers of Territorials or in which the TA could be a basis for expansion, the government signalled a major review. The TA role would now be to provide key individuals and a few units for immediate reinforcement of the army in a 'come as you are' limited war, which would offer no opportunities for large-scale reinforcement. A far-reaching reform plan had emerged from a controversial review of the TA's role by the Committee on the Future of Army Reserves, which first met on 30th April 1965 to discuss the implications of the conclusions of the earlier Home Defence Review Committee—chaired by Sir Philip Allen of the Treasury—that the cost of the TA could not be justified. The Director of Army Staff Duties, Major General Michael (later Field Marshal Lord) Carver produced the crucial paper for consideration. It was predicated on the assumption that the sole function of the TA was to bring the regulars from a peace to a wartime footing and that the increasing strength of the Army Reserve following the termination of national service[1] precluded the need for a 'tension reserve'. Much was made of the Home Defence Review Committee report, but that had been substantially steered towards its own conclusion by none other than Carver, who had appeared before the committee on 19th March 1965.

The committee's interim report was ready by 17th May and the overall proposals endorsed by the Army Board on 9th July, with the 'First Key Plan'

---

1. It would double in size by 1969.

OPPOSITE *Two Territorial staff sergeants from the Royal Corps of Transport carry out the 'buddy-buddy' equipment fitting checks of their Mark 3 NBC suits and S6 respirators during Exercise* PLAIN SAILING, *held at Grantham in 1989.*

COURTESY OF SOLDIER MAGAZINE

ABOVE & OPPOSITE *A Royal Army Ordnance Corps bakery in operation during an internal security exercise in Pembrokeshire, 1967.*

COURTESY OF SOLDIER MAGAZINE

for reorganisation being agreed on 16th July. As the Deputy CIGS, Lieutenant General (later General) Sir John Hackett explained to GOCs on 23rd July 1965 it was considered that, although the TA had steadily declined in strength, there was still not enough modern equipment available for it and, in any case, the force was not available for service in the most likely circumstances to arise in future. As the Parliamentary Under Secretary of State, George Reynolds MP, noted, many Territorials seemed to believe they would be serving in the front line in any conflict even though most were clearly designated for home defence.

The proposals were outlined in a White Paper on 15th December 1965. No more than 50,000 Territorials from the existing 107,000 would be retained, over half in support formations: 1,500 would be required in an 'Ever Ready' type role for logistic units, 11,000 would be required for logistic support of the Strategic Reserve in limited conflicts (which would require only two brigade groups at most), and 37,000 as reinforcements for BAOR in a more major crisis. Those brigades and divisions without a role upon mobilisation would be abolished. A total of 73 TA infantry battalions, 41 artillery regiments and 19 armoured regiments would go, leaving just 13 infantry battalions, a single armoured regiment, a single parachute battalion, four artillery regiments and the SAS units. The annual cost of the TA would be reduced from £38 million to £20 million.

The Parliamentary Under Secretary of State, George Reynolds MP, noted many Territorials seemed to believe they would be serving in the front line in any conflict even though most were clearly designated for home defence.

There was considerable opposition, notably from the Council of Territorial Associations. The Council's Chairman, the 16th Duke of Norfolk, had not been consulted prior to the announcement in July 1965. Indeed, Norfolk was especially annoyed that Hackett cancelled a lunch meeting with him immediately prior to the parliamentary announcement. The Council had established a working party to suggest its own ideas for reform on 5th April and its report, *A Study of the Role of the Territorial Army*, was forwarded to the MoD in May. For the teeth arms the ideas, based on a revised cyclical liability, had been studiously ignored so far as the Council was concerned. In fact, they had been immediately rejected as making no real savings. There was no statutory requirement to consult the Council and it was a deliberate policy to keep Norfolk and his two Vice Chairmen[2], or 'henchmen' as the Permanent Under Secretary for the Army termed them, from learning that decisions had already been reached for fear they might be 'stimulated to suggest changes'. Despite Hackett's view, expressed after a meeting with Norfolk on 5th August, that there was 'an erroneous impression of the extent to which the scheme was open to discussion', it was

2. Sir Edward Caffyn and Lord Clydesmuir.

LEFT *RAMC (V) soldiers carry casualties on board a C130 Hercules specially fitted for transporting stretcher cases on an exercise in 1967.*

COURTESY OF SOLDIER MAGAZINE

In the face of the strategic and financial arguments, the TA's defence often rested on a perceived social role—*The Daily Telegraph* spoke of Territorials' sense of doing something 'acceptable and beneficial to the rest of the community'—and upon county traditions that had no resonance for Labour politicians.

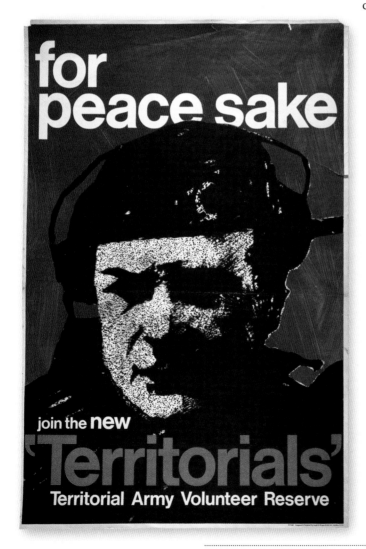

for peace sake

join the **new** 'Territorials'
Territorial Army Volunteer Reserve

agreed to establish a joint working party on reorganisation, with the meetings to be chaired by Reynolds or the DGTA&C. The first meeting took place on 11th August. In an internal memorandum in September, Carver warned that there could be 'no climate of change' and at one point negotiations broke down over the Council's attempt to have 10,000 soldiers put back into the order of battle. The Council went on to pass a resolution on 14th October that the reorganisation was not in the national interest. In time, accepting that there could be no major changes, the Council resumed negotiations.

The Council's stand was endorsed by the Conservatives, whose motion to reject the reforms was defeated by just one vote in the Commons on 16th December 1965. Six Field Marshals—Earl Alexander of Tunis, Sir Claude Auchinleck, Sir Francis Festing, Viscount Slim, Sir Gerald Templer and Lord Harding of Petherton[3]—also signed a letter condemning the proposals. In November 1967, amid economic crises leading to the devaluation of the pound, the Wilson government targeted the army as a whole in a bid to reduce defence expenditure, leading to a withdrawal from bases east of Suez. A target was set of reducing the army from 60 to 50 battalions by 1968, a process accomplished largely by establishing new multi-battalion regiments.

In the face of the strategic and financial arguments, the TA's defence often rested on a perceived social role—*The Daily Telegraph* spoke of the Territorials' sense of doing something 'acceptable and beneficial to the rest of the community' —and upon county traditions that had no resonance for Labour politicians. Many special cases were raised. G Y Mackie MP,

3. Lord Harding had begun his military career as a Territorial officer in the 1/11th London (Finsbury Rifles) in 1914.

for example, pointed out that the intended reduction of the TA presence in Caithness and Sutherland, in Scotland, would strike at the local economy as well as penalising an area which had seen good recruiting. Faced with their own hard choices, regulars had little sympathy for the TA's fate even though a War Office committee chaired by Reynolds had pointed out that reducing the TA would mean considerably fewer billets for regular officers, leading to redundancies, and the potential loss of up to 1,400 annual Territorial recruits for the army. As it happened, the future Field Marshal Sir John Chapple had initially served in 461 (Middlesex) HAA Regiment, RA (TA)[4] as a national service officer before commanding the infantry sub-unit of the Cambridge University Training Corps and then being commissioned as a regular in 1954.

A few concessions were made, it being announced in February 1966 that an additional 28,000 men would be retained in 87 'lightly armed units of infantry type', and a few signal units for home defence and in support of the civil authorities. It was also agreed to retain 'Territorial' in the title since the original intention had been to call the new organisation simply the Army Volunteer Reserve. Now the whole would be termed the Territorial Army and Volunteer Reserve (TAVR), absorbing both TA and army reserves.

Under the Reserve Forces Act of 1966, and with effect from 1st April 1967, the TAVR comprised four categories. TAVR I consisted of Ever Readies and

LEFT *The Churchill family [l-r: Colonel The Duke of Marlborough, Major the Viscount Churchill, Major Winston Spencer Churchill, Major John Strange Churchill] were closely associated with the Oxfordshire Yeomanry. Winston had been a member of the Queen's Own Oxfordshire Hussars since 1902 and became their Honorary Colonel in 1927. In planning his own funeral, Churchill lodged a sealed copy of his detailed instructions—in which he had given the honour of marching before the coffin to his old regiment—in the TA Centre in Oxford. This caused some considerable annoyance amongst Guards officers who thought that the honour should be theirs. Following Churchill's death in January 1965, as the detachment of 30 men commanded by Major Tim May formed up, a senior Brigade Major of the Guards stormed up to Major May and indignantly pointed out that his men were incorrectly positioned according to state funeral protocol. Unmoved by this outburst, Major May replied that: "In the Oxfordshire Yeomanry we always do state funerals this way."*

COURTESY OF THE OXFORDSHIRE YEOMANRY TRUST

---

4.   The lineal descendant of the Finsbury Rifles, in which Field Marshal Lord Harding had also served.

A TA RAOC (V) laundry unit on exercise in Pembrokshire, September 1967.

COURTESY OF SOLDIER MAGAZINE.

other specialists now constituting the Special Army Volunteer Reserve. TAVR II, now regarded as 'Volunteers', consisted of units with a limited war or general war role that undertook to serve outside the UK upon embodiment. Equipped to Regular Army scales, they had a substantial training commitment. Rather than the former provision for calling out the TA by proclamation in the event of imminent national danger or great emergency, TAVR I would now be called out by 'Queen's Order' when warlike operations were in preparation or progress, though only after full use had been made of regular reservists. TAVR II, however, could not be called out as individuals or selectively by unit. Distinction in TAVR II was also drawn between 'independent' units organised on a local basis and 'sponsored' units organised on a national basis. Most sponsored units were from the RAC, RA, RE, Royal Signals, RASC, RAOC, REME, RAMC, RMP, RAPC, Royal Pioneer Corps, Intelligence Corps, and Army Catering Corps. Sponsored units were intended to recruit individuals with skills and experience acquired in civilian life or previous military service, thereby requiring less training upon mobilisation, and those who felt they could not give as much time to the TA as would have been required in an independent unit or who would have had to travel too far to an independent unit of the right cap badge. Once trained, members of independent and sponsored units undertook 15 days' continuous training (usually the annual camp) and an annual range course. Independent units were liable to between six and 12 out-of-camp days' training at weekends in order to qualify for the bounty, whereas members of sponsored units only undertook four out-of-camp days' training. The training bounty was set at £20 (taxed) and the liability bounty at £60 (tax free).

TAVR III—'Territorials'—comprised the home defence units with light equipment and a much reduced training commitment of just an eight-day camp, five days' out-of-camp training and 27 drill periods. Moreover, TAVR III units were to be armed with the old .303-inch No 4 Lee Enfield and wear battledress, while TAVR I and II received the 7.62mm. Self-Loading Rifle and combat dress. Camps and some weekend training were unpaid, leaving it as a private venture, and all permanent staff were also withdrawn. TAVR IV was a miscellany of units such as elements of the Royal Signals, RE and RAOC, bands, and OTC. The latter were classed as TAVR IV (a), Training Corps at universities having become University Training Corps in 1948 and OTC once more in 1955.

The concept of county associations just survived extinction; a total of 23 (subsequently reduced to 14) larger regional groupings[5] only being retained, the Council of Territorial Associations successfully arguing that substituting enlarged district headquarters for associations would be more wasteful. In fact, the original idea had been to retain only six regional groupings. After some wartime amalgamations in 1943-44, amalgamation had again been suggested in 1950, such as Denbighshire with Flintshire, and Roxburgh with Berwick and Selkirk on the northern border with England and Scotland. The TA Advisory Committee had also accepted the need for grouping of associations in 1954 and the number had declined to 66 by February 1965, of which 36 had units below establishment. This, however, was far more radical. In the case of the Eastern Wessex TAVRA, the new arrangements meant a merger of the former associations for Berkshire, Buckinghamshire, Dorset, Hampshire, the Isle of Wight and Oxfordshire. Western Wessex TAVRA now embraced Cornwall, Devon, Gloucestershire, Somerset and Wiltshire. The largest of the new TAVRAs, however, were the Lowland TAVRA with 14 former associations, and the Highland TAVRA, with 21 former associations. Moreover, TAVRAs would no longer have an administrative function (though this was not the eventual outcome), being intended purely to maintain contact with local interests, especially employers and the trades unions. The sponsored units were administered through a series of Central Volunteer Headquarters (CVHQ).

Though technically most units were disbanded on 31st March 1967, in practice existing TA units were substantially reduced to sub-unit size

ABOVE *108 (Welsh) Squadron, Royal Engineers—a TAVR II unit—responded to Bridgend's need to divert traffic from its congested streets by building a 65-foot Bailey Bridge over the River Ogwy in under eight hours. The bridge, built in May 1968, was only one of the Military Aid to the Civil Authorities (MACA) tasks undertaken by the Squadron throughout South Wales.*

COURTESY OF SOLDIER MAGAZINE

---

5. Now to be Territorial and Army Volunteer Reserve Associations (TAVRAs).

COURTESY OF SOLDIER MAGAZINE

ABOVE *The No 2 slams a 120mm High Explosive Squash Head round into the breech of a MOBAT recoilless anti-tank gun belonging to the 1st Battalion, 51st Highland Volunteers during an exercise on Stanford Training Area in 1973. MOBAT crews nicknamed it the 'VC Gun' because their position would be given away instantly by the fearsome backblast.*

and status when transferred to TAVR III. In January 1968, however, despite continued efforts by the Council of Territorial Associations led by Norfolk and its Secretary, Brigadier Hugh Tyler, to preserve at least cadres for future expansion, TAVR III was axed and Civil Defence was placed on a care and maintenance basis. Then, in November 1968, it was announced that the first two TAVR categories would be effectively merged, with all liable to serve overseas upon embodiment, though the training commitments varied. TAVR I and TAVR II would now be TAVR Group A and TAVR IV would be TAVR Group B. With the new organisation taking effect on 1st April 1969, all TAVR III units were formally disbanded, though 90 former units were retained as cadres of eight officers and men within Group A units. Not surprisingly, overall numbers fell significantly from 116,500 in December 1964 to 54,800 by March 1968. In 1969 there were 945 personnel in TAVR I, 34,833 in TAVR II, 10,767 in TAVR III and 3,010 in TAVR IV—a total of 49,555 against an establishment of 61,000. Numbers went down further to 47,589 by March 1970.

The Territorials were revived somewhat by the return of a Conservative government in 1970. It was announced in July that 10,000 men would be added to the TAVR in Group A to 'make provision for an uncommitted reserve of formed units and men' for NATO. The role generally was to provide a national reserve capable of reinforcing British forces in NATO, securing the home base and providing a future means of expansion. A total of 20 new battalions[6] were formed from April 1971, of which 15 were allocated to a 'General Reserve' and trained for home defence; the cadres retained in 1969 providing the nucleus of companies in these battalions. In 1974 it was resolved to provide the General Reserve battalions with headquarters and reconnaissance elements by reducing some under-recruiting units and cadres that had not been drawn upon previously. The establishment remained at 74,000 but, in fact, strength was only about 54,000 at the time and it was increasingly difficult to persuade men to stay beyond two years. Moreover, General Reserve battalions retained the air of a second-class tier, having no anti-tank weapons or sustained-fire machine-guns.

....

6. So-called 'Heath battalions'.

BELOW A GPMG gunner from the 5th Battalion, The Royal Anglian Regiment takes up a fire position in a German street.

COURTESY OF RON MCDAID/CHRIS ST JOHN

The beginning of 'The Troubles' in Northern Ireland in 1969 posed an interesting problem for the TAVR. No difficulties had actually arisen with the TA or TAVR units in Northern Ireland by 1969. With the escalation of the military presence, however, questions began to be raised as to the possible use of the Territorials in the province, TAVR premises themselves being commonly utilised by regular units from the beginning. In May 1971 a company of the 5th Royal Anglian (Volunteers) applied to accept the invitation of the 1st Royal Anglians to undertake its annual camp with them in Northern Ireland. In August, Ian Gow, later a Conservative MP murdered by the IRA in 1990 but at the time simply on the party's list of approved parliamentary candidates, applied with a fellow TA officer to undertake his annual training on attachment in the province. Permission was refused in each case. In the autumn the Northern Ireland government raised the issue of whether Territorials could join the new Ulster Defence Regiment (UDR). It was pointed out that the TAVR was a reserve for the army as a whole and could not legally take on other operational duties on a part-time basis. Its responsibilities were very different from those of the UDR, which had replaced the former Special Constabulary Reserve and was intended to reinforce the military on a part-time basis. Territorials could guard their own centres and even help train the UDR, but that was the limit of potential involvement, fears also being expressed as a result of press coverage of circulating rumours that any hint of being engaged in an active role in Northern Ireland would have a detrimental impact on the TAVR on the mainland. In November 1971, therefore, it was made clear that men could not belong to both TAVR and the UDR and, if they wished to have a role in aid of the civil power in the province, they must resign from the TAVR before joining the UDR. The then GOC in Northern Ireland, Sir Harry Tuzo, expressed disappointment with the decision. Individual Territorials, however, did subsequently deploy with regular units in Northern Ireland by discharging from their Territorial unit and re-engaging with regular units for the duration of their service there. TAVR training in the province continued as usual until a Territorial travelling in uniform was shot in Belfast, after which personnel travelled to units in plain clothes. One officer of 74 (Antrim Artillery) was issued with a pistol and ten rounds to defend his squadron headquarters, but the ammunition was boxed, wrapped in paper and heavily sealed, with strict instructions that the seal should not be broken until he was fired upon.

COURTESY OF IMPERIAL TOBACCO

PLAYER'S CIGARETTES

ARMY VETERINARY CORPS.
1908

The notion that the TAVR was a reserve for the army as a whole reflected the increasing emphasis upon integration between the army and reserves. In 1977 the last remaining all-arms volunteer brigade[7] was broken up as a formation, though its constituent elements remained. Now, two combined regular and volunteer brigades (briefly referred to as field forces) would contain two volunteer infantry battalions and supporting units. In 1979, however, following the Shapland Report on wastage rates in the TAVR by Major General Peter Shapland, the Director of Volunteers, Territorials and Cadets, Mrs Thatcher's new government announced that the title of Territorial Army would be revived. In the event, it was not until 7th April 1982, under the provisions of the Reserve Forces Act of 1982, that this actually took effect, the earlier Reserve Forces Act in 1980 merely replacing surviving legislation from 1921 and consolidating the various reserve forces measures since the 1960s. While the overall title had been revived, TA infantry units still continued to be styled 'Volunteer Battalions'. Shapland, who reported in 1978, had noted a 30 per cent turnover in the TAVR and, taking a realistic view of the paradox that a volunteer must give priority to his family and employment before the TAVR, his committee had urged giving the Territorials specific missions, improved benefits, better training and more modern equipment. Much was done to address Shapland's recommendations and, as a result of this and other subsequent reports by the MoD and outside consultants, a 'Volunteer Reserve

TOP *Lieutenant Colonel Brian Martin, CO 4 (V) PARA, addresses the battalion after a FIBUA exercise in Bonnland, Germany in 1987. The enemy forces, played by Bundeswehr soldiers, are formed up in the background.*

INSET ABOVE *Major Norman Hodges of 4 (V) PARA issues some fairly direct instructions to his fellow Territorials after 'endex'.*

COURTESY OF RICHARD WATT

7. 44 Parachute Brigade.

ABOVE *Privates Crowther, Dale, Hill and Hatton of B Company, (Oldham) 4th. (V) Battalion The Parachute Regiment wait to do their first jump at RAF Hullavington in Wiltshire, 1979.*

RIGHT *The barrage balloon, based at RAF Hullavington in Wiltshire, which was used up until the mid-90s during parachute training to take soldiers to the height of 800 feet for their first jump. Subsequent descents were from C 130 aircraft.*

COURTESY OF RICHARD WATT

Forces Campaign', with an initial budget of £1 million was launched through the auspice of a new National Employers' Liaison Council (NELC) (later the National Employer Advisory Board or NEAB) in 1986.

The reassessment of the TA role owed much to the far more positive defence posture of Mrs Thatcher's administrations as espoused at the 1979, 1983 and 1987 elections, as compared to the anti-nuclear and minimalist defence position of the Labour opposition. The June 1981 Defence Review, *The Way Forward*, envisaged that, after providing for the nuclear deterrent and home defence, priority should be given to central Europe. This emphasis was subsequently challenged by the Falklands War but, in the shorter term, it meant an expansion

"There are many other hobbies, which offer similar attractions in terms of challenge, fun and adventure (though not pay), against which the TA has to compete, and in which you become a fully paid up member of the club more quickly."

BRIGADIER R P G WILLIAMS

programme announced in June 1981 to bring the TA back up to 86,000 by 1990 and to provide a complete reserve division for the I (British) Corps in BAOR, although one brigade would be a regular one. The two TA brigades, with headquarters at Topcliffe in Yorkshire and Chilwell in Nottinghamshire, would be responsible for protecting the corps rear areas in Germany. In addition, amid calls in some quarters for the revival of a kind of Home Guard or for conscription for Territorial service, a Home Service Force was created for defence of vulnerable points. It was classed as Group C since the TA had retained the concept of Groups A and B from the TAVR. The intention was to reach a strength of 4,500 by 1990 in some 47 infantry companies that would be sponsored by TA units. Men aged between 20 and 55 with some form of military experience would be accepted with a liability of six days' compulsory training per annum and up to four days' voluntary training.

Constituting some 28-30 per cent of the army's mobilised strength (and costing less than five per cent of the army's budget) including 50 per cent of the infantry for I (British) Corps and some 50 per cent of those forces available for home defence, the TA averaged 88.9 per cent of its establishment between 1979 and 1989. An average of 76.9 per cent was trained at any one time during the same period. Many older attitudes remained, however, in terms of the relationship between regulars and Territorials. The incentives and disincentives were also consistent with the past, with the annual turnover running at 17 per cent for officers and between 25 and 30 per cent for soldiers. Moreover, despite the efforts of the NELC, many of the old difficulties with employers prevailed and public awareness of the TA remained low. A report for the MoD in September 1985 by consultants Grandfield Rork Collins concluded that, while there was a broad awareness of the TA, 'it is very superficial awareness with scant knowledge'. Indeed, it was estimated that 55 per cent of TA recruits became aware of the force through family, friends or colleagues at work. In 1989-90 the 72,823 serving Territorials represented just 0.12 per cent of the British population as a whole and only 0.65 per cent of males aged 17 to 30. The

In 1989-90 the 72,823 serving Territorials represented just 0.12 per cent of the British population as a whole and only 0.65 per cent of males aged 17 to 30.

consultants' report in 1985 suggested high wastage was a result of inadequate bounty levels, repetitive training and inordinate administration. Unfortunately, repetitive training—also highlighted by the consultancy report 20 years earlier —was a likely consequence of a high turnover. In 1985, 29 per cent of the TA had less than a year's training, 46 per cent had less than two years and 59 per cent less than three years. Wastage was also seen as a result of 'age group volatility', characterised by one TA officer in 1987 as 'Change job, change girlfriend, change hobby'. The Shapland report in 1978 had seen TA membership as 'a demanding hobby to the virtual exclusion of other hobbies' and, as Brigadier R P G Williams put it in 1988: 'There are many other hobbies, which offer similar attractions in terms of challenge, fun and adventure (though not pay), against which the TA has to compete, and in which you become a fully paid up member of the club more quickly.' Similar solutions to those in the past were advocated. The Blythe report on wastage conducted for the Army Personnel Research Establishment in 1984 suggested better bounties and Neil Thorne MP in May 1989 also called for a better bounty for Territorials 'to encourage their wives to want them to continue'. It was also pointed out that there was no retirement package for Territorials and they received the lowest pay in their rank while regulars got increases each year they served in a rank.

Recruiting still relied upon an almost traditional appeal as illustrated by an open day programme for 201 (Herts and Beds Yeomanry) Battery, RA in 1983 which emphasised the need for 'bright, hardworking, fit young men' and stressed that employers actively encouraged TA involvement as it 'helps to increase self-confidence, makes men more responsible and mature and builds character'. Women, too, had increasingly joined the TA since 1947, the continuation of mixed anti-aircraft units with ATS personnel being agreed in September 1946 and signalled publicly by the Secretary of State for War, Frederick Bellenger, on 21st October 1946. Subsequently, women were eligible for entry into the Women's Royal Army Corps (WRAC), which replaced the ATS in 1949, and also the Royal Signals, RAMC, Queen Alexandra's Royal Army Nursing Corps and the RASC, which became the Royal Corps of Transport (RCT) from 1965. Subsequently, the WRAC became part of the Adjutant General's Corps (AGC) in 1992 and the RCT part of the Royal Logistic Corps (RLC) in 1993. Lieutenant Colonel Jean Blackwood became the first woman to command a TA unit when taking over 37 Signals Regiment in March 1982 and Colonel Kathleen Clarke was the first to reach the rank of Colonel when taking over 201 (Northern)

COURTESY OF IMPERIAL TOBACCO

PLAYER'S CIGARETTES

1ST/4TH BN. THE KING'S OWN
(ROYAL LANCASTER REGT.) 1918

General Hospital, RAMC in April 1982. In October 1997 a range of remaining restrictions on the role that women could fulfil within the TA were lifted so that they could serve in any regiment or 'discipline'. When 100 Field Squadron of The Royal Monmouthshire Royal Engineers (Militia) deployed to Iraq in 2003, 15 out of 172 members were female including three of the five troop commanders.

The TA's short-lived significance for government in the 1980s, however, was soon to fade for these were also years of considerable change in global affairs with the collapse of communism in Central and Eastern Europe between 1989 and 1991. Moreover, just as the Labour government had imposed further defence cuts in 1974 and 1975, the Conservatives' effort to improve defence was ultimately undermined by the impact of world depression on the economy, the need for tight monetary control on public expenditure, and escalating costs on major defence equipment projects. Accordingly, in anticipation of a 'peace dividend', the Minister of Defence, Tom King, announced the review *Options for Change* on 25th July 1990. No final decision had been made with regard to the TA by the time the implications for the Regular Army were unveiled in July 1991, but it was anticipated that the TA would not recruit above 60-65,000. The Regular Army itself was to be reduced to 155,000, a total subsequently raised to 159,000 by King's successor Malcolm Rifkind.

ABOVE *Men of the 6th Battalion, The Royal Anglian Regiment brew up during a Home Defence exercise.*

COURTESY OF RON MCDAID/CHRIS ST JOHN.

In December 1991 it was announced that the TA establishment would be reduced from 74,000 to 63,500 while the Home Service Force, which had reached a strength of 3,297, was to be disbanded. In fact, given the level of under-manning in the TA, the reduction would only amount to about 10,000 and only five battalions would be lost through amalgamation, leaving 28 committed to home defence and six to the proposed Rapid Reaction Corps. One interesting consequence of *Options for Change* was that it was felt that a number of units such as the London Scottish could no longer be affiliated to far-flung units such as the 51st Highland Volunteers, resulting in the reformation of The London Regiment in 1992 as a four-company regiment: briefly comprising six companies before reverting to four, the 'Londons' were moved into the Household Division in 2005.

Expectations of the 'New World Order' following the end of the Cold War were somewhat set back by the new demands for peacekeeping and 'small wars'. The First Gulf War in 1990-1991 immediately revealed the disadvantages of the reduced size and capability of the Regular Army. For the first time since 1956, ex-regular reservists were called up and volunteers were sought from the TA.

BELOW *Troopers of A Squadron, 21 (V) SAS abseil down a rock face in Brecon Beacons during their continuation training.*

COURTESY OF THE MILITARY PICTURE LIBRARY

A total of 272 Territorials were already serving on full-time engagements on a voluntary basis and 98 of them were deployed to the Gulf. Another 651 were mobilised on a voluntary basis. Of these, 529 served with the RAMC, 39 with the RMP and four with the Intelligence Corps. The Territorials of 42 Survey Engineer Group and 8 Map and Air Chart Depot offered operational support of a different kind while 873 Movement Light Squadron ran a series of intensive battlefield illumination and searchlight operators' courses for 1 (British) Corps Lighting Troop being deployed to the Gulf. In the case of the RAMC, 205 (Scottish) Field Hospital was mobilised[8] and, augmented by volunteers from other units, was established in a disused terminal at King Khalid International Airport, Riyadh in Saudi Arabia. When questions were raised as to why Territorials were still there after many regulars had left following the conclusion of the war in February 1991, the field hospital was sent home but, as they were not formally attached to it, the volunteers from other units remained—some serving up to six months in theatre.

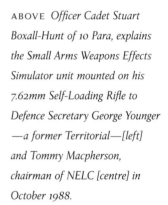

ABOVE *Officer Cadet Stuart Boxall-Hunt of 10 Para, explains the Small Arms Weapons Effects Simulator unit mounted on his 7.62mm Self-Loading Rifle to Defence Secretary George Younger —a former Territorial—[left] and Tommy Macpherson, chairman of NELC [centre] in October 1988.*

COURTESY OF SOLDIER MAGAZINE

Under the 1980 legislation, which envisaged only general war, it was not possible to call out the TA until substantial use had been made of ex-regular reservists and, of course, since the changes in 1967, there had been no provision for calling out selected units or individuals. Yet the concept of integration meant that many regular units could not be sustained in the field without the anticipated TA element. In effect, the changes to the army and the TA had made the army dependent upon the TA in circumstances falling well short of a national emergency. Gaps were only made good by drawing upon regular units not required for the Gulf. It was not surprising, therefore, that a new review of reserves was ordered amid demands in some quarters that the 'one army' concept be made meaningful. An Open-Government Document entitled *The Future of Britain's Reserve Forces*, heralding even more far-reaching changes in the TA, was published in March 1992.

❖

8. The first complete TA unit to be so mobilised since the end of the Second World War.

HACKETT AND CARVER

BELOW *(Richard) Michael Power Carver, Baron Carver photographed by Bernard Lee Schwartz, 1977.*

COURTESY OF THE NATIONAL PORTRAIT GALLERY, LONDON

THE REDUCTION OF the TA in 1967 was popularly attributed to Sir John 'Shan' Hackett, the Deputy CIGS from 1964 to 1966, and Michael Carver, Director of Army Staff Duties from 1964 to 1968. Some TA officers took to wearing a tie with crossed hatchet and carving knife. Both were intellectual soldiers and had exemplary active service records. Hackett, who later became CinC of BAOR and then Principal of King's College, London, had commanded 4 Parachute Brigade at Arnhem while Carver, who was to become Chief of the Defence Staff in 1973, had been the army's youngest brigade commander at only 29 when taking over 4 Armoured Brigade in Normandy.

Carver was later to complain that his 'superiors in the Army Department were pusillanimous in failing to fight harder for the reorganisation' and letting the odium be deflected on Labour politicians 'and, to a considerable degree, on myself'. In fact, the actual plan for reorganisation originated with Lieutenant Colonel (later General Sir) Hugh Beach within Carver's directorate, but Carver was not prepared, as he put it, 'to apologise for the proposals'. He believed the TA too large to be recruited, equipped, trained or 'even clothed', and was so geographically scattered that it 'wasted the little money that could be spared'. Carver saw the primary aim of the reforms 'to bring the Regular Army from a peace to a war footing' and was highly critical of the decision to call the organisation TAVR rather than the Army Volunteer Reserve and also of the subsequent revival of the title of TA.

It was also Carver, as Chief of the General Staff from 1971 to 1973, who articulated the 'one army' concept in a speech to the Council of TAVRAs on 13th July 1972, remarking: 'When we talk about the army as a whole, it is a good thing to remind ourselves that, in spite of many different outward appearances—and some minor differences—we are one army—Regular, Reserve and Volunteer Reserve.' Primarily, the speech was concerned with establishing a context of scarce resources, in which to emphasise that it had been possible to devote a 'modest proportion' to the TAVR. He also trailed the introduction of a UK Land Forces Headquarters, whose GOC was also to be Inspector General of TAVR, but the essential message was that, if the Army Board appeared 'hard-hearted', it had a duty to ensure the resources available were 'used in the most effective and efficient way'. He ended with an allusion to 1940 by stressing another duty to avoid soldiers being 'chucked into battle with inadequate training, inferior equipment and without proper fire and air support'. The speech had a certain ambiguity, with many regulars seeing it simply as a sop to the Territorials' wounded pride after the restructuring. Territorials, on the other hand, argued that regulars had not kept their side of the bargain by providing the TAVR with the same front-line equipment as the regulars. Others have argued that Carver meant simply that there was a single chain of command—'one family' rather than one army—and that regulars and TAVR would be integrated in time of war.

ABOVE *Sir John Winthrop Hackett photographed by William Bird, 1966.*

COURTESY OF THE NATIONAL PORTRAIT GALLERY, LONDON

"When we talk about the Army as a whole, it is a good thing to remind ourselves that, in spite of many different outward appearances—and some minor differences—we are one Army—Regular, Reserve and Volunteer Reserve."
GENERAL SIR MICHAEL CARVER, 1973.

EXERCISE LIONHEART

ABOVE *Territorials from the*
10th Battalion, The Parachute
Regiment prepare to board
a CH3 Chinook on Exercise
LIONHEART. *Although it seemed*
to be possible to get the infantry
to the forward edge of the battle
area in a matter of hours, the
same did not apply to the rest
of their kit. The succession of
deployments and redeployments
meant that backpacks, containing
warm clothing and sleeping bags,
sometimes took the best part of
two weeks to catch up with their
owners.

COURTESY OF SOLDIER MAGAZINE

T HE EMPHASIS UPON improving the war-fighting capability of BAOR in the 1980s brought attention to the TA in a series of large-scale exercises. The first, CRUSADER, in September 1980 tested the speed with which the TA could be deployed both to BAOR and to guard vulnerable points at home against Soviet special forces. ETERNAL TRIANGLE held around Kassel in Germany in 1983 involved 18,000 men and tested the TA's ability to guard key headquarters and critical installations in rear areas. BRAVE DEFENDER in September 1985 was the largest conventional exercise held in the UK since the end of the Second World War, involving 65,000 regulars and Territorials to test home defence capabilities further. The exercise with the highest profile, however, was LIONHEART from 3rd September to 5th October 1984, representing the largest British troop movement exercise by sea and air since 1945.

Some 35,000 Territorials took part, the whole exercise involving more than 131,000 British, US, Dutch and German personnel. Eighteen months in the planning and costing £31 million—compared to £8.5 million for CRUSADER—LIONHEART comprised two separate but overlapping exercises. SPEARPOINT was a field force exercise for 1 (British) Corps from 17th-27th September and FULL FLOW, from 3rd September to 5th October, a base support and rear area exercise testing maintenance of the line of communications, logistic support,

Some 35,000 Territorials took part, the whole exercise involving over 131,000 British, US, Dutch and German personnel.

out-loading of combat supplies and casualty evacuation. Both were undertaken in the context of a simulated Soviet incursion, in which US, Dutch and German troops, as well as the British 5 Airborne Brigade, played the opposition 'Orange' forces.

LIONHEART was timed to avoid peak holiday traffic, but still had to lessen the impact in Germany, not least for farmers. Cross-channel and North Sea ferries were taken up with, for example, 3,000 vehicles and 7,800 troops passing through Dover alone during the TA movement weekend. Territorials represented 59 per cent of army and RAF personnel sent out from the UK. Most home-based units arrived at their wartime stations within 48 hours, though some took 72 hours in the traffic congestion through Belgium and, of course, none were actually under attack. Inevitably, perhaps, press coverage tended to highlight 'human interest' stories, such as the TA units participating with the largest number of family members: 202 (Midland) General Hospital from Birmingham had a father and daughter and three married couples, while 7th Battalion Light Infantry from Durham fielded four pairs of brothers, a pair of sisters and a married couple. Attention was also drawn to the anomaly that female members of participating OTCs were permitted to carry weapons while the WRAC could not.

❖

ABOVE *A private soldier from No 1 Company, 5th Battalion, The Royal Anglian Regiment in Complete Equipment Marching Order and carrying his SLR and scrimmed 1944 pattern steel helmet, stands ready for the next move during* LIONHEART. *Having lived for two weeks in their NBC suits, soldiers were often amazed at how colourful their camouflage clothing seemed when revealed at Endex. Camouflage NBC suits did not appear on general issue to the TA until the early 1990s.*
LEFT *Embarking at Dover.*

COURTESY OF RON MCDAID/CHRIS ST JOHN.

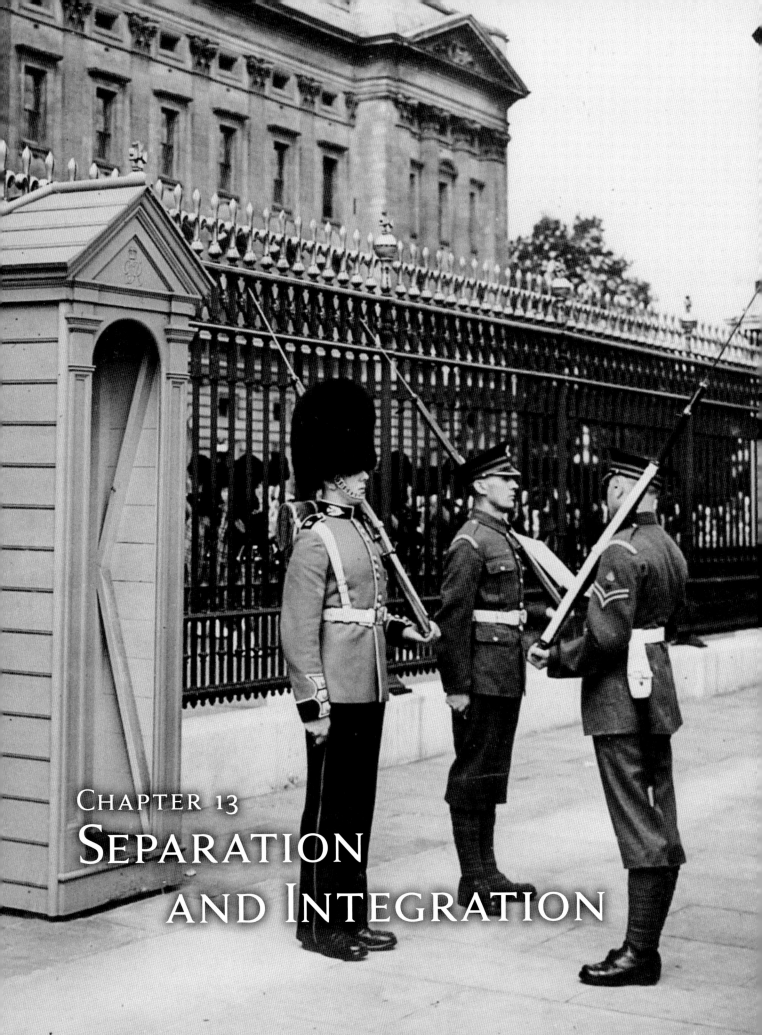

CHAPTER 13
SEPARATION AND INTEGRATION

Much might be made of the common contemporary usage of STABS (Stupid TA Bastards) and ARABS (Arrogant Regular Army Bastards) by regulars and Territorials respectively. Operational deployment, however, has always resulted in a substantial decrease in antagonism and an increase in mutual respect.

THERE HAS OFTEN been an uneasy relationship between regulars and auxiliaries. There is an assumption on the part of the professional that the amateur cannot attain the highest standards and, on the part of the amateur, that the hidebound professional cannot comprehend the special value of the amateur approach. Thus, at a time in the 1860s when most regulars believed the volunteers 'at the very best as harmless lunatics and, at the worst, as utterly valueless as a military force', Lord Ranelagh of the 2nd Middlesex (South Middlesex) RVC was so dismissive of the lack of ability of regulars to realise volunteers' capabilities that he held that they 'should form a distinct and separate force from the Army'. Rifle volunteers were only permitted to wear silver lace on their uniforms as gold lace was deemed to be the exclusive mark of regular soldiers. Far from being taken as a snub, the volunteers welcomed the ruling since it would ensure that they would not be mistaken for the 'dregs of society'. In one scene in *The Way Ahead* (1944) William Hartnell's regular Sergeant Fletcher says of David Niven's Territorial officer, Lieutenant Perry, that he is as 'good as a regular, almost', very much reflecting the inter-war regular view of the 'Saturday Night Soldiers'.

When resources have been scarce—a not uncommon occurrence in terms of military expenditure—it is also not surprising that competition is enhanced still further. Thus, in January 1922 a meeting of GOCs at the War Office concluded that the TA could not fulfil any of the essential military tasks required for the defence of the empire. Indeed, 'On the contrary, it is absorbing money to fund which regular units are to be abolished. It is impossible, therefore, to justify the retention of the Territorial Army in its present form on military grounds'. At precisely the same time, speaking of the Army Council, the Earl of Scarbrough remarked: 'I have little doubt that they would welcome abolition and if thereby they can save something substantial for the Regular Army they will probably press for it and, if successful, destroy the one thing that keeps the voluntary spirit alive in the country'. Interestingly, the National Audit Office (NAO) report in 2006 suggested that the TA was good value for money, costing £10,000 per soldier per year when not deployed compared to a regular costing £55,000 per year.

In some respects, the old competition holds some of its power even with the increasing emphasis since the 1990s upon integration rather than separation, the expectation being that it would increase the sense of involvement and commitment on the part of Territorials towards regulars and thus also enhance

OPPOSITE *On 6th July 1938 The Honourable Artillery Company became the first Territorials to form the guard at Buckingham Palace.*
COURTESY OF THE IMPERIAL WAR MUSEUM.

> "At the beginning I thought that because they were part-timers I would be better than them but they soon changed my mind. I would honestly work in any environment with them again, and I made some really good mates."

REGULAR SOLDIER FROM 1 PWRR
Iraq 2004.

their willingness to volunteer for operations. In 1988 US Colonel Wallace Earl Walker, conducting a study of the TA, was told by one regular training major that a TA unit judged a regular commanding officer 'not on how good a job he has done, but on how little harm he has done'. Similarly, in June 1992 Major General Murray Naylor, who had just ceased to be DGTA, expressed the view that 'ignorance, envy and disdain on both sides all too often show themselves and for those who care to look for them, tensions between the two halves of the "One Army" are all too evident beneath the surface'. In May 1999, Bruce George MP, Chairman of the Commons Defence Committee detected 'an undercurrent of distrust, and, on occasion, disdain from some sections of the Regular Army and MoD when dealing with the TA'. Certainly, the NAO in 2006 concluded that reservists needed access on deployment to officers and NCOs who understood their particular problems.

Much might be made of the common contemporary usage of STABS (Stupid TA Bastards) and ARABS (Arrogant Regular Army Bastards) by regulars and Territorials respectively. Operational deployment, however, has always resulted in a substantial decrease in antagonism and an increase in mutual respect. In the Great War, when first sent to the front, Territorial units were usually initially attached to regular units for experience. Whatever prejudice Territorial officers encountered throughout the war, accounts universally attest to the good relationship quickly developed between other ranks. Thus, when attached to 2 Brigade in 1st Division in 1915 the men of the 1/9th King's (Liverpool Regiment) found that far from assuming an air of superiority, ordinary regulars 'displayed a sense of admiration that Territorial soldiers could have so quickly learnt the profession of arms'. Similarly, joining 88 Brigade of 29th Division, men of the 1/4th East Lancs found men of the Worcesters 'always ready to show us how things should be done, and we for our part were equally keen to be shown'. Within a week the battalions were firm friends and 'the Worcesters actually spoke of their battalion as the Worcester-Lancs'. Much the same still applies, with one regular in 1 PWRR in 2004 saying of Territorials in his company in Iraq: 'At the beginning I thought that because they were part-timers I would be better than them but they soon changed my mind. I would honestly work in any environment with them again, and I made some really good mates.' As one of the Territorials with 1 PWRR also noted: 'prejudice is prompted by ignorance and was normally dispelled by exposure'.

OPPOSITE *A waiting detail from Salonika Company prepare to practice compound entry drills at Camp Bastion. The Company, raised by 7 Rifles, contained Regulars, Territorials and Reservists and, like Somme Company raised by The London Regiment before them, proved to be a robust mix. Within weeks of arrival, all four platoons were operating outside Bastion, some in observation posts overlooking Musa Qal'h.*

COURTESY OF JON DOLPHIN.

CHAPTER 14
ONE ARMY
1992-2008

"...the men who went out to Mesopotamia in 1916 had joined up in 1914 because the country was at grips with Germany. If to-day, out of a cloudless sky, there came a demand for 100,000 extra men to go out to Mesopotamia in a localised campaign, would they be found so easily, at ordinary infantry pay?"

LIEUTENANT COLONEL J K DUNLOP MC TD
The Problems and Responsibilities of the Territorial Army, 1935.

COURTESY OF IMPERIAL TOBACCO

The *Future of Britain's Reserve Forces* in March 1992 promised 'fundamental changes' in the way the TA and other reserves were organised and deployed. It was informed by the MoD study of the 'regular/reserve mix' undertaken in the light of the First Gulf War, which suggested that it had been difficult to gain access to the categories of reservists in those support areas most needed for such 'out of area' operations. While Britain had mobilised around 2,000 reservists of all kinds for the Gulf, the United States had mobilised 230,000 reservists. Consequently, there would be legislative changes to enable deployment in more limited conflicts, for UN peacekeeping and humanitarian operations overseas, and for 'back-filling' when regulars were deployed overseas. It was suggested that new legislation would revive the concept of the Ever Readies so that selected individuals and units could be called out at short notice 'through the assumption of voluntary liability for this status', and that all reserves could be called out compulsorily as individuals or units as required. As a further MoD paper, *Britain's Reserve Forces: A Framework for the Future* put it in October 1993, it was also intended 'to supplement the existing regular capability on a broader front to meet temporary increases in commitment'. A further document in December 1994, *The Territorial Army, a Direction for the Future*, also emphasised the change from a 'threat-based' army to a 'capability-based' army. It was the most far-reaching change to the very basis of TA service since the establishment of the force in 1908, representing to a large extent the fulfilment of the 'one army' concept enunciated by Carver in 1972. Ironically, just as the Golden Jubilee in 1958 had celebrated the TA on the brink of change, so the Royal Review of the Yeomanry for its 200th anniversary in Windsor Great Park on 17th April 1994 echoed a very different past.

The Reserve Forces Act of May 1996, which came into effect on 1st April 1997, established a High Readiness Reserve equivalent to the former Ever Readies. This would be a 'Ready Reserve' of individuals prepared to undertake full-time reserve service with regular units for short engagements up to a maximum duration of 42 months in peacetime, which meant that Territorials would no longer have to be discharged from their TA engagement to serve with regulars. Secondly, it established a Sponsored Reserve of civilian specialists from defence industries and support agencies who, by agreement with their employers, were prepared to undertake maintenance and support functions. The High Readiness Reserve was specifically intended to provide 1,500 specialists such as interpreters, civil affairs officers and press officers—for which duties regulars

OPPOSITE *Rifleman Chris Grant from A Company 7 Rifles mans a defensive position in Patrol Base Oscar 44 in December 2007, during Salonika Company's six-month tour in Helmand Province, Afghanistan. The 20-man base was attacked twice in one week. Water rationing in this spartan and inhospitable location—which can only be supplied by air—makes shaving a luxury.*

COURTESY OF CHRIS GRANT.

COURTESY OF IMPERIAL TOBACCO

were not trained—on seven days' notice, for which a higher bounty was offered. Also incorporated were safeguards for employers, under which they could claim exemption for key employees or financial compensation, employment and financial safeguards for reservists having been included in the earlier Reserve Forces (Safeguard of Employment) Act in 1985.

The most important aspect of the legislation was the new power to call out the reserve. Members of the reserves could still be called out by Queen's Order in the event of imminent national danger, great emergency, or actual or apprehended attack on the UK. Reserves, however, could also now be called out by order of the Secretary of State for Defence in circumstances short of those required by Queen's Order if it appeared 'warlike operations are in preparation or progress', or if it was felt desirable to undertake operations outside the UK for 'the protection of life and property', the 'alleviation of distress', or 'the preservation of life and property in time of disaster or appended disaster'. Serving reservists could elect to be bound by the new legislation or would become liable to it when re-engaging or being commissioned.

The new legislation rather begged the issues of just how far a government's response to particular conflicts would find general public acceptance, and of the consistency with which a government would react to similar contingencies in different circumstances, seemingly weighting more perhaps the ethical dimension of one conflict as opposed to another. Abstract declarations of internationalism do not matter overly much when military intervention on such grounds results in a minimum commitment of short duration. It matters a great deal when military forces have been committed to a seemingly open-ended conflict and are sustaining significant casualties on what appear to be dubious or even manufactured grounds for seemingly intangible objectives. The national interest needs to be articulated in effective terms for, as Professor Sir Michael Howard once wrote of allied war aims in the Great War: 'the flower of British and French manhood had not flocked to the colours in 1914 to die for the balance of power.' From the point of view of

BELOW *Corporal Bev Cheema mobilised in 2005 to give administrative support to Roebuck Company on Operation* TELIC *6.*

COURTESY OF CHRIS FLETCHER

the Territorials, the potential sacrifice of employment, family life and life itself was now being asked of them for a much lower level of conflict than had been traditionally regarded as vital to the national interest.

Reactions to the 1996 legislation varied. The TA had been made responsible for finding the Falkland Islands Resident Infantry Company (FIRIC) in 1994 on a trial basis, but it did not prove popular. Thereafter, only TA platoons were sent there on an occasional basis though, in recent years, the TA has provided a signal squadron for service there and FIRIC is making its way back onto the TA Operational Commitments Plot (OCP). In 1995, in advance of the new legislation, arrangements were also made for Territorials to volunteer for six-month tours with regular units and many did so. As indicated in a major study of the views of more than 18,000 reservists undertaken by Lieutenant Colonel William Townend in 1998, some Territorials welcomed the possibility of compulsory mobilisation as freeing them 'from the responsibility of having to justify themselves to their employers and families'. However, many remained to be convinced that employment safeguards would be upheld since employment was far more volatile than in the past. While the legislation protected those already in employment, it could not guarantee employment for those with a mobilisation liability who were seeking jobs. The legislation also required the individual Territorial to obtain a certificate from an employer that he or she was available to be mobilised. Spouses and families were less tolerant of the possibility of separation and bereavement—marriages and family life being far

ABOVE *Private David Lucas from Leicester, a Territorial from The East of England Regiment, attracts some good-natured attention from some Kabul locals. The joint platoon raised in 2002 by The Royal Rifle Volunteers and The East of England Regiment deployed in support of the Royal Anglian battlegroup on Operation* FINGAL. *They were welcomed by the locals for many reasons including the fact that they were among the few foreign soldiers who bothered to get out of their vehicles and patrol through the streets on foot thus providing a visible deterrent to criminals.*

COURTESY OF CHRIS FLETCHER

COURTESY OF IMPERIAL TOBACCO

BELOW *Lance Bombardier Simon Lamb from 266 Para Battery RA (V) on attachment to No 7 (Sphinx) Commando Battery, 29 Commando Regiment RA during Exercise* SAIF SAREEA II *held in the Omani desert in 2001.*

COURTESY OF THE MILITARY PICTURE LIBRARY

less stable than in the past. Most Territorials were ready to volunteer, but for a realistic role rather than back-filling. Interestingly, the least popular scenario for mobilisation or volunteering was in support of an allied nation outside Europe, precisely the model for 'expeditionary operations' the MoD envisaged.

The 1996 legislation was not concerned with force structure since, in July 1994, it had been announced that the TA's establishment would be reduced to 59,000 —its role now defined as providing a general reserve for the army, reinforcing it as required and providing a framework for expansion in national emergencies. The emphasis was very much on support units, the infantry being reduced to 29 General Reserve battalions. All mortars and MILAN firing posts previously allocated to battalions were to be concentrated in four fire support battalions. For the time being, the artillery organisation remained the three squadrons of the HAC, two field regiments, three air defence regiments, a light battery, a parachute light battery, and a commando light battery. One of the field regiments was converted to a Multiple-Launch Rocket System (MLRS) regiment in 1998.

Further restructuring came with the new Labour government's Strategic Defence Review in July 1998, which saw the main emphasis for the future being one of using military force to promote British interests globally in peace and stability. 'Foreign-policy led', the review suggested that Britain 'must be

prepared to go to the crisis, rather than have the crisis come to us', with tri-service Joint Rapid Reaction Forces spearheading the response. A new mission, therefore, was to be 'defence diplomacy', by which forces would be available 'to dispel hostility, build and maintain trust, and assist in the development of democratically accountable armed forces'. Rather more familiarly, it was intended 'to give Britain robust and modern defence at a reducing cost in real terms', achieved through greater cost-effectiveness and efficiency.

Beyond domestic security, the intention was to provide for the deployment of up to an armoured division for combat operations on a similar scale to the First Gulf War, or sufficient

forces for a more extended deployment on a smaller scale while still being able to field a combat brigade for a second substantial employment. In the latter case, it was assumed that neither of the lesser deployments would involve major combat or last more than six months. At the time, it was assumed that just over 19,000 reservists, including more than 7,000 for medical units, would be needed for a large-scale combat operation. Another underlying assumption was that any large-scale threat in the longer term, from perhaps a resurgent Russia, would provide sufficient warning time for preparations. It was not unlike the assumptions behind the Ten Year Rule of 1919 without the acknowledgement that, if smaller-scale conflicts such as the Falklands War and the First Gulf War had occurred unexpectedly in the recent past, it was not impossible for a large-scale threat to develop unexpectedly too. Moreover, as has been pointed out, modern weapons systems have a long procurement genesis and rapid expansion to a mass army is equally problematic given the time required for training and equipping such a force.

It was noted that the TA remained at around 80 per cent of its strength at the end of the Cold War, with units still largely earmarked for home defence or a NATO role. Consequently, it was to be reduced further to 41,200 by 2001, comprising 33 'teeth' units and 43 support units, the overall total also including 3,000 members of the OTC and 1,200 Non-regular Permanent Staff, both these latter groups being non-deployable. Moreover, the provisions of the 1996 legislation would be fully utilised 'for situations well short of a direct threat to the United Kingdom' so that Territorials should be under no doubt that they should expect to be mobilised in the future. In November 1998, therefore,

ABOVE *Padre Jane Ball from Devizes, officiates at her first service for The Royal Wessex Yeomanry whilst on Exercise* GLOWWORM, *held at Fort Hood, Texas on 22nd October 2006.*

COURTESY OF THE MINISTRY OF DEFENCE.

"The Territorial Army has punched well above its weight with its remarkable contribution to the campaigns in Kosovo, Iraq and Afghanistan. The country should be proud of its achievements."

HOUSE OF COMMONS PUBLIC ACCOUNTS COMMITTEE
18th June 2007.

ABOVE *Corporal Neil Attridge*
of A Company, The 5th Battalion,
The Royal Green Jackets, fires
the Battalion's first missile on
Exercise DEADLY IMPACT, *the*
1996 MILAN concentration held
in Otterburn. This particular
missile caused a real 'mobility kill'
by disabling the moving target
mechanism.

COURTESY OF THE MILITARY PICTURE LIBRARY

the role of the TA was defined as providing 'formed units and individuals as an essential part of the army's order of battle for operations across all military tasks in order to ensure that the army is capable of mounting and sustaining operations at nominated state of readiness'. It was also, however, to 'provide a basis for regeneration while at the same time maintaining links with the local community and society at large', suggesting something of a sop to the past. War Establishment Reinforcement training units were to be organised for the RAC and RA while the infantry would be trained within General Reserve battalions.

The infantry was to be cut to 15 battalions, of which five would be allocated to home defence. Only two battalions remained TA battalions of a single regular regiment, these being 3rd (Volunteer) Battalion, The Princess of Wales's Royal Regiment and 4th (Volunteer) Battalion, The Parachute Regiment. All others were to be widely spread, multi-badged TA battalions, in which companies were affiliated to different regular regiments. Thus, The Royal Rifle Volunteers incorporated three separate regimental identities, with one rifle company badged as The Princess of Wales's Royal Regiment, one as The Royal Gloucestershire, Berkshire and Wiltshire Regiment, and two as The Royal Green Jackets[1]. The TA's artillery order of battle would comprise a MLRS regiment, three close air

1. The other regiments would be The Rifle Volunteers, The London Regiment, The King's and Cheshire Regiment, The Lancastrian and Cumbrian Volunteers, The Tyne Tees Regiment, The East and West Riding Regiment, The East of England Regiment, The West Midlands Regiment, The 51st Highland Regiment, The 52nd Lowland Regiment, The Royal Welsh Regiment, and The Royal Irish Rangers.

defence regiments, a surveillance and target acquisition regiment, and two war establishment reinforcement training regiments. In the case of engineers, the expansion from seven to ten regiments that had occurred after *Options for Change* was reversed, with just six engineering regiments surviving, of which one was 101 (London) Engineering Regiment (EOD) (V), tasked with explosive ordnance disposal. The number of engineering sub-units under command of the regiments was cut from 62 to just 27. The Conservative Opposition opposed the cuts, but the motion to reject them was lost in the Commons on 18th May 1998.

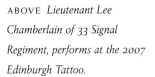

ABOVE *Lieutenant Lee Chamberlain of 33 Signal Regiment, performs at the 2007 Edinburgh Tattoo.*

COURTESY OF THE MINISTRY OF DEFENCE

In another change, the TAVRAs became Reserve Forces and Cadet Associations (RFCAs) in April 2000, tasked with recruitment and publicity, maintenance of accommodation for the reserves, liaison with employers, and administration of the Army Cadet Force. The number was also reduced from 14 to 13 by merger of the former South East TAVRA with Eastern Wessex TAVRA. The property portfolio still remained large at this time, the Highland TAVRA, for example, responsible for maintaining 61 TA properties, 88 ACF properties, eight Combined Cadet Force properties, and eight ranges spread over 17,210 square miles. The London TAVRA was responsible for 310 properties across 32 boroughs. The value of the associations had been confirmed by the Chiswell report in 1988, though it recognised that their functions had sometimes become

LEFT *165 Regiment RLC (V) provides the British Army with a reserve capability in port, maritime and railway expertise which is available for deployment worldwide in support of expeditionary operations.*

COURTESY OF THE MINISTRY OF DEFENCE

COURTESY OF IMPERIAL TOBACCO

> "The days are gone of having two armies, one Regular and one TA. We are one Army, with full-time and reserve soldiers operating closely together. As the demands on the Army increase, so those Reservists are proving more and more valuable."
>
> LIEUTENANT GENERAL JOHN MCCOLL
> *Commander of the Army's Regional Forces and Inspector General of the Territorial Army.*

blurred 'in the higher peacetime profile cast by the Regular Army'. Indeed, two association chairmen had commented in August 1990 that only associations could provide the 'supportive local environment in which our independent Reserve units can flourish'. The work was, and remains, low profile but essential. As Richard Holmes observed in 2001: 'As a subaltern I thought the TAVRAs were useless; as a major I knew they were useful, and as a Commanding Officer I found them far more responsive to many of my day-to-day problems than my own [regular] chain of command.' Inevitably, however, what has sometimes been a subtle behind-the-scenes influence on the part of the associations, and also the Council of RFCAs, has been eroded by their lack of real political significance given the politicians' lack of sensitivity towards traditional forms of local governance.

Something of a test for the new TA structure came with the repercussions of the on-going crisis arising from the collapse of the former Yugoslavia in 1991. A UN peacekeeping force, UNPROFOR, was established in Croatia in January 1992 and then further deployed to Bosnia in August 1992, and to the Former Yugoslav Republic of Macedonia in December 1992. Some 2,000 British troops were contributed to UNPROFOR. With the escalation of NATO involvement in Bosnia, UNPROFOR was replaced by a NATO Implementation Force (IFOR) of 60,000 men following the Dayton peace agreement in December 1995. In turn,

RIGHT *Members of 212 Field Hospital RAMC (V) receive another casualty at Camp Bastion, Afghanistan. The field hospital can accommodate up to 25 patients and offers care levels comparable to a UK hospital. In this fourteen week deployment, the professionally-qualified staff of 212 treated 1,500 coalition, civilian and Taleban patients suffering everything from sprained ankles to blast and gunshot injuries.*

COURTESY OF ANNE STAVELY

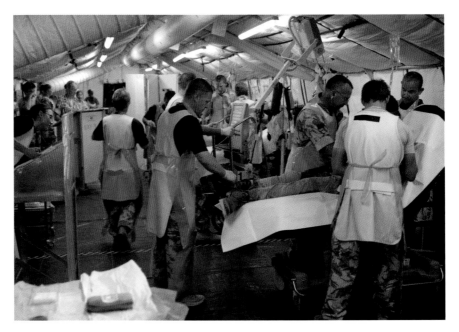

ABOVE *Corporal Mark Williams and Lance Corporal John Aitchison from 100 Squadron, 128 Pioneer Regiment, building a store room at Duckensfield Early Childhood Institution near Spanish Town, Jamaica in September 2006.*

COURTESY OF SOLDIER MAGAZINE.

IFOR was replaced by a NATO Stabilisation Force (SFOR) of 32,000; this being reduced to 7,000 in 2004. NATO became involved when conflict spread into Kosovo in 1998, with the Kosovo Force (KFOR) being established in June 1999.

At the height of its involvement in peacekeeping and peace implementation operations in the former Yugoslavia, around 15 per cent of British forces were provided by the reserves, including the TA, on a voluntary basis. A larger scale mobilisation of the TA using the compulsory powers of the 1996 legislation was contemplated in 1999 but averted by the Serbian withdrawal from Kosovo. Between 1995 and 1998 there was a requirement in Bosnia for around 850 specialists at any one time and, during that period, 835 reservists and 2,799 Territorials served there, many serving more than one tour. The specialist support provided included, for example, the Engineer and Logistic Staff Corps, RE (V), who advised on the reopening of quarries and the repair of a geothermal well near Sarajevo. The Corps, all of whom are officers, had equally advised on quarrying, water supply, geotechnology, electrical problems and airfield construction after the Falklands War, and on infrastructure, water supply and tackling petroleum fires after the First Gulf War.

By 2005, the British presence had been significantly downscaled to around 1,000 in Bosnia and 200 in Kosovo, with the main battlegroup being withdrawn from March 2007. By 1st June 2007 a total of 7,890 reservists of all categories had been mobilised for duty in the Balkans since 1992. There were 22 Territorials deployed to the Balkans on 1st June 2007. Subsequently, some reservists also

RIGHT *On 27th May 2006,*
the 25 cadets of Territorial
Army Commissioning Course No
61 became the first TA officer
cadets to wear No 1 Dress and
carry swords on their pass out
parade, taken by the Adjutant
General, Lieutenant General
Freddie Viggers CMG MBE, *at*
the Royal Military Academy,
Sandhurst. The parade marks an
important milestone for the TA.
While No 1 Dress has hitherto
been the sole domain of Regular
Army cadets, TA cadets have
previously paraded in No 2 Dress
or, exceptionally, working dress.
TACC 61 were also the first TA
course to follow the tradition
of their regular counterparts
by marching up the steps and
through the front door of Old
College at the end of the parade,
followed by the Adjutant on his
horse.

COURTESY OF SOLDIER MAGAZINE

served on a similar basis in Sierra Leone, to which British forces were committed in May 2000 following escalating violence in the country. In 2001 there were 51 reservists serving in Sierra Leone—the number falling to just two by 2005. Similarly, a few reservists served with UN forces in the Democratic Republic of Congo.

The emphasis upon the use of specialists in Bosnia and Kosovo reflected the emergence of 'specialist pools' alongside independent and sponsored units within TAVR from 1967 such as the Pool of TAVR Observation Officers (later the TA Pool of Information Officers and today the Media Operations Group (V)). Initially just two strong, it had grown to 56 members by 1994. Others were the All Arms Watchkeepers and Liaison Officers Pool, the RA Specialist Pool, the geologists of the Engineer Specialist Pool, and the Army Air Corps TA Pool of Pilots, from which 666 Squadron (V), AAC was formed in 1986.

As a result of the Strategic Defence Review in 1998 other specialist units emerged, such as the Land Information Assurance Group (LIAG), composed entirely of commissioned officers, formed for information warfare duties. The renamed Media Operations Group (V) exists to provide media training, advise on media relations, provide escort officers, media planners, analysts, and spokesmen and women. Other new units that have emerged include the Catering Support Regiment, formed within the RLC in 1993 to deploy chefs for units on active operations and on training exercises. The RLC also includes 88 Postal and Courier Regiment, RLC (V) and 162 Movement Control Regiment, RLC (V). In the case of the Catering Support Regiment, this rather unique unit had 40 per cent of its strength deployed on operations in 2003. Sponsored units generally continue to demonstrate their special skills, as in the case of 170 (Infrastructure Support) Engineer Group, which is offering consultancy support to the MoD Counter Proliferation and Arms Control Directorate in the ongoing destruction of chemical weapon stockpiles in Russia.

> "Generals may conceive the most brilliant plans. Their staffs may issue the most perfect orders, but in the end it is the Platoon Commander who will be the deciding factor between victory and defeat."

LIEUTENANT COLONEL W E GREEN DFC TD
Infantry Training and Drill, 1938.

The first significant recourse to the compulsory provisions of the 1996 legislation came in 2002 when a number of Territorials were called out for service in support of operations in Afghanistan following the 9/11 attack on the World Trade Center in New York in September 2001 and the US-led operation to oust the Taleban from the control it had exercised over the country since capturing Kabul in 1996. The operations, beginning on 7th October 2001, led to the requirement for more personnel in the UK to collate and analyse intelligence and it was deemed that the posts could not be filled on the basis of six months' voluntary service or for longer periods of full-time reserve service. Thus, under an order signed by the Secretary of State on 11th October 2001, 75 personnel from 3rd (Volunteer) Military Intelligence Battalion were called up compulsorily for six months from mid-January 2002, together with some medical personnel. The order was then renewed for a further year with effect from 1st October 2002. Under the legislation, the Secretary of State deemed warlike operations to be in preparation or progress 'following terrorist activities in the United States of America'. Since then, the UK has continued to contribute to the International Security Assistance Force (ISAF) in Afghanistan, the separate operational activities there being consolidated in 2005 as Operation HERRICK.

In advance of anticipated operations against Iraq, the 1996 legislation was again invoked on 7th January 2003 to compulsorily mobilise some 4,500 reservists for the Second Gulf War. Three TA units were formally mobilised—131 Independent Commando Squadron, RE (V), 165 Port and Maritime Regiment, RLC (V), and 202 (Midlands) General Hospital (V). Volunteers also came forward for service, active operations commencing on 20th March 2003. One sub-group of 60 soldiers from The Royal Yeomanry working with 131 Independent Commando Squadron, RE (V) made a heliborne landing on the Al Faw peninsula at the very start of the invasion of Iraq before securing crossing points over the Khawr az-Zubayr river and enabling armoured units to advance on Basra. Territorials have also been utilised for the subsequent ongoing stability operations in Iraq (Operation TELIC). Iraq, indeed, has represented the largest deployment of

BELOW *Signaller Lesley Aitken from 2 Signal Squadron, takes a break during the newly adopted seven-week Exercise* SUMMER CHALLENGE *run by 51 Brigade in 2006. Starting as a newly attested recruit, Lesley emerged as a fully trained soldier ready to undertake her specialist training. Under normal circumstances, an average recruit could expect basic training to take a minimum of twelve weeks—and, in reality, much longer.*

COURTESY OF THE MINISTRY OF DEFENCE

Kingsman (later Lance Corporal) Michael Davison, a 22-year-old builder from Liverpool in The King's and Cheshire Regiment became the first Territorial since 1965 to win the Military Cross when dragging a wounded officer to safety after an ambush in Basra on 4 July 2003.

reserves of all kinds since the Suez affair in 1956, for which only regular reserves were utilised. In April 2007 it was also announced that TA soldiers would be mobilised to support UN peacekeeping operations on Cyprus (Operation Tosca), with drivers of 152 (Ulster) Transport Regiment RLC (V) being amongst the first to be deployed there. On average Territorials have made up around 10-12 per cent of the army on active operations since 2003. In the case of Iraq, 18 per cent of those deployed on Telic 2 between July and November 2003 were Territorials and 15 per cent on Telic 4 between April and November 2004, the proportion falling to eight per cent on both Telic 6 and 7 between April 2005 and April 2006. In individual units the proportion could be much higher. Reservists made up 27 per cent of 6 Regiment Group, RLC on Telic 1, the commanding officer commenting: 'When one considers that these soldiers came from a wide range of units and different cap badges, that they had little notice of their deployment and that many had never worked in the supply area before their performance was all the more remarkable.' The overall average of reservists in Iraq from January 2003 to April 2006 was 11 per cent.

By 1st June 2007 a total of 13,510 reservists had been called up for service in Iraq since 2003, those proceeding on active operations being signed on as regulars for the duration of their tours. The number then actually mobilised after failure of medical and dental inspection (this being the most common reason) or rejection from other causes, was 11,568 reservists, of whom 10,869 were Territorials. In June 2007 approximately 280 TA personnel were deployed on operations there. In the case of Afghanistan, 1,730 Territorials had been mobilised since 2001, with approximately 270 deployed there on 1st June 2007. Overall, between 2004 and 2007, the TA effectively deployed the equivalent of 21 battalions in Iraq or Afghanistan. Kingsman (later Lance Corporal) Michael Davison, a 22-year-old builder from Liverpool in The King's and Cheshire

ABOVE *Roebuck Company undergo public order training prior to deploying on Operation* Telic 6. *This training was put to the test when a four-man Immediate Response Team commanded by Corporal Frazer Bakas (3 PWRR) was brought in to support the operations around the Al Jameat police station. Corporal Bakas was awarded a Mention in Despatches for rescuing casualties from rioters.*

COURTESY OF KEITH MINDHAM

Regiment, became the first Territorial since 1965 to win the Military Cross after dragging a wounded officer to safety following an ambush in Basra on 4th July 2003, the MC itself having become available to all ranks since 'democratisation' of gallantry awards in 1993. Between January 2003 and February 2007 a total of five reservists died on active service in Iraq and one in Afghanistan. A further 14 reservists were injured in both theatres between January and December 2006.

Participation has been variously in the form of composite TA companies, regular companies with an integral multiple of Territorials, 'cohorts' of individuals deployed together to regular units, or deployment to individual posts. Thus, Y Company of 1st Princess of Wales's Royal Regiment (PWRR) serving in Al Amarah in Iraq in 2004 included a platoon from The Lowland Regiment, with men ranging in service experience from ex-regulars to one recent recruit who had attended only four training weekends and a two-week camp prior to mobilisation. The battalion formed part of a PWRR Battle Group, including a squadron attached (as infantry) from The Queen's Royal Lancers, in which there was also a contingent from The Royal Yeomanry. Other Territorials were attached to the Battle Group as the major part of the Civil-Military Co-operation Team (CIMIC). Major Andrew Alderson, a former merchant banker, for example, was responsible for the economic planning and development of all four southern Iraqi provinces under British control in 2003. In a similar civic action role, 225 (City of Birmingham) Plant Squadron, Royal Monmouthshire RE (M) sent 36 personnel to Basra as part of 100 Field Squadron Royal Monmouthshire RE (M) to assist in rebuilding roads and bridges

ABOVE *TA REME soldiers such as Sergeant Andy Cleveland [above], played a key role in the destruction of many illegally-held small arms confiscated by coalition forces in Iraq, which could not be refurbished and re-issued.*

BELOW *A small museum quickly grew out of the thousands of weapons handled by the REME armourers, including this ceremonial AK-47 and gold-plated Tariq 9mm pistol.*

COURTESY OF SERGEANT CLEVELAND, REME.

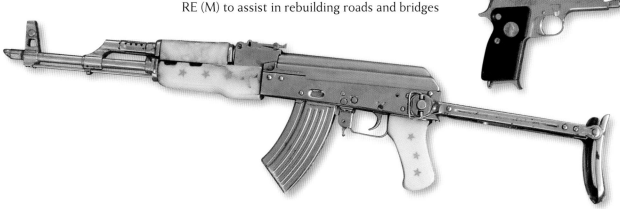

"...it appears that it might be necessary for the Territorial Army to be prepared to throw off, as it were, small bodies of short-term mercenaries, while retaining at home the cadre aspect of the normal Territorial Army."

LIEUTENANT COLONEL J K DUNLOP MC TD
The Problems and Responsibilities of the Territorial Army, 1935.

as well as water and sewage plants. 75 Engineer Regiment also contributed personnel. A major undertaking was the repair of Aldershot Bridge, a floating bailey bridge over the Shatt al Arab waterway, which had been badly damaged by an explosion. It had to be repaired again almost immediately when an Iraqi operator of a 150-ton crane tried to use it as a short cut home. In 2004, 507 Specialist Team, RE helped get Iraq's railway system working again.

In the case of The London Regiment, a number of men were compulsorily mobilised in 2002. In 2004 Cambrai Company was sent to Basra, being replaced by Messines Company in 2005, with Somme Company then deploying to Afghanistan in March 2007 for a six-month tour on force protection duties at Camp Bastion in Helmand as part of the 1 Worcester and Sherwood Foresters Battle Group in 12 Mechanised Brigade. The company comprised 140 soldiers from 11 different TA units from London and within the M25 area, reinforced by regulars and other reservists. The task involved protecting both the base and also the airfield that sustained all operations within Helmand. In another case, 26 TA drivers drawn from 151 (London) Transport Regiment and 158 (Royal Anglian) Transport Regiment were mobilised in 2007 to augment The Royal Marine Commando Logistic Regiment at Camp Bastion. Similarly, The Rifle Volunteers provided 55 men for service with the Royal Gurkha Rifles Battle Group in Afghanistan in November 2003, losing one man who was killed in a suicide bombing on 28 January 2004. Subsequently, The Rifle Volunteers (later 6th Battalion, The Rifles) provided Salamanca Company for the 1st Cheshire Regiment Battle Group in Iraq in 2004 and Peninsula Company for service with 3 Commando Brigade at Camp Bastion in Afghanistan in 2006.

Most Territorials have preferred formed or sub-unit deployment, which also provides greater opportunities for Territorial officers and NCOs. A Regular Army itself short of manpower and stretched to the limit, however, has favoured what might be regarded as the cherry-picking of junior ranks to fill gaps in the regular order of battle. In particular this has the potential to damage cohesion

ABOVE *Engineers from the Royal Monmouthshire RE (V) clear wreckage from a bridging site on the Shatt al Arab waterway before building 'Aldershot' Bridge.*

COURTESY OF THE CASTLE AND REGIMENTAL MUSEUM, MONMOUTH.

OPPOSITE *A team from 103 Regiment RA (V) LAD REME (V) manufacture a makeshift distributor for a Landrover TUM (HD) during a timed competition on Exercise* WESTERN APPROACHES *held at Swynnerton Training Area, 1997.*

COURTESY OF THE MILITARY PICTURE LIBRARY.

ABOVE *With the number of types of weeapons in the platoon group increasing, it is important that every man remains proficient with each one. Private Doherty from The Royal Rifle Volunteers, fires the 5.56mm Minimi light machine-gun (LMG) whilst on deployment to Afghanistan as part of the NATO Allied Rapid Reaction Corps.*

COURTESY OF MIKE HUGHES

by leaving more senior Territorials with little reason to continue to serve. In some respects, it is almost a reversion to the function of the militia prior to 1908 as primarily a quarry, simply a draft-finding body for the army, shorn of its wider social significance.

In the light of 9/11 a *New Chapter* to the *Strategic Defence Review* revisited the home defence role to some extent, recognising that the geographical spread and local knowledge of the TA 'could be an asset in home base security'. A discussion document, *The Role of the Reserves in Home Defence and Security* was published in June 2002, suggesting that TA personnel could reinforce brigade headquarters in the UK, but also that a 500-strong 'reaction force' be established in each of the 14 brigade areas. Effectively informal groups of reservists, all trained personnel would be considered available for this tri-service Civil Contingencies Reaction Force (CCRF), unless they opted otherwise—and might be called out at 24 hours' notice in the case of terrorist attack, major accident or natural disaster. The TA could still not be used for aid to the civil power, but aid to the civil community was technically a different matter, enabling some TA personnel from the CCRF to man operations rooms in support of regulars deployed during the firefighter's strike in the West Midlands in November 2005. Of course, Territorials had often assisted in civil disasters such as at Aberfan in 1966 and during the foot and mouth epidemic in 2001.

A further Defence White Paper, *Delivering Security in a Changing World* on 11th December 2003, together with the *Future Army Structures Review*, fixed the

COURTESY OF IMPERIAL TOBACCO

Regular Army's establishment at 102,000, with further reductions in the number of infantry battalions and a 'rebalancing' of manpower to other areas. The White Paper was predicated on the assumption that a large-scale conventional attack on the UK was now unthinkable and, indeed, any operations of a high-intensity nature against opponents in Europe armed with advanced weapons systems equally unlikely. Consequently, only 'small wars' and expeditionary operations, albeit throughout the world, were to be assumed. While a number of very different missions might be undertaken simultaneously in any particular operation, from peace support to counter-insurgency, they would usually be in co-operation with other allies and partners.

On 21st July 2004 a Command Paper, also entitled *Delivering Security in a Changing World*, announced a reduction of regular infantry battalions from 40 to 36. In turn, in order to support the new structure, the TA's infantry was to be reduced to 14 battalions between April 2006 and April 2008, with all companies reduced from three to two platoons. The TA footprint had already been substantially reduced since 1992 and this reduced it still further, the then Director of Reserve Forces and Cadets (DRFC), Brigadier Richard Holmes, having already pointed out in 1998 that TA centres were often the only military presence in an entire area. There were only two in mid-Wales, five north of the Highland line and half a dozen west of Exeter. As Holmes observed, TA strength 'reflects the size of its national footprint, and the reduction

ABOVE *A team medic teaches fellow Territorials to canulise each other at Camp Bastion in 2006. Getting fluids into a wounded soldier rapidly may make the difference between life and death.*

COURTESY OF MIKE HUGHES

of this footprint reduces recruiting potential'. Holmes also suggested that campaigns by the TA to save itself before restructuring had a baneful effect after restructuring had been completed: 'The public, having been told vociferously that the TA is under threat, is then too easily persuaded that it has indeed been disbanded.' The TA's profile within the MoD was increased, however, in 2004 by the establishment of a new post of Assistant Chief of the Defence Staff (Reserves and Cadets), with more access to the Minister and reporting directly to the Chiefs of Staff. Its initial incumbent, the Duke of Westminster, became the first Territorial to be promoted to major general since the Second World

ABOVE *A five man patrol from Cambrai Company, drawn from the West Midlands Regiment, shelter from the rotor wash of the Sea King that has just landed them, Iraq, 2005.*

COURTESY OF NEIL EDDINGTON.

War. Major General Simon Lalor succeeded the Duke in 2007. The process had begun with the appointment for the first time of a reservist[2] as DRFC in 1997 with the rank of brigadier (or equivalent), and the subsequent addition of a Territorial full colonel as Colonel Reserves DGS within the General Staff, the only previous representation being of a colonel within the DRFC directorate. In 2006 further posts for Territorial brigadiers were established at regional divisional headquarters.

The *Future Use of the UK's Reserve Forces* paper on 7th February 2005, building upon the earlier policy documents, defence planning assumptions and the MoD's *Defence Intent for Reserves* outlined the purposes of the TA and other reserves as augmenting the Regular Army for 'enduring operations', providing additional capacity for 'large-scale operations', providing specialist capacity, providing civil contingency reaction capability in the UK, and maintaining links between the military and civil communities. On 23rd March 2006 further efforts at rebalancing the TA by 2010 were announced under the TA *Future Structures Review*. Without reducing the overall strength of the TA from approximately 38,500, the intention was to reduce the number of infantry by 850, the number of artillery by 507 and the number of the army medical services by 1,598—the latter reflecting the difficulties in recruiting up to establishment. The numbers thereby released would be channelled into the RE (1,594), the Intelligence Corps (196), the Army Air Corps (394), and the provost sections of the Adjutant

2. Brigadier Richard Holmes.

General's Corps (239). An infantry battalion would be reduced, but there would be a new engineer regiment, a new medical general support regiment, a new national transport regiment, a new national supply regiment, a new military intelligence battalion, a new military provost service company, and a new AAC regiment. All TA units would also be paired with one or more regular units with the intention that these units would train together where possible and also that, when mobilised, Territorials would be attached, where possible, to the paired regular unit. Restructuring, however, is likely to be delayed by the current level of deployment overseas.

The TA and the other volunteer reserves have become in official parlance the 'reserve of first choice' ahead of regular reservists. The deployments to Iraq and Afghanistan, however, have created undoubted strains. In order to sustain the effort, TA mobilisation has been kept at around 600 personnel every six months, or 1,200 per annum. The 1996 legislation specified that no TA soldier should be mobilised for more than one year in three, but the *Future Use of the UK's Reserve Forces* paper in February 2005 outlined a 'defence intent' that no TA soldier be mobilised for more than one year in five unless they volunteered. It also undertook to give Territorials and employers at least 28 days' notice of mobilisation wherever possible since the 1996 legislation had specified no

COURTESY OF IMPERIAL TOBACCO

LEFT *Territorials from Somme Company, the force protection company mobilised by the London Regiment in 2007, watch a coalition airstrike on Taleban positions in Helmand Province, Afghanistan.*

COURTESY OF THE LONDON REGIMENT

COURTESY OF IMPERIAL TOBACCO

minimum period of notification. The difficulty has been that, even without such an undertaking, the level of deployment has been such that more than 8,000 Territorials—around a third of the TA—are not currently available for redeployment for some years. Indeed, in November 2005 the House of Commons Public Accounts Committee (PAC) estimated that only 63 per cent of the trained TA personnel necessary to support a large-scale military operation would be immediately available as a result of the level of mobilisation since 2003. As, at any given time, there will be newly recruited and partially trained Territorials as well as those also unavailable as a result of physical fitness or for other reasons, the burden of current deployment falls upon an ever smaller proportion of junior officers and soldiers.

There was a sense among regulars that the Territorials serving with 1 PWRR in 2004 had been 'used and then thrown away' in terms of after-service care if affected by their experiences. As one regular officer put it: 'They watched our backs—who would now watch theirs?' One of the Territorials also indicated that, as they were a composite group that then dispersed, it took time to readjust to civilian life, as they did not have the opportunity to wind down with fellow soldiers, as regulars would have done. In Bosnia, too, regulars had expressed the need for better welfare support for Territorials deployed with them as TA units did not then have the equivalent of a Unit Families Officer for the volunteer or his dependents. Similarly, regulars or ex-regulars were entitled to use welfare organisations such as the Royal British Legion and the Soldiers, Sailors, Airmen and Families Association (SSAFA), to which the TA at the time had no access. St Dunstans and the British Limbless Ex-Servicemen's Association (BLESMA) would provide support for injuries sustained on duty but regimental charitable funds varied enormously in their scope for assisting Territorials. Subsequently, Regimental Operations Support Officers (ROSO) have coordinated welfare and employer support for those deployed. In the case of The London Regiment, a welfare fund was established

BELOW A gunner from 103 Regiment RA prepares himself to take part in a 'gun run' event at the 2005 Southport Air Show and Military Display.

COURTESY OF THE MINISTRY OF DEFENCE

in 1984 with donations from the City Livery Companies and regimental associations. More recently, the financial support given to the 7th Battalion, The Rifles by The Worshipful Company of Goldsmiths in 2007 enabled the Battalion to bring the soldiers' families—spread between Cornwall and the East End of London—together during Salonika Company's deployment to Helmand. Generally, the closure of many TA centres and the reduction of the footprint'in the locality has made it sometimes difficult for individual reservists to find sufficient local support immediately available.

The results of a major study of reserve forces undertaken by the National Audit Office (NAO) were published on 31st March 2006. These informed the subsequent examination of reserve forces by the PAC, the report of which was published on 18th June 2007. The NAO report included a survey of 4,722 reservists, of whom 3,122 were Territorials. It found that the majority of reservists were satisfied with their experience of deployment, and that the personal challenge represented by reserve service and the opportunity to learn new skills were the highest rated factors in recruitment. There had been a distinct cultural shift in that most reservists joined because they wished to go on overseas deployment. Nonetheless, 16 per cent of those reservists questioned expressed an intention to leave within a year: 41 per cent of this group had been mobilised. Among reservists as a whole, most intending to leave cited that service was 'no longer fun' though, significantly, most Territorials intending

ABOVE *Private James St Clair-Jones, team captain, takes part in the Field Kitchen Competition during the Combined Services Culinary Challenge held at Sandown Park in Surrey on 31st October 2006. The event encompassed all aspects of catering. In the Field Kitchen Competition teams of chefs were challenged to use field kitchens and operational rations to produce a 2-course meal for 20 people, whilst in the Parade de Chefs team competition, one Service team per day prepared, cooked and served a VIP meal for 64 diners.*

COURTESY OF SOLDIER MAGAZINE

ABOVE *Responsible for the protection of key points from air attack, 104 Regiment RA (V), seen here in 1996, were equipped with the Javelin shoulder-launched anti-aircraft missile, effective out to 4,500m.*

COURTESY OF THE MILITARY PICTURE LIBRARY

to quit cited personal or family pressure as a primary reason. Some 41 per cent of respondents intending to quit, however, cited 'lack of support' as a contributing reason.

It appeared from a report, commissioned by the MoD from King's College, London, and published in *The Lancet* in May 2006, that reservists were more likely than regulars to suffer mental health problems as a result of active service: the NAO's own survey found that 22 per cent of its respondents had found deployment 'traumatic'. The NAO report noted that some improvements had been made in post-deployment welfare and health provision, with the intention of introducing a new Reserve Mental Health Programme from November 2006. Currently, reservists suffering from post-deployment mental problems were the responsibility of the NHS. The NAO recommended that procedures for diagnosis and treatment should be available through Defence Medical Services. Similarly, the 'fast track' system on the NHS for regulars was not available for reservists wounded, injured or traumatised on operations. The NAO urged, therefore, that all reservists should have 'adequate dedicated provision of welfare support', with particular attention to be paid to the families of those deployed. In turn, while noting that it had been announced in May 2006 that mental health assessments would now be available to all those reservists deployed since 2003, the PAC recommended, in turn, that the diagnosis of physical injuries be speeded up. It also wished to see all units encouraged to develop dedicated support organisations.

The NAO noted that other problems had been addressed by a new remuneration package for reservists on operational deployment, which was introduced in April 2003, while a Statutory Instrument, Reserve Forces (Call Out and Recall) (Financial Assistance) Regulations, in 2005 provided for mobilised reservists to make up the difference where a civil salary exceeded the Regular Army pay received on operations, and for an allowance for loss of benefits.

There was criticism, however, of the state of health and physical fitness of many reservists, since it appeared that some had been able to join the TA without actually passing the requisite fitness tests, and that medical and physical procedures at the centralised Reserves Training and Mobilisation Centre (RTMC) at Chilwell, established on 1st April 1999, had been inadequate. It was acknowledged that new fitness procedures would be introduced in November 2007 and that mobilisation procedures had much improved, but that too many reservists were being deployed without having had the opportunity to undertake either routine or pre-deployment training with regular units. Though the contribution of reservists had often been valuable, they would be able to perform even better if trained, mobilised and integrated with regulars. Some 40 per cent of after-action operational reports mentioning reservists seen by the NAO had indeed praised their adaptability and skills although levels of mental and physical fitness for challenging operational tasks had been questioned in some reports. Commissioned reservists had proved good in headquarters' roles but, through lack of experience in the field, had taken time to adjust to more active command.

Training generally presented problems, with too many course cancellations and a lack of equipment. Just 37 per cent of reservists said they were satisfied with the equipment available for training, though 62 per cent of the Territorials were satisfied that the training they had received was sufficient for the tasks they were asked to perform on operations. Nonetheless, the NAO found that reservists such as Territorial Royal Signals units were often trained on a narrower range of equipment than regulars. It recommended more worthwhile and challenging core training with proper equipment levels to maintain enjoyment as well as more adventurous training to improve fitness. Notwithstanding the existence of specialist units, reservists were generally called

COURTESY OF IMPERIAL TOBACCO

BELOW *The padre gives thanks for the return of Somme Company from Afghanistan. The service took place in the London Scottish drill hall, Buckingham Gate. The Regimental War Memorial can be seen in the background.*

COURTESY OF BRIAN FAHY

up for their military skills, with little information available in advance as to additional civilian skills that might prove useful in theatre. These skills, however, had proved invaluable, especially where it was too dangerous for civilian contractors to operate.

Recruitment and retention also exercised the NAO and PAC. The TA's establishment was 38,430, but its strength at 31,260 showed a shortfall of 19 per cent, with above-average shortfalls in nationally recruited units of the Army Medical Services (AMS), Royal Signals, REME and RLC. In the case of the AMS, the strength was 3,049 when the establishment was 5,176, the significance being that the TA has provided more than 50 per cent of the medical personnel deployed to Iraq since 2003. It was suggested in June 2006 that 16,000 soldiers had left the TA since the invasion of Iraq in 2003, including 1,280 officers who had resigned their commissions. To some extent, this reflected what would have been a normal pattern of turnover since this had always been high within the TA, but there had also been data cleansing by the new Joint Personnel Administration to remove old records from the system. Numbers, however, did decline steadily until the latter months of 2005 before showing a gradual increase, with strength reaching 32,150 in April 2006, or 84 per cent of establishment. As the PAC report indicated, a TA Manning Action Plan had been implemented whereby all army advertising material provided information on the TA, there was greater emphasis upon pairing and training affiliations between regular and TA units (under the *Future Structures Review*) and recruits would be 'nurtured' through initial training, with more full-time staff available to support TA units, the provision of special occupational health services, and as much warning time as possible given for mobilisation.

In June 2007 the All-Party Parliamentary Reserves Forces Group, formed in June 2006 with Conservative MP Julian Brazier and Labour MP Bruce George as co-chairmen, published its own report, *Recognising the Opportunities*. The report was critical of the shortage of man training days (MTDs) within the TA since, typically, units received an annual budget of just 27 MTDs per person which, after deduction of 15 days' camp and, say, ten days for weekly training evenings, allowed only one weekend training a year when between eight and ten were really required given the multiplicity of roles within infantry and yeomanry units. Indeed, the report suggested that a basic unit structure seemingly intended to be 'collections of spare parts for regular units' was not conducive to recruitment and retention. Shortfalls in officer recruitment were

ABOVE *Mark Lancaster, Conservative MP for North East Milton Keynes and a serving Territorial officer.*

COURTESY OF SOLDIER MAGAZINE.

OPPOSITE *The Anti-Tank Platoon of The 7th Battalion, The Rifles train with the new Javelin Weapon Effects Simulator against a BTR-70 belonging to the 1st Mechanised Infantry Battalion of the Macedonian Army on the Krivolak training area, June 2007, where the temperatures regularly rose above 45°C.*

COURTESY OF 2LT PATERSON/7 RIFLES.

"I pay a huger tribute to the Territorial Army for what it has done and achieved... the equivalent of 19 or 20 infantry battalions deployed on operations is a huge achievement and speaks volumes for their ability, commitment and dedication."

FIELD MARSHAL LORD INGE
Speaking in the House of Lords, 19th January 2006.

BELOW *Soldiers of the
4th Battalion, The Duke of
Lancaster's Regiment taking part
in the 2007 Derby Trophy—
an arduous military skills
competition held at Catterick for
TA units based in the North of
England.*

COURTESY OF THE MINISTRY OF DEFENCE

also highlighted. Since OTCs were generally over strength, the report suggested incorporating parts of the TA commissioning course into summer vacations for students, with greater efforts to track OTC members once they had graduated to inform them of opportunities in their local TA units, plus officer gap year schemes. A more radical suggestion was a new reserve engagement scheme whereby a year's service in the Regular Army would be followed by four years' reserve liability, with enhanced student loans for those successful in a TA officer training course.

The All-Party Group also expressed doubt over the intended transfer of recruiting from RFCAs to brigade and divisional headquarters, it being felt that RFCAs remained an underused asset in terms of local expertise. The Group was most concerned that the suggested replacement of the title Territorial Army with Army Reserve would cause greater problems given the confusion that already existed among employers and the general public about the TA and its role. Integration with the Regular Army, it concluded, 'must never be done at the expense of integration with the civilian world'. The Group's report was aired in a Commons debate on 12th June 2007, in which it was again stressed that there was a danger of reducing the TA's local footprint too far and that it would be a considerable error to dispense with the title of Territorial Army.

The TA's capacity to meet the aims of the intended restructuring and, at the same time, to maintain its capability in the face of the current unprecedented level of peacetime deployment is certainly a testing challenge. Moreover, in July 2007 Conservative MP Mark Lancaster publicised an intended reduction of £5 million over two years in the TA's budget, which would involve cuts in weapons training and in a recruitment freeze in all units not supporting operations in Iraq or Afghanistan. The All-Party report in June had already expressed concern that a proposal appeared to be circulating to reduce MTDs for those units and sub-units not required for Iraq or Afghanistan when no one could be clear of the future requirements. It pointed out that The Royal Yeomanry

had been the only unit in the army for many years with a chemical defence role when its services were suddenly in demand in Iraq in 2003. A total of 79 MPs, including all but one member of the Commons Select Committee on Defence, signed an early day motion on 7th July 2007 opposing any cuts. Quite what the future holds for the TA, therefore, is uncertain.

As it approaches its centenary, the TA is arguably under greater pressure from operational deployments than at any time since its creation, certainly outside of the two world wars. At the same time, it is smaller than at any time in its history though, to echo an overused phrase, it is more 'fit for purpose' from the point of view of the Regular Army than at any time in the past. In the process it may even finally lose the very title of Territorial Army that symbolises its past and traditions. Clearly, it is not the Territorial Force envisaged by Haldane for, as time passes, strategic circumstances, perceptions of national interest and, indeed, societies and public expectations change. There are continuities, however, alongside the discontinuities and the TA has always seemingly faced many challenges at every period of its history. In its survey in 2006, the NAO noted that, alongside the motivations of personal challenge and learning new skills, 72 per cent of reservists cited a desire to contribute to the defence of the UK as a reason for joining. That at least would have been understood by Territorials at any time since 1908, and by all those part-time soldiers that had preceded them since the first systematic organisation of local forces in the mid-16th century.

ABOVE *Captain Georgina Myles of 208 Field Hospital got a huge welcome home when she returned from Afghanistan. Her three-month tour was followed by one month of post-operational leave before she had to return to work.*

COURTESY OF THE MINISTRY OF DEFENCE

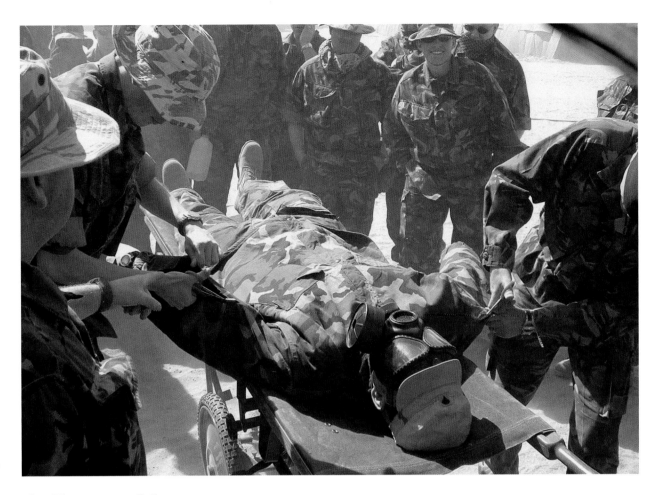

A FIELD HOSPITAL
IN THE SECOND GULF WAR

ABOVE *With the land war only a matter of days away, medics needed to know how to deal with casualties arriving from a contaminated battlefield and still in possession of dangerous ordnance. A simulated casualty is used to demonstrate the correct drill for removing clothing without unnecessarily exposing either the staff or patient to further chemical, biological or radiological hazards.*

COURTESY OF LANCE CORPORAL PRICE

ORIGINALLY ESTABLISHED AT Dawberry Fields Road in Birmingham in 1967 as 202 (Midland) General Hospital RAMC (V), 202 (Midland) Field Hospital has detachments at Birmingham, Oxford, Shrewsbury and Stoke-on-Trent and was re-roled as a field hospital under *Options for Change.* Mobilisation papers for the Gulf were issued in February 2003 and vacancies filled by other TA medical staff from Liverpool, London, Manchester, Newcastle-upon-Tyne, Northern Ireland and Scotland. After mobilisation at Chilwell, pre-deployment training was undertaken at York for other ranks and in Nottingham for officers before the unit arrived at Camp Coyote in Kuwait on 13th March 2003 in advance of the commencement of active operations against Iraq. It formed part of 102 Logistics Brigade. As the unit's history puts it, the medical facility at Camp Coyote 'had already been built by a regular unit who, much to their anger, had to wait in reserve and not man the hospital themselves. This caused a good deal of bad feeling towards the Territorials who, for their own part, would have been happy to have changed places with them.' With the fear of possible

ABOVE *A helicopter door-gunner's view of Shaibah airfield.*

COURTESY OF WEST MIDLANDS RFCA/202 FD HOSP

nuclear, biological or chemical attack, conditions were often unpleasant, with three hours being spent in trenches wearing the hot and claustrophobic chemical, biological, radiological and nuclear (CBRN) protective suits on 21st March 2003, which became known as 'Scud Thursday'. At Coyote, 202 treated 1,366 patients between 19th March and 21st April, with 63 requiring intensive care. The operating department carried out 320 procedures on 160 patients—23 of them children—while the burns unit dealt with 60 cases.

202 moved to Shaibah just south of Basra during the week of 8th-15th May to take over a 200-bed facility from 34 Field Hospital and then to help construct a more permanent British Military Hospital at Shaibah, where the temperature frequently hit 45°C. After nine weeks there, the unit returned to Britain in August 2003 having been responsible for supporting 50,000 troops and civilians—the hospital having become 'something of a "beacon" for locals with all manner of complaints, as well as for military casualties'. At Shaibah, many of the medical staff suffered from gastroenteritis: 'although unpleasant in all but a few extreme cases the virus had run its course in between two and seven days, and the patient returned to duty somewhat thinner!' Fortunately, the unit suffered only one serious injury after a vehicle collided with a camel.

LEFT *The ever-present Scud threat to the rear areas meant that all hospital staff were no strangers to the air raid trenches. This image, taken the day before 'Scud Thursday', shows the conditions in which many uncomfortable hours were spent. The soldier holding up the black waterbottle is carrying out the CBRN drinking drill.*

COURTESY OF WO1 TITMUSS

Force Protection
in Iraq and Afghanistan

ABOVE *Sergeant Howard Roger of the Royal Rifle Volunteers, serving with Roebuck Company on Op* TELIC *6, briefs a multiple before heading out on a routine Snatch patrol. By the end of their tour, Roebuck Company were being tasked by HQ MND(SE) in preference to a number of regular units operating in the same role.*

COURTESY OF SOLDIER MAGAZINE.

FORCE PROTECTION DESCRIBES the range of measures employed to preserve the combat capability of a force on operations. In Iraq and Afghanistan it has implied both static and active guard duties by Territorials and other reservists, enabling regulars to be deployed on other tasks. The experience of the Royal Rifle Volunteers in Iraq and Afghanistan since 2003 may serve as an illustration of modern soldiering on active service undertaken by Territorials. Between its formation on 1st July 1999 and October 2005, more than 300 officers and soldiers from The Royal Rifle Volunteers served on mobilised or full-time reserve service with the regulars or joined the regulars in Afghanistan or Iraq, representing 67 per cent of the battalion's strength.

Initially, the regiment provided 54 soldiers on a voluntary basis for the Kabul Patrols Company at Camp Souter from February to May 2003 on what was then classed as Operation FINGAL. Two Territorial platoons were formed; each platoon consisted of two 'multiples' which contained three four-man fire teams. Twelve days were spent in fortified sentry posts, or 'sangars', and on gate guard duties. This was followed by five operational phases, each of three days' duration, consisting of patrols, quick reaction force, escorts, guards, and training

"A recent letter to The Times spoke of the voluntary system having broken down. It has done nothing of the sort. The voluntary system to-day provides 130,000 men under circumstances so onerous that it is a wonder any such number come forward. All that is wrong with the voluntary system is that it has been working too well, and that the overstrain on loyal men has been so little apparent."

LIEUTENANT COLONEL J K DUNLOP MC TD
The Problems and Responsibilities of the Territorial Army, 1935.

in reserve. Ten patrols, each lasting an hour, were undertaken every 24 hours in both urban and rural areas. Those in daylight were carried out in consistently high temperatures with each soldier carrying more than 50lbs of equipment. Vigilance was required throughout. A grenade thrown over the perimeter wall wounded one soldier, but quick thinking by a sentry gave sufficient warning to prevent higher casualties and led to the apprehension of the attacker.

In Iraq, the regiment found half the composite Eden Company deployed between October 2003 and April 2004, the remainder being found by The East of England Regiment. Eden Company served as the force protection company for the headquarters of 20 Armoured Brigade at Basra Palace, manning static positions and mounting 'framework' patrols beyond the complex, some by boat or raised tracks through marshland. The regiment also provided most of the personnel for another composite, Roebuck Company acting as force protection for the headquarters of the Multi National Division (SE) in Basra between May and November 2005, taking over duties from Normandy Company of The East and West Riding Regiment. It involved checking passes, searching vehicles and carrying out ground clearance patrols to deter attack or infiltration. Other tasks undertaken included providing a guard force for the Allenby Lines accommodation site, involving quick reaction in the event of incidents, and armed escort duties for convoys between Basra and the Kuwaiti border, for the movement of divisional staff and visiting VIPs. Each task was undertaken for three days

at a time on a nine-day rotation. Members of the company were involved in one high media profile incident, helping to rescue burning crewmembers of a Warrior armoured vehicle after it was attacked and set alight by a hostile crowd at Al Jameat on 19th September 2005. The regiment was succeeded in November 2005 by Cambrai Company from The West Midlands Regiment.

In addition, individuals from the regiment have worked in such areas as media operations, and psychological warfare and information operations.

ABOVE *Members of Salonika Company practice with the 40mm underslung grenade launcher (UGL) in Helmand Province. This weapon, along with certain other items of equipment, are not issued to peacetime TA units thus the majority of Territorials have to train from scratch on mobilisation.*

COURTESY OF JON DOLPHIN

CIVIL-MILITARY CO-OPERATION

ABOVE *Lieutenant Colonel Simon Wilkinson, Chief of Humanitarian Operations, uses a crib card to communicate with some local youths from Az Zubayr about the availability of food during Op* TELIC 1.

COURTESY OF SIMON WILKINSON

THE CIVIL-MILITARY CO-OPERATION (CIMIC) Group was established within the TA in 1996 to ensure co-operation and coordination between the military and 'in-theatre civil actors' such as non-governmental organisations (NGOs). The social, political, cultural, economic, environmental and humanitarian aspects of intervention operations had become apparent in the Balkans where various organisations—both governmental and non-governmental—had become involved in military action. Originally established as the Civil Affairs Group within the orbat of Central Volunteers HQ, RE (Field and Works) (Sponsored Units), there were three categories: staff augmentees, who joined formation headquarters on operations; field teams who provided project managers and liaison officers for civilian organisations; and specialist teams with expertise in a variety of civilian disciplines. The tri-service Joint CIMIC Group (JCG) was then established in July 2004, becoming fully operational in January 2006 with a cadre of 27 regulars and a pool of 72 reservists, of whom 65 per cent have already been deployed operationally.

CIMIC has been involved in Iraq since 2003. Indeed, there was a significant TA presence in the UK Joint CIMIC Group in Basra tasked with humanitarian support and working with NGOs and other agencies to rebuild infrastructure,

restore utilities and plan for development and financial stability. In 2006, the Group helped staff the UK Provincial Reconstruction Team (PRT) in Basra; provided expertise on banking, policing and civil aviation; established links between the UN, the Southern Iraq Donor Group and the Iraqi Provincial Council; as well as leading and augmenting CIMIC teams in Al Muthanna and Maysan provinces. Similarly, in Afghanistan, assistance has been provided to the PRT in Lashkar Gah, and in supporting all those brigades and manoeuvre groups deployed to Helmand province. Training has been undertaken in Belize, Nepal and Ghana to hone CIMIC skills, as well as helping to train host-nation defence forces, while pre-deployment briefing in civil-military liaison and civil-military operations is offered to units deploying to Iraq and Afghanistan. Since 1998 CIMIC personnel have also served in Kosovo, Macedonia, Bosnia, East Timor, Sierra Leone, Indonesia and Cyprus.

ABOVE *This newsletter, written by a local Iraqi journalist in Maysan Province, was printed and paid for by the Information Operations team attached to the 1 PWRR battle group in 2004. It not only publicised local CIMIC projects being carried out by coalition forces but also helped to counter inflammatory propaganda spread by insurgent groups.*

COURTESY OF JOHN HOLE.

LEFT *A Territorial serving with the Allied Rapid Reaction Corps in Afghanistan trains local policemen in personnel search techniques in 2006.*

COURTESY OF MIKE HUGHES

EPILOGUE

BY BRIGADIER GREG SMITH TD DL LATE RGJ
DEPUTY INSPECTOR GENERAL TERRITORIAL ARMY

I N WRITING THIS epilogue my aim is two-fold. First, I seek to do credit to an institution that has its unique place in our nation and, second , I hope to paint a vision for its future.

Looking back we can see that Haldane's concept of a professional, first-line Army, suitable for expeditionary warfare, supported by a volunteer second line, which is embedded in the nation, but organised and trained in the same way as their Regular Army colleagues, still holds good. His ideas have stood the test of time remarkably well, and the integrated British Army of today is a direct product of this thinking. His implicit assumption is still that the volunteer force should be relevant, useful and fully integrated into the Army, ready and able to be used but, at the same time, retaining the unique characteristics that have underpinned the organisation throughout its first century.

The 'volunteer ethos' is still the chief distinction that marks out the Territorial. We go out of our way to play our full part in the army and, are trusted to do so by our regular colleagues. It brings a 'can-do' attitude with flexibility, enthusiasm and willingness, but it must never be taken for granted. The TA will continue to need the three types of people it generally attracts: those who are able and willing to volunteer at short notice for operational service in peacetime; those who find it almost impossible to mobilise because of particular family responsibilities or career pressures and those who are somewhere in the middle. This latter group are either in training, or they are in positions that 'enable' the organisation. Others are at a stage in their TA careers where they have reached its leadership (the 'management'). In essence, they are the glue that holds the TA together. Each part relies on the other and, without one, the others fail to thrive. Together the TA continues to perform, usually way above and beyond expectations.

The TA has moved away from being a strategic reserve to a tactical resource, able to plug gaps and extend the capacity of the Regular Army. As a result, expectations on both sides have changed. There is a risk that, if we fail to meet those expectations, the confidence and goodwill that we have built over the years may be replaced by frustration as the constantly changing strategic threat alters the demands, and the TA might become less credible. The modern

OPPOSITE *Rifleman Ceesay— one of the new generation of Territorials—seen here on the Combat Infantryman's Course at the Infantry Training Centre, Catterick, deployed with Salonika Company on Operation* HERRICK 7 *in October 2007 six months after completing his Phase 2 training.*

COURTESY OF JOHN SKLIROS.

ABOVE *A member of Normandy Company near Basrah Air Station on Operation* TELIC *8.*

COURTESY OF CHRIS BARKER

PLAYER'S CIGARETTES

1ST CITY OF EDINBURGH RIFLE VOLUNTEER CORPS, 1859

COURTESY OF IMPERIAL TOBACCO

TA soldier not only needs to be fit, able and trained, but must also be available to deploy at short notice. The TA soldier must do this without the benefit of living on a military base with training circuits and gymnasia, and a daily routine geared to military training. Furthermore, Territorials might be paid the same pro-rata as their regular equivalent, but they and their dependents certainly don't enjoy anything like the employment package available to a regular. There are difficult (and expensive) ongoing questions to be faced about the nation's duty of care to its part-time soldiers and their families.

Modern British society is not well-informed about the military. First-hand military experience is restricted to a relatively small number of former regulars and volunteer reservists. Most employers have no personal experience of it either, and find it difficult to imagine why someone should want to devote their spare time to soldiering. Maintaining the support of employers is crucial to the continued survival of the TA. Related to this, we must not overlook the important role that the TA has to play as the 'army in society', effectively providing the essential link between the military and wider society.

It is hard to predict where the TA will be in the next five years, let alone the next 25, except that the dynamic of change will continue to dominate. I foresee a future where it will become increasingly integrated with the Regular Army, and the military covenant will be extended to embrace Territorials and their families. I can envisage a 21st century TA that will be well recruited at all levels, well led and providing rewarding experiences and intelligently managed careers for its people. Respected by both military and civilian populations, it will enjoy an enhanced image and status. There will be stronger, recognised relationships with employers, including those through novel constructs such as strategic partnerships.

The future TA could not thrive without the work done by the Reserve Forces and Cadets Associations. This long relationship has been mutually beneficial—if not without occasional tension—and they are as vital today as they were in the past. Their role must develop and change as ours does and we remain vital partners into the future.

ABOVE *A London Irish Piper serving with Somme Company on Operation* HERRICK *6.*
COURTESY OF THE LONDON REGIMENT

Today, the TA is engaged in operations on the streets of Basra and in the hills of Helmand Province showing that we have all learnt to adapt to the changing world. Meanwhile TA centres up and down the country continue to thrive. What binds them is commitment and pride in serving their country. A steady flow of young men and women are needed and, to maintain this flow of the willing, we need to ensure the understanding, trust and support of society. We need to convince the community of families, friends and employers that Territorials, who live among us, perform a vital and worthy purpose. And we need the continued affirmation of the Regular Army in order to validate, treasure and nurture this voluntary resource to the battlefield. The recruits of tomorrow will be the interested and curious individuals looking for a challenge. In their turn, they will become the Territorial Army of the next one hundred years, and they will serve their country in the same way as their predecessors: as soldiers, in a Reserve with Pride.

It is hard to predict where the TA will be in the next five years, let alone the next 25 but I am certain that the dynamic of change will continue to dominate the life of the TA.

ACKNOWLEDGEMENTS

A GREAT MANY INDIVIDUALS have assisted in the production of this volume. First and foremost, my thanks go to Brigadier Greg Smith for giving me the opportunity to contribute to the celebration of a great British institution at a moment when, like so many others, it is under enormous pressure. While only a century old, the Territorial Army still represents a much longer 'amateur' military tradition that was part of the very fabric of the county system. I have thus been able to continue my original research interest in the Territorials and their predecessors by extending my knowledge to the post-1945 period. Second, I am most grateful to the invaluable support of the TA100 Centenary Book Committee: Colonel Angus Taverner, Colonel Alastair Bruce of Crionaich, Major John Skliros, Major Alan Frost, Liz Heasman, and David Reynolds of DRA Books. In particular, Liz was responsible for picture research and John for both photography and design while David has proved an excellent publisher with whom to work. Additional assistance was also received from Lieutenant Colonel Simon Wilkinson, Major Lynda Black and from Professor Richard Holmes, who was kind enough to read and offer sound advice on the text as well as to contribute a preface. It has been a long time since our membership of the Sandhurst escape committee and it has been a particular pleasure to work with Richard again after our separate emergence from under the wire.

I am also grateful to two fellow long-time students of the auxiliaries, Colonel John Sainsbury and Dr Bill Mitchinson, for allowing me to plunder their work. John's detailed background general histories in his publications on the TA units in Hertfordshire saved me much initial work on the post-1945 period, and Bill generously gave me sight of the manuscript of his forthcoming book, *England's Last Hope: The Territorial Force, 1908-14*. For specific assistance on aspects of the TA and the generous provision of privately produced unit histories, I would like to thank Colonel Anthony George and Colonel Heidi Doughty. In the past, Colonel Wallace Earl Walker (US Army) and Lieutenant Colonel Will Townend were also kind enough to give me copies of their important work on the TA. Field Marshal Sir John Chapple provided help on London Territorials and Colonel Rex Stephenson on the Council of Reserve Forces and Cadet Associations. I am also grateful to Dr Alan Guy, Dr Peter Boyden and Juliet McConnell of the National Army Museum, Rod Suddaby and Dr Simon Robbins of the Imperial War

PLAYER'S CIGARETTES

THE LAW ASSOCIATION
VOLUNTEERS, 1803

COURTESY OF IMPERIAL TOBACCO

Museum, and Andrew Orgill and his staff at the Library of the Royal Military Academy, Sandhurst.

COURTESY OF IMPERIAL TOBACCO

General Sir Garry Johnson and Brigadier Colin Sibun of the Army Museums Ogilby Trust kindly allowed me to hijack one of their events at the National Army Museum to appeal for help from regimental curators. The latter, as well as those charged with the care of regimental archives in local authority collections and those who gave us access to their personal or commercial archives, have been especially helpful and the thanks of Liz Heasman, John Skliros and myself in particular go to James Armstrong, David Blake, Zoe Bramham, Martin Brown, Doreen Cadwallader, Nick Channer, Charles Cooper, Michael Cornwell, Paul Evans, Martin Everett, Brian Fahy, John Fensom, Colonel Stephen Foakes, Lesley Frater, Jonathan Ferguson, Ken Gray, Charlotte Hughes, Derek Harwood, Gavin Henderson, James Hereford, Ian Hook, Chris Hobson, John Keyworth, Patricia Lynesmith, Nigel Mogg, Andy Murkin, Major Michael O'Beirne, Stuart Robinson, Peter Russell, Chris St John, John Sainsbury, David Stanley, David Tetlow, Gwyn Thomas, Colonel Ian Thompson, Clem Webb, Cliff Walters, Alan Watkins, Mike Webster, Mike Weston, Major Stephen Wright and Melanie Young of West Midlands RFCA. I would also like to thank Major Seth Ellett for allowing us to consult his encyclopaedic knowledge of military hardware in order to identify some of the more obscure weaponry and Jamie Wilson for his careful guidance on publishing this volume.

None of the foregoing, of course, is responsible for any of my errors in the text and the views expressed are those of myself alone and, therefore, do not represent those of the Ministry of Defence.

SELECT BIBLIOGRAPHY

The following are those studies that have proved most useful in the compilation
of this history.

GENERAL STUDIES

Alex Alexandrou, Richard Bartle and Richard Holmes, eds.,
    Human Resource Management in the British Armed Forces (Frank Cass, 2001)

Stanley Simm Baldwin, *Forward Everywhere: Her Majesty's Territorials*
    (Brasseys, 1994)

Ian F W Beckett, *Riflemen Form*
    (Ogilby Trusts, 1985; reprinted by Pen and Sword Select, 2007)

Ian F W Beckett, *The Amateur Military Tradition, 1558-1945*
    (Manchester University Press, 1991)

Ian F W Beckett and Keith Simpson, eds., *A Nation in Arms: A Social Study of the
    British Army in the Great War* (Manchester University Press 1985; reprinted
    by Tom Donovan, 1990, and by Pen and Sword Select, 2004)

Brain Bond, *British Military Policy between the World Wars*
    (Oxford University Press, 1980)

Lindsay Boynton, *The Elizabethan Militia, 1558-1638* (David & Charles, 1971)

John Buckley, *British Armour in Normandy* (Frank Cass, 2004)

Michael Carver, *Out of Step* (Hutchinson, 1989)

L J Collins, *Cadets* (Jade Publishing, 2001)

J E Cookson, *The British Armed Nation, 1793-1815* (Clarendon Press, 1997)

Jeremy Crang, *The British Army and the People's War, 1939-45*
    (Manchester University Press, 2000)

Hugh Cunningham, *The Volunteer Force* (Croom Helm, 1975)

Peter Dennis, *The Territorial Army, 1907-40*
    (Boydell Press for the Royal Historical Society, 1987)

David French, *Raising Churchill's Army* (Oxford University Press, 2000)

David French, *Military Identities* (Oxford University Press, 2005)

Austin Gee, *The British Volunteer Movement, 1794-1814* (Clarendon Press, 2003)

Peter Liddle, ed., *Home Fires and Foreign Fields* (Brasseys, 1985)

S P Mackenzie, *The Home Guard* (Oxford University Press, 1995)

Timothy Harrison Place, *Military Training in the British Army, 1940-44*
    (Frank Cass, 2000)

P J R Mileham, *The Yeomanry Regiments: A Pictorial History* (Spellmount, 1985)

K W Mitchinson, *Defending Albion: Britain's Home Army, 1908-19*
    (Palgrave, 2005)

K W Mitchinson, *England's Last Hope: The Territorial Force, 1908-14*
    (Palgrave, forthcoming)

Adrian Preston and Peter Dennis, eds., *Swords and Covenants*
    (Croom Helm, 1976)

L V Scott, *Conscription and the Attlee Governments* (Clarendon Press, 1993)

Hew Strachan, ed., *Big Wars and Small Wars* (Routledge, 2006)

W A H Townend, *Reserves for the 21st Century: Mobilisation in the TA of the
    Future* (Unpub. Army Service Fellowship Dissertation, Oxford, 1998).

Wallace Earl Walker, *Reserves Forces and the British Territorial Army*
    (Tri-service Press, 1990)

J R Western, *The English Militia in the Eighteenth Century* (Routledge, 1965)

UNIT STUDIES

Ian F W Beckett, *Call to Arms: Buckinghamshire's Citizen Soldiers*
    (Barracuda, 1985)

Peter Caddick-Adams, *By God They Can Fight! A History of 143rd Infantry
    Brigade* (143 Brigade, 1995)

Anthony George and Tony Green, *The Truth of Tears* (Lulu, 2006)

Tony Green, *A Jolly Good Show* (Lulu, 2006)

Tony Green and Mark Wareing, *There and Back Again* (Lulu, 2006)

Richard Holmes, *Dusty Warriors* (Harper Press, 2006)

Jill Knight, *The Civil Service Rifles in the Great War* Pen & Sword, 2004)

Helen McCartney, *Citizen Soldiers: The Liverpool Territorials in The Great War*
    (Cambridge University Press, 2005)

Charles Messinger, *Terriers in the Trenches: The History of the Post Office Rifles*
    (Picton, 1982)

K W Mitchinson, *Gentlemen and Officers: The Impact and Experience of War on a
    Territorial Regiment* (Imperial War Museum, 1994)

Gerald Napier, ed., *History of The Corps of Royal Engineers: Volume XII,
    1980-2000* (Institution of Royal Engineers, forthcoming)

Tim Jones, *SAS: The First Secret Wars* (I B Tauris, 2005)

Jonathan Riley, *The History of The Queen's Royal Surrey Regiment, 1959-70*
    (Privately published, n.d.)

J D Sainsbury, *The Hertfordshire Yeomanry* (Hart Books, 1994)

J D Sainsbury, *The Hertfordshire Batteries, Royal Field Artillery* (Hart Books, 1996)

J D Sainsbury, *The Hertfordshire Yeomanry Regiments, Royal Artillery. Part 1: The Field Regiments* (Hart Books, 1999)

J D Sainsbury, *The Hertfordshire Yeomanry Regiments, Royal Artillery. Part 2: The Heavy Anti-Aircraft Regiment and the Searchlight Battery; and Part 3: The Post-War Units* (Hart Books, 2003)

J D Sainsbury, *Herts V.R.* (Hart Books, 2005)

Mike Scott, *The Royal Rifle Volunteers: On Operations* (Royal Rifle Volunteers, 2005)

Glenn Steppler, *Britons to Arms: The Story of the British Volunteer Soldier and the Volunteer Tradition in Leicestershire and Rutland* (Alan Sutton, 1992)

Hew Strachan, *The History of the Cambridge University OTC* (Midas Books, 1976)

Anthony Verey, Stuart Sampson, Andrew French and Simon Frost, *The Berkshire Yeomanry* (Alan Sutton Publishing, 1994)

Graham Watson, *Militiamen and Sappers* (The Castle, Monmouth, 1996)

Index